David Guttmann, PhD

Ethics in Social Work
A Context of Caring

"Without an ethical foundation clinical practice is at best an amoral technology. In their education and practice, clinicians tend to experience ethics courses as external to them, a set of rules and guides to action that provide answers as to how to behave properly. In *Ethics in Social Work,* David Guttmann thoroughly shatters this notion. He convincingly demonstrates that ethics cannot be acquired passively but must be personally and meaningfully engaged by the practitioner. He does this by examining the philosophical underpinnings of ethics, cross-cultural similarities and differences, and the fact that many ethical dilemmas involve legitimate standards that are in conflict. Those who read this book will appreciate that conflicts between legitimate standards are insoluble and that it devolves on the practitioner to make a decision as to a defensible course of action.

This text is a welcome addition to the literature on practice ethics. It is clearly written. Yet, it has high-level content, especially in examining ethics' philosophical base, providing comparative cross-cultural benchmarks, and unraveling the dilemmas involved in handling legitimate differences that are in conflict. This book makes consideration of ethics forever problematical but provides the practitioner with the tools necessary to make optimal ethical decisions."

Harris Chaiklin, PhD
Professor emeritus,
University of Maryland
School of Social Work

More pre-publication
REVIEWS, COMMENTARIES, EVALUATIONS . . .

"*Ethics in Social Work* has several important elements for the field of social work and for members of other helping disciplines. First, and foremost, it offers a comprehensive theoretical foundation for the integration of three interrelated components of professional practice: what we know—our systematic knowledge base; what we do—the foundation of effective service delivery; and why we do it—the dimension that incorporates our ethics and values. Second, this book offers a comprehensive developmental and contemporary perspective about the development and foundations of social work ethics and values. Third, this book serves equally well the needs of practitioners, program and agency directors, social work educators, and the social work leadership at the local, state, national, and international levels. Fourth and finally, it provides an important comprehensive information source for the constant review and implementation of our Social Work Code of Ethics."

Zev Harel, PhD
Professor,
School of Social Work,
Cleveland State University

The Haworth Press
New York • London • Oxford

Ethics in Social Work
A Context of Caring

THE HAWORTH PRESS
Social Work Practice in Action
Marvin D. Feit
Editor in Chief

Ethics in Social Work
A Context of Caring

David Guttmann, PhD

The Haworth Press
New York • London • Oxford

For more information on this book or to order, visit
http://www.haworthpress.com/store/product.asp?sku=5577

or call 1-800-HAWORTH (800-429-6784) in the United States and Canada
or (607) 722-5857 outside the United States and Canada

or contact orders@HaworthPress.com

The Haworth Press, Inc., 10 Alice Street, Binghamton, NY 13904-1580.

PUBLISHER'S NOTE
The development, preparation, and publication of this work has been undertaken with great care.
However, the Publisher, employees, editors, and agents of The Haworth Press are not responsible
for any errors contained herein or for consequences that may ensue from use of materials or information contained in this work. The Haworth Press is committed to the dissemination of ideas and information according to the highest standards of intellectual freedom and the free exchange of ideas.
Statements made and opinions expressed in this publication do not necessarily reflect the views of
the Publisher, Directors, management, or staff of The Haworth Press, Inc., or an endorsement by
them.

Identities and circumstances of individuals discussed in this book have been changed to protect
confidentiality.

Cover design by Jennifer M. Gaska.

Library of Congress Cataloging-in-Publication Data

Guttmann, David.
    Ethics in social work : a context of caring / David Guttmann.
        p. cm.
    Includes bibliographical references and index.
    ISBN-13: 978-0-7890-2852-5 (hard : alk. paper)
    ISBN-10: 0-7890-2852-2 (hard : alk. paper)
    ISBN-13: 978-0-7890-2853-2 (soft : alk. paper)
    ISBN-10: 0-7890-2853-0 (soft : alk. paper)
    1. Social workers—Professional ethics. 2. Social service—Moral and ethical aspects. I. Title.

HV40.G98 2006
174'.93613—dc22

                                                                    2005029269

CONTENTS

PART II: APPLIED ASPECTS OF THERAPEUTIC WORK

Acknowledgments

I wish to acknowledge with gratitude the technical assistance I received from the staff of the Scientific Library, at the Institute of Medicine in Budapest, Hungary, and by the staff of the library and the School of Social Work at the University of Haifa in Israel in preparing this book for publication.

This book is dedicated to the hundreds of students of social work I have had the pleasure of teaching at the Catholic University of America's National Catholic School of Social Service in Washington, DC, and at the University of Haifa in Israel as well as to those I taught in many other parts of the world. I dedicate this to the new generation of social workers and other practitioners in the caring professions, many of whom are my former students who have reached important positions in the health and welfare services in their respective countries and continue to develop services valuable to their professions and societies.

I wish to express my thanks and gratitude to Tara Davis, Copy Editor, for her excellent and professional work. In editing the content of this book the employees of The Haworth Press invested much effort in disseminating information according to the highest standards.

I hope that this book will make a contribution to professionals in the caring professions beyond social work, and I hope that all those who read this book about ethics will adopt its principles, rules, and values, and will live by them.

Ethics in Social Work: A Context of Caring
© 2006 by The Haworth Press, Inc. All rights reserved.
doi:10.1300/5577_a

ix

ABOUT THE AUTHOR

David Guttmann, PhD, is the former Dean of the School of Social Work at the University of Haifa, Israel. He is an international expert on logotherapy and received the Grand Award for lifetime achievement in logotherapy from the Viktor Frank Foundation in 2003. He is co-editor of *Exemplary Social Intervention Programs for Members and Their Families* (Haworth) and author of *Logotherapy for the Helping Professional, Meaningful Social Work*. Dr. Guttmann's work has also appeared in several books and journals, including *Issues in Global Aging* (Haworth).

Introduction

The first decade of the twenty-first century seems to be a proper time to investigate anew the philosophy, values, and guiding ethical principles of social work in light of the many changes that characterized the past century. At the beginning of the past century emphasis was placed on developing a system of values as a position for the social mission of a profession. At that time it seemed as if the purpose and fate of social work was clear, for it took the position of aiming to achieve social justice, particularly for the poor and downtrodden. In the early 1900s "private practice" was nonexistent, for example, and few questions resulted in serious debates about the professional conduct of the practitioners. Today it is customary to consider ethical dilemmas and conflicts of interest because of the various perspectives that exist based on theories of ethics, codes of professional conduct, and the law, not to mention threats of malpractice and potential lawsuits.

The development of the profession of social work, as attested to by its ever-growing literature, has resulted in ethics occupying its rightful place as a legitimate and necessary subject in relation to services provision. This development began in the seventies, at a time when social work had come to be recognized as being among the major caring professions in welfare, health, and mental health.

Since 1960, the formulation of the National Association of Social Workers (NASW) Code of Ethics has hastened the change in the image of the profession in the eyes of the public and improved its standing. It has also helped the profession to gain power and prestige, albeit at a lower level than medicine. Today ethics is not only taught in all professional schools of social work, but is also respected by all practitioners whose main interest lies in resolving the various conflicts and dilemmas life brings to people in general. This is documented by a vast array of publications and international conferences, which reevaluate not only the worth of human existence but also the

Ethics in Social Work: A Context of Caring
© 2006 by The Haworth Press, Inc. All rights reserved.
doi:10.1300/5577_01

ways to improve it. We may even say that ethics has been rediscovered as a practical and applied philosophy.

WHAT IS ETHICS?

Ethics, or moral philosophy, is a branch of philosophy that deals with the study of what is good and bad, right and wrong, and includes values, principles, and theories. Ethics is connected to several scientific disciplines, such as anthropology, psychology, and sociology, but the concept is much broader in application. It concentrates on values and virtues rather than on facts. Ethics includes not only moral matters but also the qualities of human character and spirituality that make an individual a good person, someone who in his or her development has achieved a moral status and understanding of what is good for himself or herself and others and actually lives by those measures.

Ethics is also an enterprise of disciplined reflection on moral choices. It confronts questions about principles that underlie judgments and rules. Ethics, Pellegrino (1989) states, is a discipline with its own content, methodology, and literature; it is the branch of philosophy that concerns itself formally, systematically, and critically with the rightness and wrongness of human character (Pellegrino, 1989, p. 491).

Agnes Heller (1994), a foremost authority on ethics, delineated three perspectives in moral philosophy that are relevant today: the *understanding or explaining,* the *normative,* and the *therapeutic or educating* perspective. Each of these perspectives tries to answer a central question in general ethics. The explaining perspective tries to provide an answer to the question of what the content of ethics or moral philosophy is. The normative perspective deals with the norms of behavior that constitute one an ethical human being, or with what human beings should do in order to be ethical. Finally, the educational or therapeutic perspective tries to offer ways to shape the natural inclinations of human beings so that they can respond to the moral expectations of the societies in which they live and prevent human misery and lack of happiness in life.

These three perspectives on moral philosophy correspond to Pellegrino's (1989) concept of ethics as being analytic, descriptive, and normative. He maintains that ethics begins when we are able to provide reasons for our moral judgment, and that these reasons should be anchored in some ethical theory or set of principles or values rather than in religion or unexplained morality. The analytic aspect of ethics thus deals with making ethical decisions that can be examined critically and systematically, delineating the process used to arrive at the decision and that gave the decision its rational basis and philosophical justification. The descriptive function of ethics, Pellegrino (1989) claims, deals with reality the way it is. This function describes the various actions that individuals and societies present in making moral choices. The normative function, similar to Heller's (1994) concept of the normative perspective, deals with the derivation and definition of the norms that aim to lead toward a good life along with the principles, rules, and duties that should shape ethical conduct.

Moral philosophy requires a strong connection between one's soul and one's behavior. Intellectual capacities alone are not sufficient for becoming an ethical person. Whoever is interested in undergoing an inner transformation that aims to transform the whole of the human being, and not just at the professional self, will no doubt benefit from the wisdom inherent in it. One of the most important lessons professional helpers can obtain from studying works on ethics, particularly virtue-based ethics, is that one must be armed with goodwill toward the partner in the dialogue. The great Greek philosopher Plato felt that a real exchange of views on any subject can occur only between friends. The basis for this friendship is not what is commonly regarded to be—namely mutual attraction or interest in something—but the intention to attain something good. This maxim applies to the relationships between social workers and their clients. True human communication is based on goodwill and morality.

Charles Levy (1972), one of the early pioneers in teaching and writing about ethics in social work, has stated that ethics rests on categories and rules of conduct. This statement is important not only for social workers but also for all who regard themselves as members of the caring and helping professions. Levy explained that the three necessary categories in ethics are the following:

1. The first deals with *moral commitment* in relationships between individuals and groups, such as the relationships between parents and their children.

2. The second category relates to the *rules of behavior* that are prevalent in each organization, such as the rules guiding the relationships between worker and manager or between a member and the organization. This category is called "the ethics of organizations."
3. The third category is *professional ethics*. This category is aimed at the professional and moral behavior of the helping professional in five areas: the clients, the role, the colleagues, the employer, and the profession itself.

Ethics is a humanistic enterprise, a study and discipline in itself. It is not reducible to mechanical calculations, nor is it applicable automatically to rules and regulations. Rather, it is relationships among human beings as measured by human yardsticks of love, respect, mutual obligations, and responsibility. Central to the ethical practice of social work is a willingness to listen carefully to clients, engage in dialogue with them, and to avoid the likelihood of harm coming to anyone.

Ethical dilemmas exist in all the helping professions and human services. They emanate from the services offered to individuals, groups, families and communities. Professions, such as medicine, psychiatry, psychology, social work, nursing, law, teaching, ministry, etc., enjoy the public's trust because they are seen as being based on a body of knowledge, values, and skills gained through professional education. Today all practitioners in the various helping professions recognize the importance of ethics and its necessity in professional work. Ethical issues, problems, conflicts, and dilemmas affect the daily lives of people everywhere, including those of the practitioners. They influence the social atmosphere of a given society. Knowledge of ethics is therefore necessary for the development of harmonious relations between service providers and consumers of services, because all issues related to ethics require choices to be made from among various options.

Ethical choices are related to actions. These need to be based on a clear knowledge of what is right or wrong ethically despite the demands of the field and the reality of a given profession. Therefore ethics must be learned in all professional schools in social work, as well in the other professions that deal with the health and welfare of people in the broadest sense.

The decision whether to continue to learn or to stagnate, McCracken (1999) emphasizes, is the responsibility of the student and the practitioner. It can be mediated by others. Learning, similarly to forgetting, affects not only the intellect but also the soul. The changes that life constantly brings in its wake necessitate learning and studying anew knowledge that has already been acquired in one way or another. Learning something, such as ethics for practicing therapists, is as if being reborn, according to Socrates. He said:

> We are never the same even in respect of our knowledge, but . . . each single piece of knowledge has the same fate. For what we call "studying" exists because knowledge is leaving us, because forgetting is the departure of knowledge, while studying puts back a fresh memory in place of what went away. (as cited in McCracken, 1999, p. 365)

RATIONALE FOR WRITING THIS BOOK

My main purpose in writing this book is to spread knowledge of ethics among social workers in order to enhance their skills in dealing with ethical problems and dilemmas. Social workers and other helping and caring professionals need a strong moral philosophy base to guide them in their services to their clients. They must be armed with, in addition to their theoretical knowledge and practice-based skills, an ability to choose among many different perspectives on the place and value of ethics in their approach to clients, and they must be able to utilize, defend, and explain their perspective to clients, colleagues, supervisors, administrators, and to the general public, including the courts, if needed.

Another purpose is to enhance the sensitivity of the caring professionals to ethical issues pertaining to their professional work as well as to enrich their souls. I believe that this book can equally be useful for students and practitioners in other helping and caring professions. I believe that reading the works on ethics discussed in this book, especially the ethical works of Plato, Aristotle, Maimonides, Schweitzer, Spinoza, Gandhi, Martin Luther King Jr. and many other outstanding philosophers and thinkers, will bring the professional immeasurable joy and a philosophical outlook on life. However, in order to reap the maximum benefit from reading these texts, one must bring to the reading an openness and flexibility to accept, or to challenge, the ideas contained in them.

Today, it is hard to describe professional work without the ethical principles and values that guide it. Professional knowledge and skills do not by themselves constitute an assurance of ethical behavior in practice. We must first have an inclination to behave ethically, to seek knowledge, and to select a "master" to serve as role model for us. The good practitioner recognizes the need to find someone who will help him or her be a better human being and professional worker. This someone can be a real person, such as a teacher, an expert, or a colleague able and willing to share his or her knowledge with the "student" who seeks knowledge. Other sources for the same purpose are the books and all other literary works that enlighten one's spirit and enhance one's knowledge.

This book is based on humanistic and secular approaches to ethics that characterize the "West" regarding the value base of all therapeutic professions. In the center of these approaches are respect of human values and cultural diversity in its broader meaning, safeguarding of human rights, dignity of the human being, and commitment to social justice and the autonomy of the individual in professional relationships. The basic concepts pertaining to ethics are discussed along with the theories, principles, rules, and values that guide services provision to clients and are based on the NASW's Code of Ethics and the NASW Standards for Cultural Competence in Social Work Practice.

It might be legitimately asked why I selected only social work and not any other caring professions. After all, medicine, nursing, psychology, education, the ministry, and many other professions all seek to achieve the same goal: to make human life upon this earth better and more satisfying. My answer is that as far as I know no other books on social work ethics deal simultaneously with both moral philosophy and professional ethics, and none provide a philosophical approach to ethics as does this book. I believe that my approach to ethics as a most valuable and necessary part of the curriculum in both the classroom and the field is an approach whose time has arrived. The more technical and machine based social work becomes, the greater the danger of it losing its soul. I can say this without exaggeration from experience with various audiences inside and out of the universities in which I have taught. I found that students, fieldwork instructors, and administrators, etc., all crave a firm philosophical basis for their activities and decisions, and only moral philosophy can anchor the ideas and the ideals of the profession.

An additional reason for writing this book on ethics is to help strengthen the commitment of the new generation of social workers to ethically serve people in pain and need. Social workers' commitment to service is based on their response to the vulnerability of the client that necessitates an ethical approach to caring.

Caring is fundamental to social work. Caring for the welfare and health of individuals, groups, and communities is central in this profession. Caring, along with advocacy, accountability, and collaboration, has important implications for professional practice. Caring provides the foundations for the actions, judgment, and professional standards and norms of behavior of the professional social worker. Caring is not just a by-product or another skill or technique to be acquired as another ingredient of professional training. It is the most binding of ethical obligations.

The caring approach is the epitome of ethical behavior. Clients come to the social worker because their illness or problem requires professional care and humane treatment. Clients expect to receive this care as part of the moral obligations of the caretaker. Caring and curing are closely connected. They stem from the same Latin root, *curo, curare,* meaning "to cure," "to take care of," "to take trouble," "to treat" (medically), "to heal," or "restore to health" (Pellegrino, 1985).

The care that denotes the social work profession refers to four different senses in which the term is used. The first is compassion, or seeing in the person who is ill or troubled a fellow human being and the center of attention and intervention. Doing for others what they cannot do for themselves is the second sense in which care is expressed. For example, assistance with ADL (activities of daily living) is an integral part of that care. Taking care of a social problem is the third aspect of care. The client assumes that the professional will marshal all of his or her knowledge and skills to find a solution to the problem. Finally, carrying out the necessary procedures competently is the fourth sense of the concept of care that is common to and characteristic of all caring professions, including social work. Thus, caring is a moral obligation for the social worker, and must take priority above one's own interest.

Care has an ethical dimension. It is not business. It is not technique. It is not a "routine" enterprise. If care resembles these then it is no longer ethically and professionally valid. Care is, as Pellegrino (1985) aptly points out, "the moral base upon which our professional obligations, our ethics, are to be re-formed . . . what we are all about, the common devotion of all health professionals" (Pellegrino, 1985, p. 30).

This book is intended to serve as an introduction to general and professional ethics for both students and practitioners in social work as a caring profession. For the former, the book can be helpful as they enter the world of ethics and its many ramifications, both in theory and in practice. For the latter the book may provide a resource for dealing with the day-to-day conflicts and ethical dilemmas that need solutions. An old Jewish proverb states that a man who has studied his Torah (the law) a hundred times is unlike a man who has studied it one hundred and one times. . . .

THE STRUCTURE OF THIS BOOK

This book is based on more than twenty years' experience of teaching ethics in schools of social work around the world. I have selected for presentation the topics I found to be helpful for and needed by social workers in order to behave in what is considered an ethically correct way.

The book is divided into two parts: The first deals with theoretical and conceptual approaches to professional ethics, and the second part with the applied or practice-related aspects in daily work. The subjects covered in this book are divided in the following way:

Chapter 1 discusses definitions of ethics and its purpose and importance in professional work. Theories of ethics are discussed in Chapter 2. All the necessary theories of ethics for the practitioner are briefly presented in this chapter. The discussion centers on the philosophies behind the theories of ethics, with emphasis being given to the leading theories, such as deontology and teleology.

Chapter 3 is devoted to a thorough discussion of the virtues important for practitioners in their work. Without these virtues and continuing efforts to acquire them, professional work worthy of that title cannot be achieved. The values that guide social work as a helping profession are dealt with in Chapter 4. Different approaches to the concept of values and compromises between opposing values are presented and discussed in detail along with an illustrative case.

Professional etiquette, seldom discussed in relation to social work practice, is the subject of Chapter 5. The etiquette of the ancient Greeks and Romans is compared to present-day approaches to etiquette in professional practice. Discussion centers on the behaviors that are mandatory for all professionals in their dealings with one another and with their clients. Issues such as advertisement and counseling in terms of what is permitted or prohibited are presented in this chapter.

Chapter 6 is devoted to questions of "good" and "bad" according to various philosophers. The discussion centers on age-old approaches to moral philosophy regarding good and bad behavior toward one's fellow human. Responsibility as a major issue in professional work is also discussed in this chapter. An effort is made to present moral and professional responsibility and the ethical dilemmas related to the practitioners' truth telling.

The concept of social justice constitutes the content of Chapter 7. Social justice in ancient Greece and among the Jews is discussed. The teachings of Maimonides regarding charity and justice are presented in relation to their importance in modern social work, along with the theory of social justice advocated by John Rawls (1971), one of the most influential philosophers in America during the second half of the twentieth century.

Distributive justice in social work opens the second part of this book. Chapter 8 deals with practice-related aspects of the concept, including the distribution of resources in accordance with the principle of social justice as specified and envisioned by Rawls. Chapter 9 presents the subject of mutual trust in professional relationships between client and practitioner. These relationships are anchored in the concept of fidelity, for example, fiduciary relationships between clients and social workers. Mutual trust is necessary in caring, for without such trust no therapy can occur.

Secrets and confidentiality is a highly charged subject in therapeutic work. Chapter 10 deals with confidentiality and informed consent in social work and with keeping secrets. Two cases regarding keeping secrets and their consequences in professional relationships are presented.

Ethical dilemmas and the necessity to choose between opposing values is the main subject of Chapter 11. Ethical dilemmas can arise in conflicts between religious and secular values and between rules and the law. Common to all ethical dilemmas is that they cause emotional hardship and spiritual anguish to the practitioner who is forced to choose the best way, ethically speaking, to deal with such a situation.

Chapter 12 offers approaches to the resolution of ethical dilemmas. Included in this chapter is a discussion of the principles that are binding on a helping professional. The process of reaching an ethical decision in social work is presented in detail, including different models in decision making that can be useful for the therapists in resolving ethical dilemmas.

Chapter 13 contains various oaths in medicine and codes of ethics in social work. The Hippocratic oath and its relevance for social work are discussed in this chapter. The importance of the code of ethics in social work is analyzed, along with its implications for professional work.

The last chapter, Chapter 14, presents concepts of malpractice in real-life situations. This chapter lists ethically wrong behaviors on the part of the practitioner. The discussion of what constitutes malpractice today is necessary since many practitioners may be seen by the public as exhibiting behaviors unworthy of a professional. Malpractice is not limited to the behavior of the practitioner and the consumer of service. It is prevalent also among supervisors and staff. Whistle blowing, deceit of clients, and embezzlement are additional subjects discussed in this chapter.

Case illustrations from existing literature and from professional experience of various practitioners, including the author, without identifying the real people involved, provide the necessary backing for what is discussed in detail in this book. An up-to-date bibliography rounds out the content and offers sources of information for study and further reading for those interested in enhancing their knowledge in general and professional ethics.

PART I:
THEORETICAL AND PROFESSIONAL PERSPECTIVES

Chapter 1

Classical Ethics

THE EARLY GREEK TRADITION

Ethics comes from the ancient Greek term of *ethicos,* meaning habit or custom relating to morals. Thus an ethical person is one who has morals. Ethics is the science of duty. It deals with moral qualities in general, which are valid for everyone, and with the qualities and rules that are binding for professionals in the caring and helping professions.

The purpose of ethics is similar everywhere: Ethics is aimed at the good life. The good life has always been the expressed wish of all people, but the definition of *good* changes in accordance with values and social perceptions of given societies. Each of us has a vague idea of an overall goal in our life. This goal was expressed by the ancient Greeks from the times of Socrates, Plato, and Aristotle up to the times of the Roman philosophers by the concept of *eudaemonia,* which is usually defined as happiness or flourishing. It is the aim of all human pursuits, or the highest goal that a person can achieve by his or her actions. Today *eudaemonism* is a term used in the study of ancient philosophy to define the theory that happiness and well-being is the highest ethical goal.

What is considered good is a highly individualistic and subjective issue, whether thought of in the form of certain possessions or in spiritual terms. Aristotle raised questions of what this good is and how it can be obtained. If happiness is a form of knowledge, then can it be obtained through learning? Or is it a product of training? In Aristotle's *Eudemian Ethics* (Aristotle, 1992), it is stated that, wisdom,

Bible verses quoted in the text come from *The Holy Scriptures of the Old Testament: Hebrew and English.* Translated by Meir ha-Levi Letteris. London: The British Foreign Bible Society, 1966.

virtue, and pleasure are connected to certain patterns of living. Thus philosophical life is connected to wisdom, political life to virtue, and an amusing life to pleasure. These patterns, of course, are not necessarily divided equally among people: some aspire to all three, others are satisfied with two, and still others select one and pursue it throughout their lives.

In his *Eudemian Ethics* Aristotle said:

> Taking note of these things, everyone who can live according to his own choice should adopt some goal for the fine life, whether it be honor or reputation or wealth or cultivation—an aim that he will have in view in all his actions; for not to have ordered one's life in relation to some end is a mark of extreme folly. But, above all, and before everything else, he should settle in his own mind—neither in a hurried nor in a dilatory manner—in which human thing living well consists, and what those things are without which it cannot belong to human beings. (Aristotle, 1992, 1214b6-1214b14)

Aristotle (1997) thought that the purpose of ethics was to gain a life full of happiness in every sense. Yet, to happiness belong both complete or perfect virtue and a fulfilled life. According to him, the proper behavior, as far as ethics is concerned, should be based on aiming at the "golden path," or "middle of the road," and refraining from all extremes in behavior. In his *Nichomachean Ethics* (Ross, 1954 cited in Aristotle, 1997) Aristotle wrote:

> Now virtue is concerned with passions and actions, in which excess is a form of failure, and so is defect, while the intermediate is praised and is a form of "success"; and being praised and being successful are both characteristics of virtue. (Ross, 1954, cited in Aristotle, 1997, p. 38)

Ethics directs the decisions of those who adhere to its principles and rules. An ethical system is a system in action, and it can be judged by action—not by contemplation. Thus ethics is applied in its nature. Ethics for Socrates was first and foremost nobility of the human spirit, and it was loyalty to the virtues that should guide a person in life. Socrates was convinced that nothing bad could happen to such a person, whatever his or her end may be.

Plato (1994), the great philosopher in ancient Greece, emphasized that acceptance of philosophy and subsequently of ethics is dependent on the individual's psychic structure. He provides a valuable example of this in his book titled *Gorgias* (Plato, 1994), in which the charactor of Callicles represents those who think that the strong have naturally more rights than the weak. In Callicles's view, those who have less can by subjugated and exploited without mercy. That is what nature shows us. The weak invented the idea the satisfaction of the passions and the instincts should have limits, whereas the strong see this satisfaction as their natural right. This attitude toward ethics is condemned by Plato (via the character of Socrates), but Callicles firmly believes that his attitude is the appropriate one and rejects Socrates's well-supported contradictory arguments.

Many people live by their passions and completely identify with them. They can be characterized as lacking control of their own drives and instincts. Plato thinks that it is worthless to argue with such people, for they lack the ability to understand and accept the truth. The dialogue with Callicles ends when Socrates realizes this weakness in his opponent's psychic structure. It seems that Plato purposely depicts Callicles as a person who is immoral in the extreme. Plato seems to emphasize that we all tend to have some of the characteristics of Callicles in our souls, thus warning that we all must develop an ethical attitude toward the "rights" of the stronger to counteract the tendency to oppress the weak, and that we should adopt the ethic of what is just and appropriate as well as the ideal of the good (Szlezak, 2000).

STOIC AND EPICUREAN APPROACHES TO HAPPINESS AND ETHICS

In the historical development of ethics two important approaches should be mentioned, the Stoic and the Epicurean (de Botton, 2000). The first relates to the Greek philosopher Zeno, and later to the Greek philosopher Epicurus. According to them, moral life means avoidance of moral judgment and extreme behaviors, such as addictions to various substances or satisfaction of the senses, and leading a natural life.

Contrary to popular belief, the Stoics did not recommend poverty. They neither feared it nor despised it. They could live in luxurious surroundings similar to any rich people. However, they differed from many rich people in their attitude to a sudden misfortune, such as losing their wealth, family, or friends, or even parts of their bodies. The Stoics claimed that the wise man can lose nothing, for he is self-sufficient and is satisfied with what he has. This did not mean that they welcomed poverty or that they desired to be without friends or family, it meant that they could live on with what was left in case of a disaster rather than committing suicide, as so many people did, for example, during the great economic crisis during the twenties and thirties of the past century.

The Stoics were interested in diminishing the external influences of the material world on the soul, in refraining from the pursuit of worldly pleasures, in concentrating on the present and foregoing the temptation to predict the future, in accepting death as inevitable and as not frightening, and in achieving serenity of the soul, the kind of serenity that creates continuous happiness. They divided their philosophy into three parts: Logics, physics, and ethics. The importance of each part was characterized by a fruit garden, in which logics represented the wall protecting the garden, physics the growing tree, and ethics the fruits of the garden. Their ethics was based on the notion that only the inner attitude of humankind to what is happening to them in the outside world is in their control. The aim of a human is to live in harmony with nature and cooperation with fellow humans, and this leads him or her to a happy life. Happiness can be attained when no impulse disturbs the calmness of the soul. The Stoic ideal was apathy, meaning freedom from harmful impulses, such as gaiety, annoyance, desire, and fear.

According to Stoic philosophy, life can be divided into the good, the bad, and the neutral. The virtues represent the good and their opposites the bad, and everything else represents the neutral aspects, for these do not contribute to happiness. The neutral aspects of life were divided further into those that can be regarded as an advantage or a disadvantage, for example, health is an advantage and disease a disadvantage. Similarly, both good deeds and bad deeds exist as well as those in between. The good deeds emanate from right and true insight, and the bad from false. From the perspective of happiness, virtue is of major importance. Virtue is in its essence moral insight into the value of life. Virtue as understanding can be acquired through learning. No middle way exists regarding virtue and its opposite. One can act in accordance with one's insight, or contrary to it. If one attains a correct understanding of and attitude toward impulses and events, one is said to acquire harmony or happiness.

Perhaps the greatest philosopher among the Stoics, who did live and die according to this philosophy, was Seneca of ancient Rome. He was born around 4 BC and died in AD 65. He had a difficult life full of disasters and losses, and had to take his own life by knife at the command of the Roman Emperor Nero. Yet, Seneca never succumbed to the turns and twists of his fortune. He kept his Stoic attitude to life until his last moment, saying:

> Never did I trust Fortune [the goddess], even when she seemed to be offering peace. All those blessings which she kindly bestowed on me—money, public office, influence—I relegated to a place from which she could take them back without disturbing me. (de Botton, 2000, p. 99)

The Epicureans based their approach to ethics on the ancient Greek concept of *ataraxia,* meaning a life without pain and disruptions and with moderate satisfaction from the pleasures of body and spirit. The Epicureans (followers of the Greek philosopher, Epicurus, born in 341 BC in Samos and died in 271 BC) thought that all people have a basic understanding about the value of life and its meaning, and therefore all people everywhere are equal. They were the first group of people to express this belief.

Ethics constitutes the main part of Epicurus's philosophy and teaching, and the basis of ethics, its chief principle, is joy. All living creatures aspire to attain joy. Someone is said to attain joy by avoiding bodily pain due to unfulfilled need and spiritual pain due to worries and anxieties. It is possible to achieve joy. The needs of human beings can be divided into three parts: necessary, unneccessary, and worthless. Food and water, for example, are natural and necessary. These needs can be satisfied without causing greater joy. Natural needs that are not necessary also exist, and then occur the worthless needs, which are falsely considered needs that do not increase joy. Satisfaction with what one has leads to joy. Thus satisfaction is an important virtue in Epicurean philosophy and ethics. Humans should weigh and calculate that which is useful and that which is harmful and avoid the kinds of joy that can cause bodily pain and mental anguish. Political activity, for example, was seen by Epicurus as an activity that brings much uncertainty into someone's life. It is therefore better to refrain from it.

Epicurus's philosophy was summarized by Alain de Botton (2000). He cites on the jacket of his famous book, *The Consolations of Philosophy*, a fragment from that philosophy, which seems to me to be appropriate for all helping professionals:

> Any philosopher's argument which does not therapeutically treat human suffering is worthless; for just as there is no profit in medicine when it doesn't expel the diseases of the body, so there is no profit in philosophy when it doesn't expel the sufferings of the mind. (de Botton, 2000)

In all periods of history a will to attain increasing autonomy from the tyranny of the instincts has existed. People have tried to gain the necessary freedom to lead autonomous lives and pursue individual goals. Autonomy means freedom from the external world and to choose consciously the good rather than the bad. Therefore the purpose of ethics is to acquire mental powers that will enable one to overcome fleeting instincts and passions by means of preferring the general good over the bad, and by developing the self to a level at which the decision to be moral or ethical will come from the heart and soul and does not to be imposed by any outside power.

ETHICS IN THE WORKS
OF MAIMONIDES AND SPINOZA

The aim and purpose discussed in the previous section is also existent in Jewish ethics. Derived from classical Jewish texts, ethics stretches from biblical and Talmudic to modern times. According to Samuelson (2001), Jewish ethics can be traced back to biblical times. It combines four traditions of Jewish thought: biblical (Torah) ethics, classical Jewish philosophy, Jewish mysticism *(kabbalah),* and Jewish law *(halacha).* Each of these traditions is linked to many outstanding personalities. Thus for example, Maimonides is the representative of the classical Jewish approach to ethics and philosophy, Spinoza and the critics of his works are considered to represent the modern period in Jewish thinking up to the Holocaust, whereas the postmodern age is represented mainly in the works of Martin Buber, i.e. *I and Thou, The Way of Man, Good and Evil*, etc. Their thoughts on Jewish ethics will be elaborated in some detail in this chapter.

In the traditional Jewish approach to ethics, God revealed to the people of Israel a world in which everything relevant for human development, including all of ethics, is recorded in the Scriptures. The rules that guided the lives of the Jewish people throughout history, up to the Holocaust, and still guide them to a large degree in the twenty-first century are those that were laid down in the Pentateuch and further detailed in the Old Testament, the Talmud and other sacred writings. These rules specify the obligations of the Jewish people to themselves, to their families, to their communities, and to all larger entities up to the universe itself, and they direct them to behave as befits human beings.

Jewish ethical perspective refers to the positive aspects, such as love of fellow humans, generosity, modesty, justice, etc., and to the negative aspects, such as taking care not to be immodest in sexual matters, extinguishing the inclination to egoism, and conquering the beast in one's soul.

The religious and the moral approaches in ethics are bound together by a strong bond. The Torah demands from all men to do good deeds and to behave morally in order to promote the general good of society. According to the Old Testament, doing the right and the just thing is the essence of Jewish ethics. Therefore, the paradox of the suffering of the just and the naive, which has accompanied Jewish religious ethics since its beginnings and is emphasized by the prophets, continues to raise philosophical and religious questions until this day.

The main ingredients of Jewish religious ethics are called in Hebrew *derech eretz*, or "ethical behavior." They are divided into two parts: those aimed toward the self, and those aimed toward others. The first category includes all the characteristics of personal behavior, such as eating, drinking, clothing, and so on, and the second category includes all behaviors in all areas of life. The rules in Jewish ethics are anchored in the Torah, and especially in the lessons one can deduce from the biblical stories that encompass all areas of life. In *Jewish Wisdom* (Telushkin, 1994) one can find ethical elements that are aimed at teaching people how to behave sensibly and in ethically correct and proper ways.

The content of ethically correct behavior wanted by God is found in Psalms 15:

> A Psalm of David
> O God, who shall dwell in your tabernacle?
> Who shall live in your holy mountain?
> He who walks uprightly and works in righteousness, and speaks the truth in his heart, he does not backbite with his tongue, nor do evil to his friend; nor lift up a reproach against his neighbor. In his eyes, the reprobate has been despised, but he honors those who fear God. He has sworn to do harm, and will not change. He has not put his money at interest; nor has he taken a bribe against the innocent.
> He who does these things shall never be moved.

These eleven characteristics of moral behavior assigned to King David were reduced to three by the prophet Micah (6:8) who said: "He has declared to you, man, what is good; and what God requires from you, but to do justice, and to love grace and to walk humbly with your God." And the prophet Amos (5:4) has reduced these further and has summarized the commandments in the Torah to one: "For thus says God to the house of Israel: Seek me, and live" (Green, 1976).

The Ethics of Maimonides

The moral rules of ethical behavior, according to Jewish religious approaches, were reinterpreted by Kraus (1998). He has considered Jewish ethics from the perspective of the major Jewish sacred sources, as found in the works of Maimonides (1135-1204), the great biblical scholar, physician, and philosopher who lived in the twelfth century.

Maimonides influenced Jewish and Christian scholarship in four areas: Religion, medicine, philosophy, and psychology. In each of these four fields of scholarship he left a legacy that is influential, relevant, and significant until the present day. He is regarded as the greatest codifier of Jewish law. In his *Mishneh Torah,* a work of fourteen volumes, each representing one area of Jewish law, Maimonides clarified the complex discussion of the law and provided a framework of guidelines for living a life satisfactory to God. In his major philosophical work, *The Guide for the Perplexed,* Maimonides reconciled Aristotelian philosophy with Jewish beliefs and faith. This work of his may be seen as the beginning of modern psychotherapy, foreshadowing Freud's treatment of the anxious and healing of the perplexed in the late nineteenth and early twentieth century (Schlessinger and Schlessinger, 2000).

According to Maimonides, the purpose of ethics is to achieve moral virtues. These are noble personal characteristics. They establish in the soul the basis for doing good deeds. Ethics deals with anchoring the personality and with enhancement of its perfection. Since a human is both a social and a political entity, meaning that he or she lives in society and needs laws to prevent chaos, the welfare of society demands that its members be of good moral habits.

Maimonides did not devote a special book to the subject of ethics, but his perception of ethics is clear in all of his writings. His works that deal with ethics are *Laws Concerning Character Traits* and *Eight Chapters* that are part of much larger works on the law, the *Mishneh Torah* (1989), and the *Commentary to the Mishnah* (Weiss and Butterworth, 1975).

Maimonides was strongly influenced by the scientific and philosophical knowledge of his times, and particularly by the philosophical writings of Aristotle and of the medieval Muslim philosophers. He used Aristotle's theory of matter and form as the scientific basis of his ethical writings. Accordingly, sin and transgression come into being through matter, whereas virtue and goodness come through form. The reason for sin is the sensual passion that is created by matter. The road to virtue passes through spiritual aspirations that represent the noblest form in human activity.

According to Maimonides, ethics is concerned with the moral virtues that are noble character traits. Ethics aims at serenity of the mind and the peace and welfare of the community. It is aimed at the moral perfection of all men, irrespective of whether or not it can be reached in each and every case. He considers this purpose more an ideal than a reality. In his famous book *Hilchot Deot, or Laws Concerning Character Traits,* Maimonides refers to the eleven good deeds binding Jews everywhere as: To walk in the ways of God, to cling to those who know God, to love your fellow human, to love strangers, and to refrain from hating your brothers and sisters are the active requirements, to warn fellow humans of danger, to not shame anybody, to not torture the downtrodden, to not spread rumors and gossip, to not avenge, and to refrain from holding onto anger are the passive deeds.

All of these good deeds are explained in detail in the seven chapters of the previously mentioned book. Maimonides, who besides being a philosopher was also a physician responsible for the good health of the sultan's family in Egypt, included matters of human nature, medicine, and moral behavior worthy of a human being in his works. According to his teachings, two ways or standards of morality exist: the middle of the road and piousness, or fear of God. The law requires adherence to the former, meaning refraining from extreme behavior. The pious person does more than what is requested of him or her. He tends to be extreme only in relation to serving God. He is modest, humble, and generous. This kind of piousness soothes the spirit more than just adhering to the requirements of Jewish religious law.

Mental health, an important element in Maimonides' teachings and a most desired goal in itself, is the subject of his *Eight Chapters* (Kraus, 1998). The content of the soul is discussed in this work from his philosophical and Jewish-religious perspectives. He dwells in detail on concepts related to the healthy and to the sick soul and on therapeutic methods for the latter. This topic will be discussed in further detail later in this book.

The Ethics of Spinoza

The Ethics was the title of a famous book by the great Jewish philosopher Baruch (Benedict) Spinoza (1982), which he did not publish in his lifetime for fear of the Inquisition and because of his need to guard his personal freedom and philosophy. In his youth Spinoza suffered emotional insecurity at home and religious strife in his native Holland. His philosophy, especially his search for freedom, human dignity, and happiness as well as his ideas about God and religion, as explained with such clarity in *The Ethics,* caused great fear and furor in the Jewish community of Amsterdam and eventually led to his excommunication and expulsion. For Spinoza, faith was not legalistic disputes on the letters of the law but a matter of love. Worship was living in justice and charity. The spirit of Judaism, he maintained, was simple and straightforward: to do what is good in the eyes of God. His ideas were adopted centuries later by the Reform Judiasm movement in the United States. In Spinoza's *The Ethics* one can find a system of abstract propositions and logically necessary deductions in which reason is the sole means of constructing such a system.

Spinoza contrasted imagination with intellect, or reason, seeing the former as an unreliable resource for comprehending the order of the universe. He saw in intellect (reason) the faculty associated with adequate ideas, truth, and active formulation, as opposed to their opposites, which are derived from and by imagination. He wanted to understand the causal order of the universe, God's universe, which may be perceived as a unified system and the proper (ethical) way of life. For Spinoza, the overall goal of ethics was to provide a basis for the perfection of human beings and human nature. In his eyes no greater knowledge existed than the intuitive love for the divine principle. He detested moralizing rules and theological rituals being presented as the true road to ethics. Human happiness is the greatest, he exclaimed, when it is able to conquer the greed for riches, public fame, and unrestrained satisfaction of lust, and when its object is the knowledge of God.

Similar to Maimonides, who preceded him by five centuries, and similar to the early Greek philosophers, Spinoza wanted to free humankind from the tyranny of instincts and passions, and particularly from slavery to the passions and to imagination. He thought that when humankind rationally understands that the universe is guided by necessity, or a system of laws, they will be able to act in accordance with this knowledge. Thus they can free themselves from the slavery of the passions and be joyous, virtuous, and free. The aim of Jewish ethics, according to Spinoza, is to arrive at mental tranquility. This can be achieved by unconditional love of God, without expectation of any benefit in return. This is intellectual love of God, the final stage of human freedom, the transforming of all passion into action, and a model vision and the way one ought to live one's life.

Above all, for Spinoza freedom was the hallmark of human dignity. The free man was for him a seeker of truth. Such a man had inner happiness—virtue itself. Virtue, inner satisfaction, and truth, were in his ethics identical to the free man's contemplation of God. He was conscious of the need to teach human beings how to behave ethically:

> For he who desires to aid his fellows in word or in deed, so that they may together enjoy the highest good, he, I say will before all things strive to win them over with love . . . in his conversation he will shrink from talking of men's faults, and will be careful to speak but sparingly of human infirmity; but he will dwell

at length on human virtue or power, and the way whereby it may be perfected.

In the preface of his *A Theologico-Political Treatise,* published originally in 1670, Spinoza (1989) wrote the following:

> This book contains several treatises to verify the truth that the freedom to philosophize is not only permissible without endangering the peace of the state and piousness, but it can be ended only with piousness and the peace of the state.

In his book Spinoza claimed that Scripture and Jewish religious tradition aim at instilling a moral way of life. The narrative and the stories in these sources stand as exemplars of good moral conduct and their purpose is to strengthen one's commitment to a way of life, not necessarily to a body of truth or to a philosophy. Spinoza said:

> In those things that the Bible expressly teaches I found none that would not agree with the intelligence, or oppose it, and I saw that the prophets taught very simple matters that anybody could easily understand, and that they expressed them in such form and with such reasoning by which they could derive respect in the hearts of the multitude toward God. Then I was totally convinced that the Bible doesn't at all touch upon the intellect, and has nothing in common with philosophy, but the one and the other is standing on its own. And in order to verify it without doubt, and to decide about the whole thing, I show how to understand the Bible and all matters in relation to it and the knowledge of the soul one has to derive from it, and not from what we know from natural enlightenment . . . After that I show that his commandments . . . that God revealed to the prophets contain a simple concept of His spirit which He revealed to the prophets, meaning that we obey God with all our hearts while keeping to truth and love. . . . (p. 16)

For Spinoza the division between philosophy and theological ethics was extremely important. Spinoza saw these two subjects as standing "as wide apart as the poles, forever separate, each functioning for a different purpose" (Spinoza, 1989, p. 189). Philosophy aims at the truth, whereas theology's role is to explain faithfully what Scripture says.

In all of his works, and in particular in the fourth section of *The Ethics,* Spinoza emphasized that good and bad are not autonomous. They come into being through the interaction between our souls and the external. He saw in the greatest good something that can be perceived in relative terms, for nothing is perfect when examined from different perspectives. Whatever is created exists due to an eternal order and the laws of nature, but since the weakness of man cannot perceive this order by his intellect he grabs at any means that can lead him to this perfection. Everything that helps a man achieve this goal together with other people is called by Spinoza "the greatest good."

Spinoza's greatest good is the knowledge of the unity that connects the intellect with nature in its entirety. As long as we cling to what is passé, namely to the objects of desire and wish for material possessions to obtain, we are open to strife, sorrow, jealousy, and hatred, but if we transfer the object of our love to what is eternal, to what nourishes the soul with joy, then we can achieve the greatest good. In order to do so we need to understand from nature what is sufficient for that ideal and to develop a community that is interested in letting as many people as possible reach that aim (Boros, 1997).

Spinoza summarized his ethics, stating that his doctrine teaches us to act solely according to the decree of God and that we ought to conduct ourselves with respect to the gifts of fortune, meaning that we should await and endure fortune's smiles or frowns with equanimity. His doctrine teaches us to hate no human, neither despise, deride, envy, nor be angry with any. It tells us that each should be content with his or her lot, and explains how citizens should be governed so as not to become slaves (Runes, 1976).

EARLY GREEK AND JEWISH
PERSPECTIVES ON ETHICS

Jewish and Greek philosophers differed in their interpretations of science and morality from biblical times onward. Both used science relative to the knowledge available to them to explain the existence of the universe and humankind's place and role in it. The rabbis held the opinion a unity of science and ethics exists, and that both ethics and science teach what is good and true. The early Greek philosophers, however, had a different view about the creation and the purpose of life upon earth. These differences are briefly explicated in relation to the correlation between human purpose and happiness (Samuelson, 2001).

An important element in Jewish ethics is the idea that human beings exist in order to fulfill God's commandments. According to the Scriptures, Jews had more binding commandments than did the gentiles. The latter were supposed to adhere to seven of the Ten Commandments to which the Jews had to adhere. Of these more will be said in Chapter 4.

In Greek moral philosophy emphasis was placed on avoiding the three cardinal vices: cowardice (which the Greek philosopher Plato regarded as a moral vice), intemperance, and injustice. Both Plato and Aristotle perceived human beings as individuals whose main motivation in their existence was the pursuit of happiness. The Jewish philosophers, on the other hand, saw in the order and welfare of the community integral elements in ethics. They accepted a hierarchical order of things in which God is the absolute ruler of humankind, the earth and the universe as a whole as opposed to the form and matter that are the mainstays of Aristotle's philosophy.

Jewish classical ethics emphasized a general correspondence between moral duty and behavior (i.e., fulfillment of the commandments) and individual happiness. This happiness was subject to the rulers' duties to provide for the welfare of their subjects. The Jewish sages had stated that ethics arises as commandments, and what constituted the difference between ethically right and wrong behavior was the relations between individuals. They also claimed that the reasons for the commandments were primarily ethical, not philosophical.

In the Jewish tradition, from the days of the Bible to the present, learning and wisdom occupied a central position. There were historical differences among classical rabbis, sages, and mystics in their understanding of what comprises wisdom in Jewish religion and ethics. Yet they all agreed that wisdom consisted of attaining both the theoretical and the practical knowledge associated with the deepest interpretations of the Scriptures (Samuelson, 2001).

The ethical systems of Plato and Aristotle and their followers in Western philosophy and ethics had a different approach. They based their theories on the ancient Greek concept of *eudaemonia*. As stated previously, this concept stressed the idea of maximization of individual happiness as a moral end to the pursuit of knowledge. They saw in happiness a major motivating force in the lives of the individuals. They insisted on personal independence as a primary value. According to their philosophy, the more independent a person was, meaning prosperous, the less he or she was prone to be dependent on others. This is why in early Greek philosophy one cannot find rules about such issues as caring for the poor, the widow and the orphan, as one does in the Bible.

Two foundations comprise the philosophy of Plato: the good and the beautiful and knowledge and morality. About the former Plato wrote:

> The good and the beautiful are one, and perfection is knowledge. Man rises above the sensual world by yearning for the beautiful. He rises from the material and perceptual world to the unseen and the immaterial world of the ideas and to the highest ideal—the ideal of the good. For the human soul is eternal. It perceives, before taking on a body, the unseen and immaterial world, and after descending from it to the seen and material world it yearns for the higher world from which it came. And when it looks at material beauty it remembers "beauty for itself" which it has seen prior to being born, and it has great yearnings for its heavenly birthplace. Thus it approaches this heavenly world, the world of ideas. (as cited in Kloisner, 1960, p. 234)

These yearnings, these cravings, are the "philosophical urge." This is the platonic love in which the soul is yearning to rise from the sensual world to the world above it. This is the "real Eros," the son of heavenly Aphrodite, not the general or popular Aphrodite, for to love beautiful things is one thing, but to love "beauty for itself" is another.

According to Plato, describing the other version of Eros, "Eros is not a god but a demon that is a middle creature between what is eternal and what is mortal. The same holds true for the soul. It stands between the natural world and the supernatural, and through its wish to move from ignorance to perfect wisdom it arrives at the love of wisdom, at philosophy" (*Encyclopaedia Hebraica,* 1960, p. 231).

Plato's concept of Eros contains two fundamentally different kinds of love: One is the desire to give birth to beauty, such as in the case of heterosexual parents who wish to produce children, and the other is

Eros as virtue, such as platonic love. Platonic love in the modern sense is an affectionate relationship between two people in which sexual attraction is nonexistent. This second type of love is the true embodiment of Eros as the "heavenly Aphrodite," or love for love's sake.

Plato's first kind of love, the desire for beauty, is a love that seeks the image of the divine, which can bring out the opposite side of Eros: the demonic. Plato has emphasized that Eros as a demon, as the embodiment of erotic impulses, can undergo sublimination due to its plasticity, a view Freud adopted in his theory of psychoanalysis. However, Freud's transference love can be harnessed in psychoanalytically based psychotherapy to produce cure in various types of disturbances in behavior.

Plato's Eros as demon is an incorporeal being requiring human respect to ensure its favor, for it is capable of good and evil. A demon can be a divine sign given to an individual, or it can be a guardian spirit that acts as one's conscience. Eros as demon is artfully depicted in Adrian Leverkühn's demonic music in Thomas Mann's *Doctor Faustus,* and it is also apparent in Paganini's playing of the violin. Their music could be heavenly, seductive, and full of beauty, but it could also destroy a human being. The power of music to exorcise demons was already known and noted in biblical times in the story of King Saul's fits of depression and melancholy that could be cured or at least eased by music played on David's harp.

As a connection exists between the good and the beautiful, so does a connection exist between knowledge and morals. Philosophy, meaning the love of wisdom, is education for life. Philosophy is not philosophizing about dialectics, nor is it gaining practical knowledge, scientific education, or sophistication; it is the basis and foundation of the state, therefore the rulers must be philosophers or philosophers should be the rulers.

CHRISTIAN AND BUDDHIST PERSPECTIVES ON ETHICS

The ethical and philosophical attitudes of Maimonides and Spinoza to human life found an unexpected echo in the writings of Albert Schweitzer, one of the foremost humanists and winner of the Nobel Peace Prize in 1953. His book, published in 1999, is titled *Respect for*

Life (Schweitzer, 1999). Schweitzer has summarized his views on ethical problems in our times in terms similar to those of Maimonides. His book is very useful to the practicing helping professional because he discusses the ways in which one can successfully deal with the problems emanating from ethically wrong ways of thinking.

Schweitzer thought that it was necessary to follow the following three guidelines in order to adhere to the right path in life:

1. Not to engage in moral judgment about the world. Here one can find the influence of the Stoic attitude on his or her thinking.
2. Not to perceive the world in pessimistic terms, but to make every effort to discover the secret of the psyche.
3. Not to sink into abstract thinking about human beings, but to be ready to help all creatures with whom one comes into contact.

According to Schweitzer, ethics is created when we think positively about the world, about life, and about the need to fulfill our goals and dreams. To be an ethical human being means to be a thinking person. Thinking is a dialogue between the will hidden in a person and his or her consciousness, and all real consciousness is experience. Such consciousness comes into being in the inner world of the individual, in his or her inner will to live, and in his or her recognition that other human beings also wish to live. Thus the connection to the world is established, and respect for other human beings is formed. To be an ethical being, Schweitzer claims, means refraining from harming others and helping all in need.

Schweitzer's ethics is typically Christian, although Jewish ethical approaches to life and remnants of early Greek philosophy are involved. It can therefore serve as a representative model of Christian culture in the world. One can find in Schweitzer's teachings the influence of the philosopher Immanuel Kant (1724-1804), who thought that sacrifice, experience, personal interest, and theoretical knowledge could not serve as the basis for morals or ethics. Our deeds must be based on selfless interest and on a real sense of responsibility, and they should be anchored in certain values, chief among which is humankind itself. That is why in his "categorical imperative," or ethical command, one should act in such a way that humankind will be always the goal and never the means.

When Christianity became the dominant religion in Europe and later in the world its philosophical attitude toward life and morals were accepted by all the Christian nations. The founders of the Church adopted the Jewish biblical heritage along with their own perception of God and humankind, and did not create a new method of ethics. They built their moral teachings on the equality of humans, on the "original sin," and on God's judgment of the deeds of human beings as good or bad in the world to come. The most important Christian values include love of God and humankind, love of one's fellow human, modesty, patience, obedience, resignation, and mercy.

In Schweitzer's philosophy, the ethics of respect for life expresses the deepest religious will of men without turning it into a worldview and without perceiving resignation of riches and fame or honor as a resignation of one's independence. Schweitzer thinks that real ethics begins when we stop speaking about it and start to act toward its fulfillment. The ethics of respect for life is in an eternal dispute with reality. It cannot stop the conflicts, but it can force one to decide in every instance whether one wishes to remain ethical.

Conflicts between a person and society stem from the recognition that one has not only personal responsibility but responsibility beyond oneself: responsibility for one's fellow human. Schweitzer emphasizes that ethics exists as long as humanity exists, as long as we take into consideration the existence of others and their happiness. Where no humanity exists, no ethics exist.

THE ETHICS OF THE DALAI LAMA

Schweitzer's attitude to ethics has been reinforced by His Holiness the Dalai Lama. In one of his recent books: *Ethics for the New Millennium* (Dalai Lama, 1999), he discusses the foundations of ethics and explains the troubles that befell men in the modern era as the results of wealth and comfort, especially in the richest countries in the world, and as the price paid for neglecting the spiritual and emotional life. He maintains that all problems of individual behavior are in fact ethical problems. They reflect our perception of good and bad, right and wrong, positive and negative, proper and improper, and particularly the neglect of man's inner life.

The Dalai Lama claims that it is impossible to solve the external problems, such as violence, aggression, wars, and delinquency, and the internal problems of mental suffering, anxiety, depression, confusion, and so on without relating to this neglect. Therefore the Dalai Lama suggests a spiritual revolution, but not necessarily a religious one. It is not important to consider whether one is religious or secular when one takes into consideration that of the six billion people on earth who belong to various religions only one sixth of them could be called religious in the true sense of the word. Therefore it is much more important that an individual be a good human being than a religious person.

The spiritual revolution that the Dalai Lama refers to is a call to people everywhere to turn to the community rather than to themselves. For only in the community can one solve personal ethical problems. If we are able to exploit the special traits and characteristics of humankind, such as love and care for another human being, and if we are able to overcome the harmful instincts in ourselves, then we have made a big step forward toward ethical life. The starting point is based on wisdom rather than on religious belief, and that means that it will be possible to create binding ethical principles when we recognize that all human beings wish to live happy lives and avoid suffering and pain. This simple truth is the difference between right and wrong. If we do not adhere to the consideration of the suffering of other people and of their feelings and wishes for a happy life, if we do not respect their right to achieve their wish, we will not be able to arrive at the same goal. Whether or not a certain act is ethical or not is dependent on its result and on its influence on the happiness of others.

The Dalai Lama teaches that an act is ethical when it meets the Tibetan term of *kon lung,* meaning something that comes from the depth of one's heart that fills one with enthusiasm and expresses one's total commitment to life. If we relate to others and to life thus, then we can speak about a real revolution, about an ethical revolution.

THE ETHICS OF GANDHI

An altogether different approach to ethics was offered and practiced by the great humanist, social activist, and distinguished leader of modern-day India, Mahatma Gandhi. His whole life was built on a constant search for truth. He inspired many great scholars in sociology, psychology, and social work by his attitude to the problems inherent in living in a global context, including the struggle with the forces of imperialism, capitalism, and materialism. Yet, above all these, his ethical position, and particularly his relentless pursuit of social justice and freedom, won him the admiration, and at times the scorn, of millions all over the world. The following is a brief explication of the main ideas contained in his philosophy and ethics that can be valuable to professionals in the helping professions in general and in social work, nursing, and even medicine in particular. Whether or not he should serve also as a role model for practitioners in these professions is a question that requires more study and exploration in today's materialistic world.

Irrespective of where one stands in relation to Gandhi's personality and personal life, as well as to his ideas on ecology and world peace, the principles he has promulgated offer a rich source for thought and perhaps even an alternative approach to the ethics of the Western model that is prevalent and dominant in many parts of the world. One of the striking facts about the life of Gandhi and his attitude toward ethics is the ability he showed in combining both levels of intervention, micro and macro, in integrating social service with social action. His nonviolent method in seeking out and achieving his goals is legendary. Although he struggled against unjust rules, laws, and institutions, and demanded their reform or abolition, Gandhi was acting within the law. This seeming contradiction in his behavior stemmed from his devotion to social justice and service to others. Both of these mainstays of his philosophy were similar to Jewish, Christian, and Buddhist ethics.

In fact, Gandhi's whole life can be compared to that of Schweitzer and of the Dalai Lama. Each of these great philosophers and religious personalities lived in accordance with their ethical perspectives and principles concerning human beings as spiritual entities. Each personified what is noble in human behavior and what can provide inspiration for millions, including professional practitioners, yet neither went to the same degree of extremism as did Gandhi to achieve his personal ambition. His actual behavior helped to subdue a great empire, a feat that no other philosopher could claim.

Gandhi's ethical stance is different from the Western ethical theory and practice of utilitarianism, which originated in the Greek concept of teleology. As stated before, this utilitarian concept is still based on the idea of a democracy in which the greatest good should be given to the greatest number in society, disregarding in the process the needs of the minority, i.e., all those who do not happen to fall into the majority. For Gandhi this kind of social justice was unthinkable. He wanted to see a world in which the only inequality that could be justified was that which favors the most disadvantaged. This is a different kind of distributive justice from the one advocated in the utilitarian theory. He wanted to see justice for the most vulnerable first and freedom and well-being for all the oppressed, and he preferred to act on the basis of feelings rather than on logic alone.

Many concepts from his philosophy were accepted and incorporated into the Code of Ethics for Social Workers (NASW, 1997). They can also be traced back to the great religions of the world, which Gandhi studied for many years. Among his most important principles based on his personal philosophy we should mention those of cooperation rather than competition, interdependence rather than individualism, and compassion for others rather than pursuit of self-interest (Walz and Ritchie, 2000).

Truth is a central theme in Gandhi's conceptual system. Gandhi advocated truthful relationships among human beings. Such a relationship should be built on love and on positive acts of body, speech, and mind. He viewed people as basically kindhearted, as human beings armed with inner resources. Hence they can understand other people and refrain from harming them. In truthful relationships one has to be absolutely honest with oneself and with one's fellow human beings. Truthful relationships are expressions of unconditional love— the opposite of manipulation and deception. Such relationships should require physicians, for example, to tell the truth to patients about their condition and their chances of regaining their health without consideration of the potential harm of telling the truth in certain cases. Gandhi even went so far in his approach to truth telling as to claim that even one's opponent has the right to be informed of all of one's intentions and future actions to allow for dialogue and response (Walz and Ritchie, 2000).

Sethi (1979) emphasized in his book on Gandhi's philosophy and ethics that the essence of his approach was humankind, both as individuals and as social beings. In Gandhi's views, a person is the maker of his or her own destiny. One has freedom of choice regarding how to use that freedom. Therefore, one should listen to and utilize one's inner voice, not find a guru to chart a course of life. A person should engage in a life of service to others—an important element in Gandhi's philosophy and ethical standpoint. The social work profession discussed in this book is a service-based profession. Serving is closely connected to notions of justice. Service for Gandhi meant personal development, a moral preference. Through service one can attain the spiritual needs to develop his or her own self, an idea that resembles Maimonides' "perfection of the soul" as the purpose for human existence.

Perhaps the most difficult part in Gandhi's philosophy for Western professionals is his insistence on material simplicity and a moderation in consumption. His idea of moderation is far from the ancient Greek philosophers Plato and Aristotle's ideas about the same concept. It also is different from Maimonides' concept of the "middle of the road" and avoidance of all extremes in behavior. Gandhi not only thought and taught his concept of moderation to others, but he actually lived by this principle. He saw all excesses in material possessions as harmful to one's soul. In his own attitude toward life he believed that material simplicity leads to a spiritual life, for consuming only the minimum of what one actually needs enables others to share in the abundance of what the world produces.

Gandhi's concept of material simplicity as an ethical standard seems almost impossible in our materialistic world, particularly in the developed countries. Few professionals, if any at all, would opt for the kind of poverty in which Gandhi voluntarily lived, yet his life and thoughts give professionals abundant material to think about. It can, and perhaps should, stimulate debates about what, if anything, to include in the code of ethics of the social work profession in terms of service, global responsibilities for the welfare and health of people everywhere, and the redistribution of wealth, in theory and in practice.

"Gandhi as a person," wrote missionary E. Stanley Jones in his tribute to Gandhi, "apart from the embodiment of certain principles, is comparatively unimportant. He can be dismissed. But Gandhi brought to focus in himself universal principles, inherent in our moral universe. Those principles are as inescapable as the law of gravitation. Gandhi in falling was like Newton's apple falling, illustrating something universal" (as cited in Sethi, 1979, p. 48).

THE ETHICS OF MARTIN LUTHER KING JR.

Gandhi's philosophy and ethics found their powerful echo in the life, work, and social mission of one of the greatest philosophers, figures, and spiritual leaders of the twentieth century, the Reverend Martin Luther King Jr., who is rightly regarded by all African Americans and by others as the foremost fighter and guiding spirit in the struggle for racial justice. In his thirty-nine years of life, cut short by assassination, he achieved eternal fame and respect and was awarded the Nobel Prize for Peace in 1964.

Although King wrote and published six books and many articles and speeches during his short life, he is mainly remembered as a powerful orator. His most important speech, his "I have a dream" speech, was delivered in August 1963, when he led a march of more than two hundred thousand people to Washington's Lincoln Memorial. In this famous speech he urged the nation to rise up and live out the true meaning of its creed, that all men are created equal. The campaigns he led, states Clarkin (2000), paved the way for legal changes that ended more than a century of racial segregation.

Born in Atlanta, Georgia in 1929, and ordained in the Christian ministry in 1948, King was influenced in his attitude to social problems by, besides the Bible, many great philosophers, such as Socrates (470-399 BC) and Kant (1724-1804), and he learned much from modern day theologians such as Reinhold Niebuhr (1892-1971) and from social scientists such as Karl Marx (1818-1883). His ethics and social philosophy were further influenced by several well-known black leaders who became famous for their fight against the discrimination and segregation of black people in the United States. Among the latter was W. E. B. Du Bois, a rather controversial, yet widely respected leader among mainstream black reformers whose personal and literary contribution to black liberation left their mark on King's life.

Du Bois was credited by one of his biographers, Broderick (1959), with two major accomplishments: his struggle for and emphasis on equal rights for African Americans and his lifting of the morale of black people everywhere.

King basically agreed with Du Bois that the biggest problem of the twentieth century was the "color line," meaning the visible barrier that prevented blacks from attaining equal rights politically, economically, and educationally up to 1968. Yet, whereas this color line in Du Bois's approach resulted in an identity crisis characterized by "twoness"—an American and a Negro, with two souls, two thoughts, and two sets of desires—King saw in the color line one of the reasons for the blatant injustice to which his people were subjected. King was aware that this injustice had its deeper roots in the national and international economy and in the final years before his death he began to attack them directly (Boxill, 2001).

Du Bois believed that education was the best means to achieve parity with the white majority in every area of life. Therefore he proposed to create a body of black professionals, "The Talented Tenth," to serve as leaders for the community. In Du Bois's eyes, these people owed a debt to their own race and society, and in particular to their ancestors, for the sacrifices they made to advance the black community. The way to repay this debt was by dedicating their lives to improving the conditions of the black people as a whole. This work, Du Bois believed, would give meaning to the lives of the Talented Tenth. Their task was to serve as the guiding forces that would eventually lift the masses out of poverty, ignorance, and disease.

In his most influential book, *Why We Can't Wait* (1964), King openly disagreed with Du Bois's approach to racial injustice in America. Whereas Du Bois urged the Talented Tenth, the elites of black society, to rise and pull behind them the masses of the race, King saw in this tactic one that would benefit only the aristocratic elite while leaving behind the "untalented" 90 percent. King's attitude to the Talented Tenth was similar to the attitude black female social workers had toward it in the first half of the twentieth century and up to World War II. These women devoted their energies to breaking down the barriers that thwarted their development as black women, socially and professionally. They had no interest in forming a "talented tenth" body of black females to lift up the less fortunate. According to Martin and Martin (2002), these women had deep "spiritual strivings to break from old oppressive gender barriers and become a mass, potent, radical force for communal action and social change" (p. 166).

King looked for a different approach, for one that would benefit and be applicable to all. He found this approach in the history of the early Christians and, in particular, in the philosophy and methods employed by Gandhi against the oppression and brutality of the occupiers in India.

Gandhi's emphasis on using only peaceful means to combat oppression was crucial in King's own nonviolent resistance to evil. He used this as his method for achieving social reform. King saw evil in all injustice and insisted that people have a moral obligation to refuse to cooperate with evil. He found that nonviolent resistance and particularly civil disobedience were the best means, both morally and practically. He incorporated them in his struggle for justice. King knew that "nonviolent direct action did not originate in America, but it found its natural home in this land, where refusal to cooperate with injustice was an ancient and honorable tradition" (Martin and Martin, 2002, p. 14).

In King's perception, "the miracle of nonviolence lies in the degree to which people will sacrifice under its inspiration, when the call is based on judgment" (Martin and Martin, 2002, p. 36).

Civil disobedience was defined by Barker (1987) in the *Social Work Dictionary* as:

> noncompliance with a government's laws or demands, usually to call attention to those laws that are considered unfair and to bring about changes or concessions in them. Civil disobedience often takes the form of group actions, such as marches and assemblies; deliberate nonpayment of taxes and obstruction of the free movement of others. (p. 25)

One of the major tactics used in civil disobedience is passive resistance, defined by Barker (1987) as:

> a nonviolent form of social activism in which individuals and groups stop using or cooperating with the institutions to which they object. For example, in the late 1950s, when blacks in the South objected to the rule requiring them to sit in the back of buses, they banded together in refusing to ride the buses. Without direct confrontation, the movement passively but effectively resisted the objectionable policy. (p. 117)

Another means advocated by King for achieving legal and social equality was the economic boycotts used successfully by Gandhi. King found these means effective because they strengthened the bonds within the community. He was also aware that nonviolence requires a level of courage and self-discipline, but also contributes to the participants' self-esteem. King knew from personal experience that those who engage in civil disobedience must accept the consequences of their behavior, including imprisonment, for he was incarcerated in the Birmingham city jail on that very same charge.

As founding president of the Southern Christian Leadership Conference, King used the tactics of civil disobedience and led the marches that resulted in the Civil Rights Act of 1964 and the Voting Rights Act of 1965 that changed the attitude of the white majority to racial segregation and exclusion of African Americans from political and social life once and for all. In his "Letter from Birmingham Jail," included in King's book *Why We Can't Wait* (1964) and subsequently reprinted in several national magazines, King articulated the principles of nonviolent resistance and refuted the argument that he was an "outside agitator." King stated: "all people are bound in an inextricable network of mutuality. Therefore injustice anywhere is a threat to justice everywhere" (King, 1964, p. 79).

King's deepest convictions are not currently popular in a largely secularized profession, says Boxill (2001, p. 951). His concept of a just society lying somewhere between capitalism and communism needs further investigation. King was convinced that a just society would become reality only when African Americans assumed their rightful place as equals in society, when they would have the same opportunities as their fellow citizens, and when the legacy of racial discrimination would completely disappear from America and elsewhere in the world.

King's ethics may best be illustrated by the story of his meeting with Prime Minister Nehru of India. They were talking about the difficult problem of the "untouchables" and the attempts of the Indian government to find a solution for the problem by way of "reverse discrimination" as atonement for the centuries of injustices. Although insisting that the United States must also seek its own ways of atoning for the injustices inflicted upon African-American citizens, King did not advocate such an approach for atonement's sake, nor as a means for self-punishment, but as the moral and practical way to bring the African-American standards up to a realistic level (King, 1964, p. 148).

Chapter 2

Theories of Ethics

It is hard to erect ethical theories, for it is difficult to imagine one theory that you can't change it in a given situation in order for the theory to be a matter of authority.

C. G. Jung (1954)

The task of an ethical theory is to give people clear ideas about the overall goal of achieving happiness in their lives and the ways to gain it. The main objective of ethics is to determine what is right, what is good, and what should be done to live an ethical life, meaning a good life. There are several approaches in ethics toward these central questions, each of which tries to serve as a compass for moral acts. Ethical theories try to explain the causes of ethical behavior and the criteria by which we can determine what is a right or a wrong act.

Greek theories of ethics are basically virtue oriented. They are perfectionist and idealistic in their character. They have definite conceptions of what is good for everyone and toward what people should strive to in order to obtain the good life. Annas (2002), a well-known scholar in ancient and modern conceptions of *eudaemonia* and well-being, defined virtue as:

> a developed disposition of the agent to choose and do the right action for the right reason, with the right response to the situation. The person who does the right thing but has to force himself to do it is not yet virtuous, in any ancient theory . . . Moreover, ancient virtue is moral virtue, the disposition to be brave, just, generous and the like, and virtue is in ancient theories the locus of what we call morality. (pp. 2-3)

Ethics in Social Work: A Context of Caring
© 2006 by The Haworth Press, Inc. All rights reserved.
doi:10.1300/5577_03

Different theories of ethics disagree mainly about the method of living a good life and about the final end of man's effort to attain the most valuable life. What is common to all theories of ethics is that they try to erect principles by which we can accept or reject various deeds. In the center of each theoretical approach to ethics is the question of which criteria will help us to determine whether or not an act is moral or immoral, or simply good or bad. Good and bad are controversial concepts, and before we make such a decision whether or not a certain problem requires an ethical solution, we must know the facts pertaining to the specific problem and clarify the relevant concepts. Relying on the rules and the guidelines of a given society does not necessarily constitute a moral act, for such rules can be bad, immoral, and unjust, and can even hurt the welfare of the public.

Opposing approaches to ethical theories exist. At one end of the spectrum we find a very extreme approach that negates the possibility of knowing what is good or bad, and at the other end is dogmatism or dogmatic belief, which negates all theoretical effort and rejects any view that opposes its own. Those who adhere to the first approach doubt everything and do not believe in the possibility of knowing the good in moral terms, whereas the latter accept only what is religiously or ideally in line with their belief and cling to it even when reality contradicts it. Both of these approaches to ethics narrow one's worldview and are not useful for helping professionals in their quest to find a just and uniform approach to the needs of the individual and society.

Philosophical ethics, or moral philosophy, tries to base its concepts and principles on a universal basis and is unwilling to accept any dogma as the desirable solution. One can find in the foundation of professional behavior of physicians and social workers principles and rules that guide the profession. These are based on theories of ethics that try to enhance rational behavior, rather than on religious dogma.

In social work, four valid principles of bioethics stem from the Hippocratic oath of antiquity, of which more will be said later in Chapter 13. The following are the four principles:

1. *Beneficence:* According to this principle the social worker must do what is good and useful to the patient or client.
2. *Nonmaleficence:* This principle means that the social worker should not harm the client.

3. *Justice:* According to this principle the social worker must adhere to what is just and respect justice.
4. *Autonomy:* This principle means that social workers should respect the right of the client to self-determination in matters of their own health and life.

Controversies exist in various cultures in the world, and even in different socioeconomic levels within a given culture regarding the definition of ethical behavior. Even the ethics of the helping professions is not uniform. Each profession has its own rules about what constitutes ethical or unethical behavior within a given profession. Professional identities are grounded in ethical perspectives and moral principles, which guide professionals in their decisionmaking regarding what is appropriate or inappropriate conduct vis-à-vis the colleague or client.

Blasszauer (1995), a respected physician and medical ethicist in Hungary, lists six approaches to ethics that are relevant for the helping professions: The religious or theological, the intuitive or hedonistic, deontology, teleology, the golden rule, and the ethics of situations. During the past decades these six approaches were condensed for the most part into two: deontology—as per the great philosopher Immanuel Kant—and teleology. These are the approaches used in various parts of the world in solving ethical dilemmas. Before concentrating on these two ruling theories in ethics we shall briefly discuss the theological approach, the first theory about morals from which all other theories of ethics emanate.

THE THEOLOGICAL APPROACH

The theological approach represents the common denominator of all religious streams based on belief in one God (or in several Gods). Attitudes to ethics and morals are reflected in the sacred declarations, laws, prophesies, and rules of conduct in writing and in oral tradition that are handed down from one generation to the next. In all monotheistic religions one can find love of God and one's fellow human as a major subject; and even if their attitudes to ethics is dissimilar, common to all of them is a perception of ethics as God's command, meaning that good and bad is judged by God. The prize awarded to those who do good and the punishment for those who do bad are included in this approach, and it serves to coerce people to do what is good in the eyes of God. In the Jewish religion for example, the fifth commandment declares: "Honor your father and your mother to lengthen your days upon the earth your God gave you" (Exodus 20:12). Here one finds the prize of those who fulfill this commandment—in longevity.

All the monotheistic religions place an emphasis on morals, and particularly on virtues, values, and love and respect for fellow humans. Common to all these religions is that they investigate and explain morals without reference to reality or to the social processes that are prevalent in a given society at a certain historical time, and they do not offer a rational explanation why evil, injustice, and violence exist in the world. Is it possible that God can be merciless? In his book *Good and Evil* Buber (1953) maintains that questions exist that are impossible to answer, such as, "How can evil exist when God exists? (p. 60).

According to the ethicist and philosopher Frankena (1973), theological theories determine what is considered the final criteria of moral behavior, or the ethical value that is created as a result of an action. Therefore, a certain action is good only if it creates more good than bad, and an action that will not create more good than bad is bad. The helping professions are interested in creating more good than bad, and all of them wish to see social justice as envisioned by the prophets. In social work, emphasis is placed on "normative ethics" because of its direct relevance to practice. Reamer (1999) claims that theories connected to normative ethics comprise the two main groups of theories in ethics mentioned previously, deontology and teleology, by creating norms of behavior generally accepted as ethically right, proper, and good.

THE INTUITIVE OR HEDONISTIC APPROACH

The intuitive approach to ethics claims that all "common men" are able to recognize by intuition or by keen visual perception, and without rational thinking, what is a good action or a bad one in terms of morals. Yet, it is impossible to base this approach on science or logical theory and to explain what makes such an action good or bad.

Some two thousand and four hundred years ago in ancient Greece there appeared a new ethical approach. Its main component was the notion that a morally good deed leads to a feeling of happiness and joy. This was the hedonistic approach to ethics. Among the philosophers who adopted this approach was Epicurus who lived between the years 314 and 270 BC. This philosopher declared that, even if a person wishes to attain happiness and pleasure, he or she must refrain from the extreme pursuit of bodily pleasures. For Epicurus, spiritual pleasures were far better than sensual ones, for they last longer. The great Roman philosophers, such as Seneca and Cicero, followed Epicurus and said that peace of mind, serenity, friendship, and harmonious relationships with others are spiritual pleasures open to all people.

In his wonderful book, *De Senectute (On Old Age),* Cicero claimed: "pleasure hinders thought, is a foe to reason and, so to speak, blinds the eyes of the mind. It is, moreover, entirely alien to virtue" (Cicero, 1909, p. 60).

THE DEONTOLOGICAL APPROACH
OF IMMANUEL KANT

Deontology stems from two Greek words, *deontos* and *Logos.* The first word means duty, the second knowledge or science. Deontology is, therefore, the ethical theory of moral obligations and duties. For example, is used to denote medical ethics in Turkish medical schools (Erdemir, 1995). In the religious attitude to ethics, deontology means the duties commanded by God. The term was first used by the philosopher Jeremy Bentham in his book *Deontology, or the Science of Morality* published in 1834 (see Kelly, 1990).

Deontology existed long before Kant, the famous philosopher who turned moral obligation into an important ingredient of his philosophy. Honoring God's commandments, irrespective of existing conditions, the happiness of the individual or even of the community is the theoretical basis of Kant's deontology. In this sense, this approach to ethics is different from those of Epicurus or Cicero. The latter philosophers saw in happiness, pleasures, joys, and particularly in spiritual pleasures the final purpose of human life. Kant created the principle of "categorical imperative," which meant for him that a human being must act in principle so that his action can become a universal rule. His categorical imperative validates the law (moral) formally and absolutely. In his deontology only what can be judged by objective, universal rules can be called good or bad. Kant maintained that the human being is a rational entity. One is capable of creating one's own norms of ethical behavior. If this is indeed true, then the theory of morality is rational and any theory can gain universal validity.

If we accept Kant's approach as necessary and sufficient for normative ethics in the helping professions, then searching for other theories of ethics is unnecessary, for the moral law obligates the individual unconditionally. Thus a physician, for example, who accepts Kant's deontology as binding, believes that killing a fetus is an immoral act in itself, irrespective of circumstances, even if such an act may lead to the survival of the mother.

The same rule applies to the social worker and the doctor telling the truth to a client or patient. According to the theory of Kant, truth telling is always right. Similarly, keeping a promise given to a client or patient is necessary as per Kantian deontology, and the same applies to keeping contracts made with clients and patients, colleagues, and organizations. Deontology negates the prevalent approach that the goal sanctifies the means, especially when the means violate the law or the right of the human being.

Several problems are related to deontology. One of them refers to the language we use regarding what is right or improper, basically or as a matter of fact. Ethical conflicts can be created that are difficult to solve. For example, in the case of the doctor who is loyal to the deontological approach to ethics, and therefore will not kill the fetus in order to save the life of the mother when medically no other solution exists, the right of the patient to self-determination was not considered.

Frankena (1973) argued that Kant's reasons for keeping a promise are not always reasonable and convincing. Moreover, one cannot disregard the conflicts that can arise between opposing duties. Sometimes, keeping a promise can prevent the doctor or the social worker from giving the necessary help to the client or the patient, for example, a doctor who promises to tell the patient the truth about his or her health but is afraid that the truth will lead to the patient's suicide. Furthermore, the laws and regulations of a country or a society are not always sufficiently clear or precise and may at times conflict with each other. Some laws may be simply immoral, such as discrimination on a religious, racist, or political basis.

THE TELEOLOGICAL APPROACH

The second major group of theories in ethics more prevalent today than deontology is the teleological, or the utilitarian, approach. This group of ethics stems from the ancient Greek concept of *telos,* meaning to bring something to its end or final goal. The roots of the utilitarian approach are also embedded in hedonistic philosophy, according to which the ethical value of a certain act is dependent on its utility, and the utility itself is expressed in the result that should be the best one in the short term.

Utilitarianism is the most prominent consequence-based theory. The classical origins of this theory are found in the writings of Jeremy Bentham (1748-1832) and John Stuart Mill (1806-1873). Problems with this theory include immoral preferences and actions, for example, obligatory suicides by frail elderly, or obligatory donation of body parts such as kidneys or livers by the sick for the benefit of the healthy majority. Still another problem in this theory is unjust distribution of social resources, especially in cases in which the interest of the majority overrides the rights of the minorities (Beauchamp and Childress, 1994).

As a theory in ethics, the utilitarian approach emphasizes that the economic resources of a society should be distributed in such a way that they will bring the greatest good to the largest number of people. This theory aims at correcting several shortcomings of the deontological approach. It wishes to enhance the good for others too, not only for the individual. It is based on the question: Which act will advance the greatest good over the bad?

Frankena (1973), among others, differentiated the following three kinds of utility:

- *Act utility,* in which the central question is: What influence or result will my act exert on the balance between the good and the bad?
- *Overall utility,* in which the central question is: What will happen if all people behave in such and such a way? For example, if all physicians and social workers become private practitioners?

- *Legal utility,* in which the central question is: Which laws will advance the general good for everybody? This is the main question in social policymaking. For example, what benefits should be given to families with large numbers of children, or with elderly parents?

Reamer (1999) claims that some philosophers who adhere to utilitarian theory in ethics are naive to think that decision making can be ethical without first considering the possible results of such a decision. Therefore, the responsible approach is to try to envision the results of a certain action before doing it. "The ethics of actions" sees all actions that cause pleasure or happiness and prevent pain and suffering as being both ethical and moral.

Two versions of this theory exist: The utility of the acts and legal utility. According to the former, if a certain act promises the best results then it is right, irrespective of whether or not it violates a social law. The latter says that the properness of an act is determined in relation to the social law that stands as a criterion. The ethical purpose of the act determines not only the personal happiness of the individual who makes it but also the common good for a society.

Any act that benefits the greatest possible number of people is considered good from the perspective of the society. Thus the social worker or the doctor need always to weigh which act will benefit the greatest number of people. This approach to ethics sounds good, but it brings in its wake many dangers. For example, who decides what is best for the majority of the people, or what act will lead to the greatest happiness for them? Is it possible to make such a decision at all? What about the happiness of the minority? How can one envision and evaluate the future happiness and utility due to a certain act?

Reamer (1999) said that it is possible to use the utilitarian approach to ethics to justify opposing approaches to the "common good." He gave an illustration in which a social worker needed to decide whether to notify the authorities about a client who made unlawful use of the money received for the welfare of his family. The question raised from the perspective of the utilitarian approach is whether the utility the client receives from the fraud is equal to the laws of society or superior to them.

A main problem in the utilitarian approach to ethics pertains to different people bringing their worldview and the education they received in their respective cultures into their considerations regarding the rightness or wrongness of a certain act. Critics of the utilitarian approach, such as Zarday (1987, as quoted in Blasszaver, 1995), claim, for example, that:

> The utilitarian approach is a poor principle regarding the distribution of scarce medical resources and their use. This approach is prone to lead to serious inequality and cause substantial harm to individuals and minorities in society if it will treat the individual as "the average man" in the community. The utilitarian approach causes dehumanization in medicine and in other areas. (p. 6)

THE THEORY OF MORAL COMMITMENT

Both deontology and teleology are deficient and inadequate to serve as the most appropriate theories of ethics for the practicing professional. Both deal with moral judgments in concrete situations and are general in their natures, and both are based on subjective perceptions of what is good or bad. Ethical determinations are always relative to a particular historic time and people in specific circumstances. Samuelson (2001) said: "no matter how morality is to be judged, the judgments that is rendered is never merely opinion" (p. 225).

A theory of ethics that is based on a critic of the utilitarian approach was offered by Frankena (1973) in the 1970s. He called it "the theory of moral commitment." This theory is in fact a mixture of the two main groups of ethical theories: deontology and teleology. According to Frankena (1973), we have no moral obligation to do a thing, whether as a primary obligation (such as keeping a promise) or as a practical obligation (one that is actually right). Instead, we have to act as in the ethics of situations, meaning to do something that is not connected directly or indirectly to what makes a person's life good or bad. If not our deeds then at least our laws should have influence over the size of the good and the bad and on the balance between them, for morality exists to serve human beings—human beings do not exist to serve morality.

In the center of Frankena's (1973) theory is the principle of beneficence and justice, as mentioned previously in this book. Justice precedes utility, but no recipe or prescription can show when a certain act is just. These two principles together define the commitments of the helping professionals. Frankena is aware of the possible conflicts between the two principles and indicates that there is no satisfactory solution. These principles are prone to conflict with each other both at the individual and at the social policy level.

THE GOLDEN RULE APPROACH

In 1975 a Swiss physician, Peter Hammerly, was charged with committing passive euthanasia on ten elderly patients. He stopped the machines that supplied them with intravenous life support and thus caused their death. The doctor defended himself saying that he acted in accordance with the "golden rule" that is prevalent among physicians in medicine. He said that he never did anything wrong, never asked for any benefit from his patient, and never did anything that he would not have done for his mother or father if they would have been in a similar condition. He even added that if he were in the same situation as his former patients he would wish that his doctor would behave toward him in a similar manner (Russell, 1977).

The principle of the golden rule is based on the famous dictum of Rabbi Hillel: "What is hated by you, don't do to your friend." This same theory is proposed in Matthew 7:12 and Luke 6:31. Fletcher (1997) developed his theory of situational ethics in the late 1960s as a result of his critique of legalism and antinomianism. Legalism claims that fixed moral laws exist that are to be obeyed at all times. Antinomianism maintains the contrary, that is, that no fixed moral principles exist and one's ethics are spontaneous. Fletcher advocated a middle way between these two approaches to ethics. He maintained that "our obligation is relative to the situation; but obligation in situation is absolute" (p. 27).

Fletcher proposed a key principle with which to guide moral decision making: Rather than obeying rules one should act in the most loving way possible. In Fletcher's situational ethics emphasis is placed on the idea that people come first, not principles. His theory does not ignore the past, the tradition of the Christian heritage, but it is not entirely bound by it. Situational ethics contains six fundamental principles based on the concept of love. These principles are the following:

1. Love only is always good
2. Love is the only norm
3. Love and justice are the same
4. Love is not liking
5. Love justifies the means
6. Love decides there and then

The only time the law should be obeyed is if it serves the interest of love; law should never be obeyed for its own sake. Many doctors subscribe to this dictum and act in accordance with its message regarding ethical matters. Yet, even if that dictum expresses practical wisdom, it is insufficient as the norm in human relationships. Blasszauer (1995) explains that such a principle would negate the social moral, for each individual would be able to decide what is moral or immoral for him or herself. The golden rule can be accepted by people on the condition that both the person making and the person receiving the consequences of the decision agree to the decision.

SITUATIONAL ETHICS

The last among the various theories of ethics discussed so far is situational ethics. Many doctors call it "clinical ethics." They think that this is the only ethics that one can rely on in reality, in real practice, in which each ethical decision is dependent on the specific situation at hand. In the ethics of situations no principles or general guidelines guide the decision maker. Everything depends and is based on the immediate situation and on the existing conditions. Thus, for example, those who accept this approach to ethics would not negate, nor would they accept, the principles according to which they should decide whether or not to conduct an abortion.

The ethics of situations is an extreme one because it views any situation as unique and singular, and does not recognize any norm of behavior. Blasszauer (1995) notes that it is hard to deal with the singularity and the uniqueness of each case. The education and the experience of the decision maker will be influential. Criticism of situational ethics is based on the fact that it rejects professional rules and disregards universal morality.

This ethics does not recognize the existence of moral values and narrows down the value of morality in an extreme way. Situations exist in which it is impossible to make a decision according to only one's conscience. To base one's actions on one's conscience without reference to a body of knowledge is insufficient. The ethics of situations can become a real danger to the medical profession, for it allows one to escape from the rules of law and morality, and to engage in inconsistencies in decision making regarding the life of the patient.

A major problem with situational ethics is that it is impossible to foresee the long-term consequences of one's actions. Another problem is that decisions may be based on personal whims rather than on universally accepted moral norms. Ethical decisions cannot be based solely on love or solely on practical, functional, or ethnocentric values. One should always weigh whether an action is morally right or wrong before the action is taken. No love can make a wrong action right.

Chapter 3

Virtues

Every occupation and every investigation, as well as every action and decision seems evidently aims at some good. Therefore it is right that good is to which everything tends.

Aristotle

The word *virtue* is given to the specific human trait of extraordinary power or excellence accompanied by self-control and courage. All the great artists in music, painting, sculpting, dancing, and writing are called "virtuoso," meaning people with clearly recognizable character traits and talents that are good and outstanding. In old English, this word virtuous used to be given to the quality of a deed. It came to signify a human being who had a unique and significant talent, skill, aptitude, and/or ability. The wise, for example, were considered by all philosophers in antiquity to be virtuous because they were oriented toward wisdom, justice, and truthfulness.

The early Greek philosophers, Plato and Aristotle, thought of virtues as practical skills concerned with the mean between two extremes. Both of these great philosophers compared ethics with medicine. The former offered three junctures in which ethics and medicine may be compared. First he equated some moral defects with diseases. For Plato some diseases were said to be traceable to an imbalance of the four elements of the body. He distinguished between two diseases or disorders of the soul: madness and ignorance. The former he thought was caused by physical problems, and ignorance by a lack of proper education. Second, he equated goodness of the soul to the soundness and health of the body. Third, the knowledge of a skilled doctor was equated with knowledge the virtuous man has, using in all three comparisons the doctrine of the mean (Hutchinson, 1988).

Ethics in Social Work: A Context of Caring
© 2006 by The Haworth Press, Inc. All rights reserved.
doi:10.1300/5577_04

Plato has emphasized (in *The Republic*) that the four cardinal virtues of the soul (that were elaborated previously) can be compared with the three cardinal virtues of the body. These are health, strength, and beauty. Ignorance, one of the two major disorders of the soul, is a lack of symmetry, and is not analogous to disease. He saw in wisdom a form of virtue in that wisdom consists of having some kind of understanding, meaning that virtues were cognitive attainments. Since medicine is also a cognitive attainment, Plato considered virtue as comparable to medicine. In his virtue model of the physician-patient relationship the emphasis would be on the sort of character an ideal physician ought to have.

Two aspects of medicine were thought by Plato to be suitable for the previous analogue: first, medical science is based on analytical knowledge of the nature of life and of the elements of health and disease, and second, medicine aims at the mean in therapy and avoids what is insufficient or excessive (in accordance with Plato's doctrine of the mean).

Aristotle (1997), the ancient Greek philosopher, in his book *Ethica Nicomachea,* differentiated between intellectual virtues and moral virtues. The former is related to the results of education and teaching, and therefore it needs both time and experience, whereas the latter comes into being as a result of habit or custom. Virtues do not emanate from nature, but human beings are built by nature to be capable of acquiring and internalizing them. Aristotle has included in the intellectual virtues wisdom, foresight, and knowledge, while generosity of the heart and moderation were listed by him among the moral virtues. His method for examining whether or not a certain act is virtuous was explained in several of his writings, for example in *Ethica Nicomachea,* as "dialect." In this method the "ethicist" examines first the various views regarding the subject, both those of common opinion and the theories of the wise, then he or she compares these and determines what is right or wrong in each of the views. In most cases we find that some truth exists in each position, but without their having a clear definition and differentiation we cannot arrive at the truth.

Utilizing this method, for example in the fifth book of *Ethica Nicomachea,* regarding the subject of justice, we find that Aristotle wishes to know how *just* and *unjust* differ from each other. In what deeds are they expressed, and why does the just stand in the middle? He shows that the just refers to the psychic structure that serves as the basis for being able to do just deeds and engage in them, and whereas the unjust is the opposite. He compares the unjust person to someone who is greedy and favors an inequality that amounts to injustice. His opposite, then, is the just, who loves the law and equality. Therefore, most people agree that justice is the highest virtue, or is the virtue that contains all other virtues (Aristotle, 1997, p. 148).

VIRTUES IN EASTERN PHILOSOPHY

Virtues as concrete and pragmatic means for decent human life and as an integral part of Eastern philosophy were emphasized by Confucius (551-479 BC). According to his teachings, basic virtues exist that come into being in the relationships between ruler and clerk, father and son, older and younger siblings, husband and wife, and among friends. These are humanity, integrity, appropriateness, wisdom, and loyalty. If one wishes to lead a stable and moral life, one should begin by improving oneself. First one must attain insight in order to think frankly. This would lead one to a sincere heart, which is a prerequisite of the formation of good character. This in turn is the basis for proper family relationships. The ideal person in Confucius's teaching is wise and noble. One can attain this level through an education that encompasses both spirit and heart and leads toward true thinking.

A different approach to virtue in Eastern philosophy is represented by *Tao,* usually attributed to Lao Tzu's classical book *Tao Te Ching,* written sometime between the fifth and the third century BC. This book discusses the Tao, or way, and virtue as related to human life, and the basic principle that guides life and nature. The ruler and the sage are lead by the Tao and free themselves from all egoistic deeds. They conduct themselves according to the idea of "doing nothing." This does not mean that they refrain from doing anything, but rather that they do not interfere without need in the course of events. They limit their activities to what is absolutely essential for maintaining order in the state. The more laws that exist, they emphasize, the less virtue, or the real virtue is lost, for anybody who lives in accordance with ethics does not need rules and regulations. The wise, the sage, lives in simplicity and influences people with his or her apparent weakness. Therefore the sage is compared to water, which is necessary to all living creatures and, despite being soft, can be hurt by no hard thing (Kunzmann, Burkard, and Wiedmann, 1999).

VIRTUES AND CHARACTER IN SOCIAL WORK

The rise or death of a virtue both depend on the same reason and are achieved by the same means: behavioral habits. This rule applies to the performing arts and to mastering a certain craft or profession. Similarly, if we wish to become moral persons we need to develop morally good habits. One cannot become a good professional without properly and justly dealing with one's clients or patients. Furthermore, the purpose of virtue, according to Aristotle, is to be good people:

> Each state of character, Aristotle maintained, has its own ideas of the noble and the pleasant, and the good man differs from others, perhaps most of all, by seeing the truth in each class of things, being, as it were, the norm and standard. (Aristotle, 1997, 1113a31-1113a33)

The two great philosophers, Plato and Aristotle, differed in several aspects in their views of ethics in general. For Aristotle, virtue and the good person was the standard of everything and such a person was supposed to rely on a well developed perceptual ability to see what is appropriate. Such a person was also supposed to have the knowledge and skills that come from experience. To adopt a role, such as becoming a social worker or a doctor and working in the profession, is a voluntary act. It implies acceptance of all the responsibilities inherent in the role. Once such a commitment has been made, the stage is set. Of course one can act contrarily to the rules of the chosen profession, or engage in activities that the profession formally prohibits, but such behavior surely would be contrary to what is commonly accepted as virtue and excellence.

What constitutes excellence *(arete)*? Does a connection exist between this concept and the concept of "good"? To be good in something requires relevant virtue or excellence. In medicine, as in other helping professions, this means the development of an ingrained set of feelings and behaviors that tend to make us "act at the right times, on the right grounds, towards the right people, for the right motive and in the right way" (Aristotle, 1997, 1106b21-1106b23).

According to Aristotle's doctrine, virtue is acquired by training. The cultivation of virtue means a systematic modification and retraining of our desires and responses over a long period of time. Moreover, it means the adoption of a mind-set and commitment to the chosen profession. This attitude to one's chosen profession is beautifully expressed by Cottingham (1997) who says (in relation to medicine) that:

> To embark on a life structured by a host of commitments logically connected with the goal of promoting and preserving health. Once those commitments are made, and once the relevant emotional and behavioral dispositions have been cultivated, the ethical landscape is profoundly altered . . . This is what his life as a doctor is about; the goal of promoting the health of the patient is what gives meaning to his profession, what defines his job or function, and what provides the materials for the exercise of that professional excellence to which he aspires [that which makes a doctor a good doctor]. (Cottingham, 1997, pp. 137-138)

This is an important point to think of in social work. In this profession practical skills and knowledge are in parity with theoretical knowledge, particularly as they are the results of long periods of training and experience in the field, for without such training and experience theoretical knowledge would be useless.

Virtue is an acquired readiness to do what is good in both the intellectual and the applied sense. The good must be done rather than be discussed. Therefore the word *do-gooder,* which many people attach to social workers in jest, is in fact a word of praise as per the philosophers of antiquity. Virtue requires action, and the good person is one who not only beholds but also performs good deeds. Calculated virtue is only half virtue, said Smith (1944). Although it is true that virtue must be learned, it must also be based on spontaneity and on habit, until it becomes "second nature" for us (Smith, 1944, p. 5).

Living life according to virtue is the best proof that we are capable of overcoming our weaknesses and shortcomings and rising above ourselves for the sake of other human beings or certain ideals. Yet, whoever wishes to teach others about the virtues must be aware of their own weaknesses. Thus, the golden rule previously discussed in Chapter 2 is not meant to glorify mediocrity. On the contrary, virtue exemplifies the ideal situation compared to the "perfect good"—the true record of human existence.

CARDINAL VIRTUES

The ancient Greeks thought that people in positions of leadership, the servants of the public, needed to be equipped with four virtues. These they called *cardinal virtues*, or virtues of primacy. They were considered the central virtues that come from the heart. All other virtues are related to the cardinal virtues. First among the four virtues was *common sense*. It was not related to sophistication or to formal education, and had nothing to do with academic titles. Common sense meant the ability to learn from anybody and from any situation.

The second cardinal virtue was called *justice*. This virtue was not related to what people today think of as the justice of the courts, nor was it connected to any form of artificial or coerced justice. For the ancient Greeks justice as virtue meant the kind of justice that is a feeling deep down in our hearts, in accordance with which we differentiate between right and wrong, and decent and indecent acts.

Courage was the third cardinal virtue. The kind of courage they considered a cardinal virtue was not the courage of the battlefield, nor the courage that comes into being in situations that allow no other choice, nor the courage of recklessness and lack of restraint. Rather, courage as a virtue, for the Greeks, meant taking responsibility for our deeds.

The fourth cardinal virtue was *moderation*. This did not mean spontaneous reaction to drives and instincts, nor did it mean negation of ones fellow human just because they are different, but to refrain from extremity in action and in judgment.

In summary, we may see the four cardinal virtues as drives toward wisdom (common sense), equality in duties and rights (justice), fighting for principles and values (courage), and balance and self-discipline (moderation or temperance).

MAIMONIDES'S APPROACH TO VIRTUES

Maimonides (1135-1204), the great philosopher of the Middle Ages, considered virtues to be habits we need to develop and guide from early childhood on. His ethics are based on the scientific knowledge of his times, on the philosophy of the soul, and on metaphysics. In order to strengthen his approach to ethics, he adopted the theories of Aristotle regarding matter and form. According to these theories, sin, crime, and iniquity are formed by "matter," and the good and the virtuous by "form." Emotional wishes cause one to sin, and they are formed by the matter, whereas spiritual aspiration leads toward the virtues.

In Maimonides's "On the Management of Health" (Weiss and Butterworth, 1975), a letter he addressed to Saladin's son al-Afdal the sultan in Cairo, Egypt, as his doctor, he explained the methods of dealing with both physical and mental ailments. Mental ailments were regarded as "bad thoughts," and people with sick souls were bad people. The sick soul must repeatedly perform actions that were the opposite of his or her vice. The idea was that by repetition one attained character traits that conformed to the mean, which was regarded by Maimonides as the aim of ethics. A healthy soul, he taught the sultan, was neither excessively joyful at good fortune nor depressed by bad fortune. Maimonides advised physicians to first ensure that their patients were of a cheerful frame of mind. He stated that such an attitude produced the remedy for depression.

We may think of spiritual aspiration as a noble act of the soul. The wish is to diminish dealing with matter to the bare minimum. The aim of ethics is to perfect the personality and to repair it if necessary. Maimonides was a great physician as well, and he used his medical knowledge to clarify his ethical approach. He maintained that similarly to the physician who is expected to treat the body, the teacher of ethics is expected to treat the soul. Therefore, the teacher of ethics must know the powers of the soul and their nature and capacities—similarly to the physician who must know the anatomy and physiology of the body.

Maimonides was the first philosopher who recognized the unity of the psyche. He divided the psyche, or soul, into five traits. To each of these traits he gave a name that specified its main function.

1. The first one he called *the nourishing* or the "growing" trait, which exists in all living creatures. Its function is to enable growth and development, and it belongs to medicine.

2. The second trait was called *the sensing* or *the living soul.* It contains the five senses of sight, hearing, smell, taste, and touch.
3. *The wishing* trait is the third. This is the trait of the soul that makes a person wish or ask for something, and is the reason why we seek to attain something or refrain from doing so. According to Maimonides, feelings of anger, fear, courage, wildness, compassion, love, hate, and goodwill are all embedded in this trait, and various body parts help such feelings.
4. The fourth trait, *the imaging,* in the soul is the power that keeps the form of the matter visible even when it no longer exists in reality. This trait is capable of creating images that cannot exist or are not available in reality. Thus we can rely on this trait of imaging in matters of intellectual functioning.
5. The fifth trait, *the reasoning,* is the power by which man reflects, presupposes, erects hypotheses, and acquires knowledge, and differentiates between deeds worthy of praise or disgrace. In this part of the soul reside the theoretical and practical roles and functions. Their purpose is to engage in professions, in arts and crafts, and to investigate and weigh the methods and principles of those functions. This is why the reasoning trait is so vital in all therapeutic professions.

Two traits or parts of the soul, the nourishing and the imaging, function independently of our will, whether we are awake or sleeping, and therefore a person is not responsible for them. As for the reasoning trait, we are in doubt, for even if a person is responsible for his or her thoughts, it is impossible to deduce any conclusions or results from them. The commandments and prohibitions in the Bible are aimed only at the sensing and wishing parts of the soul, for these are the ones in need of supervision.

Maimonides adopted Aristotle's division of the virtues and moral shortcomings into two groups: Ethical and intellectual virtues, and ethical and intellectual deficiencies. He agreed with Aristotle, who claimed that the nature of our actions is such that excess or deficiency cause our ruin. For example, in the area of food consumption, bulimia and anorexia, overeating, or refraining from eating in the extreme, cause the ruin of the body.

The intellectual virtues are expressions of excellence in knowledge and wisdom, such as axioms and "pure science"—as in physics—and of a quick and sharp mind. The opposites of the intellectual virtues are the intellectual deficiencies, such as slow thoughts and inability to see abstract connections.

The moral virtues dwell in the wishing part of the soul, and the wishing part completes the sensing part. Many moral virtues exist, for example, moderation, generosity, justice, modesty, satisfaction with one's lot, and so on, whereas moral deficiencies and shortcomings occur when these traits are given too much weight or are being used in a wrong way.

We acquire virtues or deficiencies by way of constant repetition of the acts that exemplify them, until they become parts of our nature, for nobody comes into this world as a sinner, nor does anybody come as a person of virtues. The education we receive in our childhood is very important, yet even if the education we received was deficient it is possible to make up for this and to eliminate the bad traits by channeling them in the right direction. It is also important to consider how much freedom exists for someone who has left the "straight way" psychologically speaking. Priority should be given to those acts that are aimed at reversing the damage and that return equilibrium in the soul.

Man must work for the perfection and improvement of his soul, says Maimonides. The word perfection has four useful meanings, defined in the following list:

1. The first and the least important is *material perfection:* money and wealth. These are external to the essence of life of a human being.
2. The second is *bodily perfection.* Improvement in the shape and function of one's body is good for gaining proper bodily proportions and appropriate muscular strength, but it is useless to the soul.
3. *Perfection of the moral virtues* is the third. This is needed to gain moral excellence. The majority of the commandments in the Bible are aimed toward this excellence. Yet, even this improvement is nothing more than a prelude to something else, and it is not a priority in itself. Perfection of the virtues is connected to what happens between a person and his or her fellow humans. The main point to remember is to be of use to others, for without them no value exists in the virtues.

4. The fourth and final, and the truest perfection of the soul is aimed at acquiring *rational virtues*. These virtues belong to the individual alone and have no part in society.

Development of moral traits enables one to gain intellectual perfection. The Bible and ancient Greek philosophy teach us that man is capable of directing his deeds and is responsible for his achievements, failures, iniquities, and sins. If man's nature and deeds were fixed from birth then all the laws and commandments would be superfluous, for if no freedom to choose exists then no value and sense to the laws exist. As it is said in the Bible: "See, I have set before thee this day life and good and death and evil" (Deuteronomy 30:15).

Virtue is a stable trait of the soul that stands between two extremes. Maimonides calls all extremes in behavior "sins." Sins are expressions of improper measures in acquiring a positive trait. The good deed stems from achieving the proper measure, and the bad deed is the tendency of the soul toward one of the extremes. The following list illustrates Maimonides's approach to the concept of virtue:

Extreme	*Virtue*	*Extreme*
Stinginess	Generosity	Squandering
Cowardice	Courage	Endangering
Pride	Honor	Self-hate
Boasting	Yielding	Dismissal
Overambition	Contention	Indifference
Impudence	Modesty	Shyness

Many people think that extreme behavior is virtuous. Sometimes they confuse a person who is ready to take risks easily with a truly courageous person, or a person who lacks sensitivity with a balanced person, or even the squanderer with someone generous of heart, but this is a mistake. Only "the King's road," the middle, and the center are worthy of praise (Weiss and Butterworth, 1975).

Healing is not dependent on being Christian, Jewish, or Muslim. It can be practiced by professionals in other religions too. What really matters is the way in which the healing is being performed. Christian healing, according to Pellegrino and Faden (1999), involves the total person. It requires a total commitment of self to the art and knowledge of treatment. It means a giving of oneself, being truly present. It requires compassion as a normal human emotion in the face of suffering. It becomes a virtue when it is practiced to a certain end, when a genuine sharing of the burden occurs, when genuine helping and comforting occurs, and when genuine respect for the suffering human being is present. The same can be said with equal force about healing as a virtue for professionals in the other religions.

True healing follows the dictum of Maimonides regarding ethics. It is to make the sick "whole again." It is to enable them to work once again on the perfection of their soul. What then are the practical implications of such healing? In the Christian Catholic approach to healing, as explicated by Pellegrino and Faden (1999), the relationship between a patient and a doctor can never be encompassed within the confines of a contract. In terms of ethics, the need for a contract would indicate that the parties to the contract are suspicious of each other and lack the essential element, which is the heart of professional relationship: trust. In contract-based relationships no real commitment is made on the part of the healer to give himself or herself truly to the patient. Furthermore, the patient, due to illness and vulnerability, could not foresee and anticipate all the potential hazards that he or she might guard himself or herself against contractually.

Pellegrino and Faden (1999) emphasize that similarly to contract-based healing, market-inspired models also constitute a break from Christian tradition in healing. The Christian tradition is inconsistent with profit-driven care. It deplores all commercialization within the health care system and rejects the idea of "managed care and marketing approaches to healing" (Pellegrino and Fagen, 1999, p. 122). In his view, the only morally viable model would be the covenantal model.

> This is the special relationship of a sacred promise and trust between one who is ill and in need of help and one who offers himself or herself as a healer. This is the kind of relationship in which there is a primary commitment to the welfare of the sick—rather than to the person of the healer. And this suppression of self-interest is the mark of a true profession. (Pellegrino and Faden, 1999, p. 122)

VIRTUES IN PSYCHOLOGY AND PHILOSOPHY

Among the psychologists of the personality that dealt specifically with the subject of virtues was Erik Erikson (1959), a disciple of

Sigmund Freud. He devoted much effort to understanding the human life cycle and especially the phases that characterize development in maturity to which Freud did not pay much attention.

Erikson postulated eight phases in human development and divided them into two groups: The first includes the phases of childhood, and the second adolescence and maturity. To each phase of development he attached a special virtue that comes into being as a result of solving the basic conflict that characterizes the specific phase in human development. The virtue exemplifies "special strength of the ego," and follows the rest of development throughout life. If this virtue is strong enough to endure, it will exist during all other crises that are expected along the path of one's life.

1. The first virtue that needs to be developed during infancy is *hope.* It comes into this world and grows through the baby's finding the balance between basic trust and lack of trust in its main caretaker. Erikson saw in hope the primary virtue that is necessary for human existence. Hope is the continuous belief in the possibility of achieving one's wishes, despite all the anger and ambition that signify such an existence.

2. The next virtue, *will,* is connected to the second phase in human development in which little children learn to differentiate between their own will and those of others. This is the phase in which the child must develop some autonomy if he or she does not want to remain fixed in shame and doubt. It is impossible to live without a will of your own. Will is the decisiveness to choose one's options freely and to use self-control. It is the basis for acceptance of law and order that are necessary for society. A child who transfers his or her willpower to others is in fact submitting himself or herself to the will of others, and the result will be catastrophic later in life.

3. The third virtue that must be acquired during childhood is *purpose.* This virtue is created by strengthening personal initiative. The opposite of this virtue is feelings of guilt, which can lead to the child's actions being paralyzed. The virtue that is supposed to be developed in this phase of life is a feeling of purpose, meaning a directing of the growing energy toward what is considered useful and necessary to achieve and to share with others in a given society. Purpose as a virtue is the individual's courage to envision objectives of value to him or her and to try and reach them without being defeated by fears, imagination, guilt, and/or the horror of punishment.

4. *Skill and aptitude* is the fourth virtue to be acquired during childhood. Skill is the ability to do something well, to learn to work and to use the human capacity for learning. This ability stands at the center of education for children in all societies at the time when the child is considered to be able and fit physically and cognitively for systematic learning. Skill as a virtue is the ability to use one's intelligence freely to accomplish a certain task or function without being restrained by feelings of childish inferiority.

5. During adolescence the fifth virtue, *loyalty,* has the central role in human development. This is the phase in which loyalty as virtue must come into the world. Loyalty, according to Erikson, is the ability to devote one's self to a certain idea or to an ideal. Throughout history leaders of nations, religions, and organizations made use of this adolescent trait for good or bad, for it is particularly characteristic of adolescent behavior.

6. *Love* is the next virtue. This is the dominant virtue in the world, or at least it should be. Love characterizes early and young adulthood. It is important to remember that Erikson refers to love as virtue when it is based on mutuality between partners both in rights and obligations and on mutuality in devotion to each other, in a devotion that is capable of overcoming all disagreements and selfishness in individual existence.

7. The characteristic virtue in maturity, which is the seventh phase in human development, is *generosity and caring.* It is expressed in caring for others, and it is necessary to the progress of mankind. Caring stands between creativity and fixation. Erikson claims that man in his basic self is a teacher, and he illustrates his thesis by the example of mother and child. One who lives a long life wishes to be needed by someone. Lack of such a feeling is the source of many psychological disturbances. Caring is an ever-widening circle for something or someone one has acquired by love and work, and is the felt necessity to transfer to the next generation all that has been gained and achieved, along with the values and the conditions for creation and development.

8. The last of the eight virtues according to Erikson is *wisdom.* Wisdom in terms of normative crisis in psychosocial development occupies a central position between integrity and despair. Erikson emphasizes that each generation must find for itself the wisdom to come to terms with what cannot be changed, including the greatest of

concessions, the yielding of life. The virtue of wisdom is expressed in accepting one's life as a whole, without regrets. It also means the ability to perceive an idea in its entirety, and to serve as an example to the coming generations. Only this kind of entirety is capable of elevating a person above the despair brought about by the thought that death is nearing and certain to come.

The eight virtues of Erikson—hope, will, purpose, skill, loyalty, love, generosity, and wisdom—serve as the basis in the education and training of social workers and all other helping professionals, in one form or another. The transfer of emphasis in professional education of social workers, for example, from the virtues to "professional values" is, according to this author, one of the main reasons why so many new students wishing to acquire the profession see it as an opportunity to open private practice, get rich, and disregard the social mission of the profession.

Today more than ever, a need exists to return once again to the virtues, personal and professional (or cardinal), both in theory and in practice. The development of enduring virtues in students and practitioners alike would enhance the value of the profession in the eyes of the public. Such a development will add greatly to the excellence in professional work. If a practitioner lacks hope, for example, he or she will not be able to change what can and needs to be changed in the condition or behavior of the client or the patient, due to the latter's own effort and attitude to his or her problem, and he or she will not be able to instill hope in the heart of the client. The same applies to the rest of the virtues. A professional helper cannot serve as an example to others if he or she lacks the virtues or does not aspire to them. Substitutes for the virtues—values—can be learned cognitively, but this kind of learning cannot replace the former, nor can it make the worker a man or woman of virtues.

THE VIRTUES ACCORDING TO COMTE-SPONVILLE

Andre Comte-Sponville is a well-known French philosopher whose *Little Book on the Great Virtues* was published in Paris in 1955 and was translated into several languages. The virtues that Erikson (1959) defined as "special strengths of the ego," which are supposed to accompany a person during his or her life and serve as a guiding light, are not included—except for the virtue of loyalty—in Comte-Sponville's list of great virtues. Comte-Sponville noted that he did not invent the virtues in his book but instead adapted those he found in the works of the great philosophers from ancient times to the present in a sincere effort to add his own notes and observations. He tells his readers that he reflected on determining the pleasant traits that enhance his appreciation of human beings when present and diminish his appreciation when not present. Comte-Sponville (1998) has listed thirty virtues and from among them he selected traits that cannot be replaced by others, such as decency instead of love of the truth, and thus he has arrived at eighteen virtues discussed in his book.

These eighteen virtues that Comte-Sponville selected are the following: courteousness, loyalty, prudence (or common sense), moderation, courage, justice, generosity of the heart, compassion, forgiveness, gratitude, modesty, simplicity, patience, cleanliness, delicacy, sincerity, humor, and love. The scope of this book does not encompass a detailed discussion of each of Comte-Sponville's eighteen virtues. Instead, I will focus on the four virtues especially needed by all social workers and other helping professionals both as members of society and as professional workers.

Comte-Sponville begins his discourse on the eighteen virtues with the virtue of courteousness. He is quick to emphasize that this is, in fact, not a virtue, for many perfectly courteous scoundrels exist. Courteousness is quality, and the person of virtues needs it for it prepares the ground for gaining the rest of the virtues. However, it does not stand alone without the others. Nevertheless, one must learn and acquire courteousness in the positive sense of the word during childhood as an expression of the delicateness of the soul and of the capacity of empathy. Even so, one must remember that courtesy cannot cover an inner vacuum and emptiness, nor can it serve as substitute for knowledge.

The four cardinal virtues mentioned earlier in this chapter (common sense, justice, courage, and moderation) were listed to emphasize that "public servants," such as social workers, should be equipped with them. Presented in the following sections is an examination of Comte-Sponville's approach to those four virtues.

On Common Sense

Common sense means that we are able to envision in advance the results and failings of our actions, and therefore we are responsible for both. Thus, this virtue becomes practical or applied morality. In ancient Rome this ability was called being "prudential," and its gist was a careful weighing of the good and the bad in a given situation. Such a weighing and its result must guide one to act properly. Common sense should be the ethical basis in decision making of the professional.

Common sense should guide the other three cardinal virtues as well, for without it we will not know how to use courage, justice, or moderation, presuming that these have been already attained. This virtue serves as a means in the service of worthy goals and is bound to choice and decision making. The common sense that weighs and determines factors in any situation or problem according to their advantages or deficiencies is the cornerstone of virtues. It is always looking ahead to the future, to what may happen, and therefore is capable of preparing itself for any future developments. Sigmund Freud called this virtue "the principle of reality." It compels us to seek pleasure and to avoid pain intelligently. It also serves as a substitute for the animal instincts that compel the beast to behave according to its nature.

Common sense as a virtue is connected to more than what it would first seem to. It relates to all the possibilities concerning a given problem or situation. This is the virtue responsible for taking risks and making decisions, and it is particularly necessary in our times for social workers and other helping professionals. It is insufficient to just be armed with good intentions for the client's sake, nor can a "clean conscience" replace this virtue. Sound common sense, in addition to knowledge and skills, is needed to arrive at the right decisions in problem solving.

On Courage

Courage is one of the cardinal virtues with which many people tend to be fascinated, for right or wrong. Courage indeed awakens general appreciation and fascination, whereas cowardice leads to shame, scorn, and contempt. Nevertheless, we must ask ourselves to which courage we are referring, for courage can serve the good in the same measure as the bad, and a courageous villain is still a villain.

In terms of ethics, courage that is a product of necessity is dissimilar to courage that arises in the absence of necessity or self-interest. Courage that serves the welfare of others, whether partially or fully, is very different from the courage that is forced on one. In this way and in this way alone does courage resemble the altruism that motivated, for example, the early social workers in England and the United States.

It is impossible to attain the other virtues without first attaining courage. Whoever is afraid to act cannot fulfill his or her role or task. The courageous can extricate themselves from the tyranny of their impulses not because they lack fear but because they are able to overcome their fear for a noble purpose. Courage alone is the virtue that enables us to overcome dangers and to carry the loads that with which life burdens us. We tend to admire and to respect Don Quixote, Cervantes' tragic hero, for his courage despite his futile fight with the windmills, which causes us to laugh at him. Courage is a matter of personal decision and action, not polemics.

The Courage of Socrates

The death of Socrates, perhaps the greatest philosopher of ancient Greece, shows what is meant by real courage. Socrates lived in Athens during the fifth century before Christ and was regarded by many philosophers as the "father of ethics," for he laid down the ethical foundations of moral behavior and conceived the basic rules in ethics. The Roman philosopher Cicero characterized Socrates as the man who brought philosophy down from heaven to earth and who founded philosophical ethics. The foundation of his laws, or philosophy and ethics are the following:

1. Never harm anybody.
2. Keep a promise in its entirety.
3. Respect the parents, the teachers, and the laws of the state.

The first two rules are embedded in the code of ethics of many helping professions, including social work. These will be elaborated in Chapter 13.

Socrates himself did not write any book on philosophy or ethics. Instead, he devoted his main energy and life to the search for truth and to instructing the youth of Athens. His teachings were recorded by his pupil, Plato, who wrote down his master's words as dialogues. In the center of his teaching and philosophy are the Greek concepts of *agathron,* or the good, and *arete,* virtue.

The inscription on the wall of the temple of Delphi, "Know thyself," served for Socrates as the need of man to examine the knowledge and good that belong to human beings. He was interested in seeking applied knowledge, the content of which was knowledge of both good and bad and their proper definition and verification. In the discussions he conducted with anybody he met in Athens, he put his trust in *Logos,* and in the part of the human soul that helps to bring forth real understanding.

Socrates used to compare his teaching to the work of his mother, who was a midwife. Similar to the midwife who helps the mother give birth to her child, so does the good teacher help his or her student to acquire self-knowledge and understanding. Socrates maintained that each human being must find insight alone, for insight cannot be given from the outside. A person can listen to his or her *daimonion,* the inner voice that guides his or her deeds and thinking toward the good. He used to say that every bad act is caused by lack of knowledge of good and bad, and he or she who has knowledge is good.

Socrates is credited with the development of the inductive thinking and approach to discovery of the truth. His system of questioning, which is called Socratic Dialogue, is widely used by many helping professionals without their recognizing the founder of this method. He employed the method of "learned ignorance" in his questioning of the interlocutor, and demonstrated great flexibility and ability to change direction in approaching a subject and a student as the occasion demanded of him. He serves as an excellent role model for many teachers and professional helpers.

Socrates's liberal views caused a great deal of anger among some politicians, who accused him of inciting the young people against "the sacred values" of society and against the gods. He was brought before the judges for trial. The maximum punishment for the "crime" committed by Socrates—if found guilty—was death. He did not need lawyers to defend him. He claimed his innocence of the charges leveled against him, and even tried to move the judges to see the truth. Nevertheless, he was convicted and sentenced to death. Socrates was given the choice of alternative punishments of either a fine of a considerable sum of money or exile. Socrates did not avail himself of either option. He spent thirty days in jail, at the end of which he drank the cup of poison and died. He was seventy years old when he died, a remarkable age in those times when the average longevity stood at less than forty years.

The speech attributed to Socrates in Plato's book *The Socratic Dialogues* (1987b) is an emotionally thrilling document that should be studied by all therapists and helping professionals during their professional training and education. The following excerpt from this moving document illustrates courage as a cardinal virtue:

> But perhaps it is not difficult to escape death, gentlemen, but a far more difficult thing to escape the stain of evil: for it flies faster than fate. And now I who am an old man and slow have been overtaken by the slower, and my accusers, who are quick and clever, by the faster, the taint of evil. And now I depart condemned to death by you, and they, convicted of evil and wrongdoing by Truth herself. And I abide, as they do, by the decision. Perhaps these things had so to happen, and I think it is well. (pp. 62-63)

The circumstances surrounding Socrates' death strengthen Comte-Sponville's argument that courage is unique and personal. One needs courage to think, and perhaps this is the greatest courage. This kind of courage means that we are unwilling to decrease our human value and will not succumb to fear, for nothing can stand between us and truth, even when truth is horrible.

On Moderation

Voluntary restraint of the passions and their diversion into quieter but healthier channels is the essence to the virtue of moderation. Such moderation means that we are in full control of the animal drives within ourselves. Moderation is extremely hard to follow, for it requires coping with the basic tensions and with immediate satisfaction of the passions. It is very hard to defend oneself against the many temptations that exist, such as sexual attraction. It is no wonder, therefore, that some therapists fail in this regard.

As a virtue moderation demands that we be happy and satisfied with little. Baruch Spinoza said in his great work on ethics. *The Ethics* (see Runes, 1976) that the wise man is permitted to strengthen the powers of his body and soul in moderation by tasty foods and drinks; to enjoy good smells; to be awed by the beauty of nature, fine clothing, and pleasant music; and to enjoy plays and performances provided that no harm is caused to anybody. He saw in such amusements real joy. Man should not be a slave to his passions, nor should he delve into lack of feelings. Those who cannot enjoy something and be happy with some good that life brings them carry an extremely heavy weight. They are slaves to their body, their passions, and to their weaknesses.

Moderation means the independence that is necessary to autonomy and to happiness. Someone full of passions that are never satisfied to the fullest is not a happy human being. The ancient philosophers knew this maxim of life very well. Epicurus, for example, knew how to enjoy a good and simple meal of bread and cheese, and he was happy when he ate when hungry. Moderation is an ability to find satisfaction with the small in life, especially when such satisfaction is accompanied by good feelings. It is easy to satisfy the basic needs of the body, but those who are constantly dissatisfied with themselves cannot feel such satisfaction. They are too occupied with what they are lacking in order to be *really* happy. When one's imagination revolves around what one is missing in life without respite, then one's condition is similar to mental disease. The philosopher de Montaigne (1533-1592) thought that lack of moderation is similar to a plague to the body. Moderation is the spice of life when it can turn the simplest joy into the sweetest (de Montaigne, 1991).

On Justice

Justice may be perceived as the hinge upon which all other virtues turn. This perception was known to the great prophets of the Jewish people. They never tired repeating that justice is what God demands from humankind, but, unfortunately, it is very hard to satisfy this demand. Comte-Sponville claims that justice as virtue symbolizes the absolute good.

The famous philosopher, Immanuel Kant (1724-1804) emphasized that all other cardinal virtues can be good, and they can be bad, too, if they are not embedded in good will (Kant, in Kunzmann, et al., 1999). He saw in justice the embodiment of good, the good that is good per se, and therefore it is impossible not to relate to it in ethics for both therapists and clients, or for doctors, nurses, and patients. Even small children know instinctively what is just, if not in an abstract way then in practice when they speak about "fairness" in their games. Adults see the extreme differences in resources division and allocation, and in political inequities they see the lack of justice that can bring about revolutions, such as the French and the American Revolution.

Justice is the virtue that helps a person to rise above all temptations; it is the opposite of egoism and selfishness. It is the virtue that is closest to altruism and love of the stranger. "A just person" is one who is willing to give everyone what he or she deserves. From the days of Aristotle and on we differentiate between distributive and corrective justice. *Distributive justice* shares the goods or resources of the community not by the principle of equality but by the principle of relativity in accordance with the personal contribution of the giver to the welfare of the community. *Corrective* or *"substitute" justice* must guide the procedure of exchange. It deals with the exchange of goods on the basis of equality, without reference to individual differences among the partners for the exchange. If all men and all women were just, then be no need for justice would exist, neither as a virtue nor as a moral value.

Chapter 4

Values

The value of man, his real value, is decided by the spirit and relativity by which man was able to get rid of his impulses.

Albert Einstein

PERSONAL VALUES

"My ideas," wrote Einstein "that stood always in front of my eyes and filled my life with joy are the good, beauty, and truth. The banal goals of a man's life—success and luxuries—I despised early in my childhood. For me the mystic of eternity, the building of the possible and wonderful, and the modest will and effort to understand the meaning of nature are sufficient—even if this understanding will encompass but a tiny part of it" (Einstein, 1931, p. 19).

The ideas of Einstein were in fact his personal values, those that gave his life the meaning he sought. People have different values regarding life and its meaning in the same way as they have different goals to pursue and to achieve. For some, their physical existence contains the essence of life. Others are capable of giving value to the meaning of their sojourn on this earth irrespective of its length. And these differences among human beings make the whole difference. For the human being gives meaning to his or her own life and existence by trying to fulfill something of which he or she sees value.

Values can be perceived as shared common experiences that people wish to attain. In our materialistic world the values of Einstein are outdated for many people. Most people wish to gain security in their lives. Millions of people base their lives on pyramidal values, a value system in which one value is considered of excessive importance, as

Ethics in Social Work: A Context of Caring
© 2006 by The Haworth Press, Inc. All rights reserved.
doi:10.1300/5577_05

if standing on top of a pyramid. The danger with such a system of values is that when the top value fails and crumbles, the whole system on which one has based his or her existence and security may collapse. Abundant illustrations support this thesis. For example, many suicides occurred during the Great Depression, and in similar cases people who lost their fortunes overnight escaped to death rather than fight their way back to life.

In contrast to these people are those whose personal value system can be defined as *parallel*. This means that for these people not one outstanding value is the most significant, but rather they consider many values as sufficiently satisfying for life. Therefore, when one of these values is lost due to some outside force or the vagaries of fate, they have many other values to fall back upon. For the professional worker, the knowledge of the client or patient's personal values and outlook on life is very important. The worker should be aware of the differences between pyramidal and parallel values. Roughly speaking, people with pyramidal values tend to exhibit a one-sided orientation of life and have by and large unstable mental health. They are still searching for security and meaning in their lives. People with parallel values can be characterized as those who have found security in their lives. They have a varied outlook and orientation to life and rather stable mental health. These are also people who have found meaning in their lives.

Viktor Frankl (1985), the founder of logotherapy, in his *Will to Meaning,* divided values as guiding lights in the lives of people in general into three groups: Creative, experiential, and attitudinal values. These are central values one can have as they affect a person's entire outlook and involvement in life. Frankl called them "worlds of values." Each group of values contains a whole world, so to speak, within which an individual can find meaning in his or her life. The first group of values, the creative, can be characterized as those encompassing what a man or woman gives to the world via his or her creativity and creative actions. It does not matter which aspect or field of creativity, whether art, music, painting, or other, any activity that helps to move humanity forward can be regarded as belonging to the creative group of values.

The second group in Frankl's (1985) worlds of values is called experiential. These values refer to the experiences one has in meetings with others and the world at large. As opposed to the creative values, for experiential values the emphasis is on what someone is taking from the world, on passive deeds, such as listening to music or enjoying a piece of art, or feeling elated by the beauty of nature. Frankl (1986) said that "in life the summits determine the full meaning of life. And even one minute can in retrospect flood the whole life with meaning" (p. 44).

The attitudinal values, the third group in Frankl's approach to values, refers to a person's attitude to the inevitable facts of life, namely that we all have to experience the "tragic triad" of feelings of guilt, suffering, and pain, and that eventually we all must die. The way in which we face these inevitabilities makes the whole difference, for in each of these we can find meaning. When we are called to face for example a loss we cannot avoid, such as the loss of a loved one, or to undergo suffering that is impossible to ease with medication, what is important, Frankl emphasizes, is the standpoint or attitude we take. In his words:

> The opportunity to fulfill attitudinal values is always present when man finds himself opposite a fate that he has no choice but to accept. But the way in which he accepts, how he carries his cross, the courage he exhibits in his suffering, the dignity he shows in his loss and tragedy, these are the indicators of his self-actualization as a man. (Frankl, 1986, p. 44)

RELIGIOUS VALUES IN THE WESTERN WORLD

Judaism's basic principles of morality for a non-Jewish society are called Noahide Laws (Cowen, 2001) or God's covenant with humanity (Genesis 9:1-17). The text in Genesis states that human beings should procreate. This is a positive obligation that is shared with all other living things (Genesis 1:22), and one of the Noahide commandments. According to another, all other living creatures should be governed by humanity. God also prohibits humanity to eat blood and commit murder. These two Noahide commitments are interpreted in the rabbinic tradition as containing seven more specific imperatives. These laws are binding on people everywhere. They express human values geared to maintain a certain order in the world and to prevent anarchy in human relations. The Babylonian Talmud (Sanhedrin 56a) lists seven Noahide Laws. These are the following:

1. Do not deny God.
2. Do not blaspheme God.
3. Do not murder.
4. Do not engage in forbidden sexual activities such as incest.
5. Do not steal.
6. Do not eat a limb torn from a living animal.
7. Do set up courts to ensure obedience to the other six laws.

Samuelson (2001) states that both the Ten Commandments—binding on Jews—and the seven Noahide Laws are guides to what should be the law, but they are not actually law. In Hebrew they are not even called commandments but instead are called "things" or "utterances," and before they can function as law it must be explained more concretely what these laws allow and prohibit (Samuelson, 2001, p. 227).

In the covenantal model of the Jewish tradition, good and bad are values related to concrete obligations in human relations. Jewish classical philosophy and mysticism agreed on wisdom as a central value in Jewish religious life. Whether this wisdom concerned theoretical or practical knowledge was a question left open for the sages to decide.

As stated before, Jewish classical ethics include commitment to a variety of values. These values do not have a hierarchical ordering, and the precedence of one value over another may vary in individual cases. This contrasts with Rawls's ranked ordering values and ethical duties that affect the social work profession (Reamer, 1999, p. 69).

In Jewish classical ethics based on the religious law *(halacha)* sanctity of life stands above many other values. Judaism does not support the taking of human life except under a few prescribed conditions, such as punishment for certain capital crimes or for self-defense. Nevertheless, even in this tradition the value of prolonging life has its limitations and may be in conflict with other values, such as minimizing suffering. Moreover, circumstances exist under which a life may be sacrificed for the sake of keeping other values, as has been shown over and over again in Jewish history for the past two thousand years.

It has been stated previously that the ancient Greeks identified four cardinal virtues as binding on public servants in Athens. In Jewish classical ethics Maimonides, in his *Tractate on the Talmud* (see Weiss and Butterworth, 1975), listed the seven following values that the ideal public servant should exhibit in his or her behavior: wisdom, humility, reverence, hate of money, love of the truth, love of fellow humans, and a good reputation. Maimonides believed that the people who deal with the interests of the public must be equipped with these characteristics in order to be worthy of serving the public.

In the Christian religious tradition, as based on concepts taken from the Old Testament and the Gospels, emphasis was placed on values that sustained life as God's precious gift. Christian perspective sees health as an important value in itself. It is an integral part of the gift of life. The same applies to healing as value. It is not a simple matter of bodily repair. Its value lies in restoring the relationship with God. Pellegrino and Faden (1999) states:

> Reckless risk to life is not condoned, but neither is survival as the supreme good. When the outcome of treatment is so dubious or marginal as to be highly improbable, and the physical, emotional, and fiscal burdens are out of proportion to the benefits, treatment can be refused or discontinued, but the balance must be struck prayerfully, carefully, and never with intent to usurp the sovereignty of God, the creator of life. (p. 118)

The underlying value in healing according to Christian tradition is respect for the human person, for his or her dignity as a creature of God. In the Christian tradition Pellegrino and Faden (1999) state that the values of spiritual healing and providing hope are very important. These are based on New Testament examples from the life of Jesus, and their purpose is to strengthen faith.

CARING PROFESSIONALS' IDENTIFICATION OF VALUES

A major challenge facing helping professionals is to convert conceptually based values into concrete guidelines for day-to-day practice. This is very important in the sense that such identification affects the practitioner's judgments about the relative importance of different values in resolving ethical conflicts and dilemmas. As already stated, values are the expression of ethics in operation. Charles Levy (1976) explained that professional helpers, such as social workers, decide their plans of action and evaluate the results afterward on the basis of their values. Values serve as a basis for ethical decision making for both regulating professional conduct and for their adjudication. Their purpose is to encourage ethical practice. Thus, some concepts related to values will be briefly reviewed.

Reamer (1999), citing the work of Milton Rokeach on human values, distinguishes among the following three groups of values:

1. The first is *ultimate values*, whose aim is to provide general guidance to a group's goals. Values such as respect for persons, equality, and nondiscrimination constitute ultimate values.
2. *Proximate values*, the second, are more specific and center on certain rights of clients, for example refusal of treatment or clients' rights to certain benefits.
3. *Instrumental values* are the third group. Here the idea is to specify the desirable means to valued ends, for example client self-determination in treatment plans.

Sadler (1997) claims that, although in general much discussion of values and their uses in actual work occurs in the helping professions, little attention is paid to identifying them. Values are defined as descriptions or conditions that guide human action. Values can be praise- or blameworthy. They are expressed in one or more of three dimensions—linguistic, causal, and descriptive—and each has its distinctive subtypes (Sadler, 1997). Sadler has also devised a methodological process for identifying how values manifest in scientific discourse. In so doing he aimed at helping scholars identify values at work in a practical way. He based his method on two underlying assumptions. First, values are both intrinsically and extrinsically involved in science and medicine, as helping professions, and second, the public and professional discourses about medicine or science will either presuppose (imply) or explicitly state what those values are (Sadler, 1997, p. 544).

Values are always embedded in a pragmatic context. They may be descriptions or conditions. Of the three dimensions cited previously, the causal is divided into three subcategories. Knowing these subcategories can be useful to the professional helper and are therefore listed as follows:

1. *Value commitments*, the first, refers to intentional or unintentional investments in particular evaluative concepts, principles, or rules of thumb.

2. *Value entailments*, the second, involve a worldview-based set of evaluative meanings about the important, the true, and the real, or they involve what is "entailed" in one's beliefs about the world, human nature, or condition. These shape the attitudes and the perception of reality and guide how one should live.

3. *Value consequences*, the third, pertain to foreseen or unforeseen effects of a particular theory, practice, or research program. These effects can guide ongoing social actions and as such are worthy of praise or blame (Sadler, 1997).

Of the many different values expressed in the descriptive dimension, particular focus will be given to ethical values. According to Sadler, *ethical values concern achieving moral, good, or virtuous ends, and reciprocally, the opposing kinds of values such as evil or immorality* (Sadler, 1997, p. 555).

In Sadler's method of identifying values, the first step is to scan the text for possible value terms (when the text forms the basis for evaluation). In the second step, a value analysis is performed involving the three dimensions already listed (linguistic, causal, and descriptive). Identifying value consequences is the most difficult task. Without going into the pros and cons of Sadler's method, it is useful for resolving some values related to conflicts. For an enlightening illustration the reader is referred to an article by Simmons (1997) titled "On Not Destroying the Health of One's Patients."

PROFESSIONAL VALUES IN SOCIAL WORK

Professional activities are performed employing a combination of four ingredients: First, a systematic knowledge that is essential and basic for engaging in a particular profession's activities, for example, a physician has systematic knowledge of the anatomy and physiology of the human body and its functioning, and second, each profession has a set of skills that can be used to solve problems that arise in its practice.

Many supervisors in social work who work with students in training are familiar with the expression of disappointment on the face of the student when it becomes clear to him or her that the fieldwork location will be different from what he or she had expected, for example, when a student had hoped to do clinical work but the only opening available is in community service. Even when the student understands the reality that he or she must acquire experience in general social work before practicing what he or she had sought, the disappointment remains and may persist for many years. It may also affect the quality of the student's work during the training period and later as a practitioner.

Behind the disappointment a supervisor can detect hidden values and influence of which the student is not aware by observing, for example, a student's attitude to the clients. Many students think that work in psychotherapeutic service is preferable to and more prestigious than work in a "regular" social service department. Even if the students are conscious of the reason for their disappointment, they still cannot avoid the conflict between their personal values and those connected to the chosen profession. The students in such cases must learn to separate the personal and the professional aspects of their work. Their clients may come in most cases from different social, cultural, and religious backgrounds from their own. Clients bring with them values that are apt to be different from those of the social workers, thus understanding values are as important to the professional helpers as their knowledge and skills. This is the reason why social work has devoted so much effort to teaching values in the training and education of its students.

A disappointed student provides the supervisor with an opportunity to clarify with the student the values that direct professional behavior in social work. No commonly agreed upon definition of *value* exists in social work. Value in Latin *(pendo)* denotes strength, overcoming, or being worthy of something. Usually the concept of value signifies a normative standard that affects the choices people make among the different alternatives of which they are aware. Social work has maintained central interest in the values that guide the profession from its early beginnings.

According to the declaration of the International Federation of Social Workers (IFSW), which includes professional organizations of social workers all over the world, a common code of ethics is accepted, despite the unique cultures in which social workers work and serve their societies.

Close to two decades ago, two educators in social work, Morales and Sheafor (1986) pointed out that these values are not unique to social work, for other helping professions have similar codes of ethics. These educators have identified the main value orientations of social workers, such as the belief in the value and dignity of all human beings, in their ability to change, and in their will to change; the responsibility of an individual toward himself or herself and toward other human beings; the uniqueness of each individual; and the human need to belong and to avoid extreme isolation. They noted that society should provide *opportunities for individual growth and development* that would enable all individuals to use their personal potential to the fullest. Morales and Sheafor (1986) also claimed that society must give the necessary resources for meeting the needs of human beings, and that each individual should have equal opportunity to participate in and work for the development of society. They have emphasized that the professional methods employed by social workers reflect *the humanitarian and egalitarian attitude of the profession.*

More recently, Reamer (1999), a noted social work educator, teacher, and writer about ethics and values of the profession of social work, has claimed that values affect the profession in the following four ways:

1. They affect the nature and social mission of the profession.
2. They influence the relationships of social workers with their clients, colleagues, and with the members of society.
3. They affect the methods of intervention in professional work.
4. They affect the solution of ethical dilemmas in practice.

Reamer (1999) noted that it is possible to identify six trends in the values of social work: The paternalistic, the social justice, the religious, the clinical, the defensive, and the immoral trend.

Despite their different conceptual meanings we can find in them various ingredients in the development of ethics in social work. Each of these six trends are briefly explicated in the following list:

1. *The paternalistic trend* was noted especially in the beginning of professional social work. This trend was based on the assumption that the social worker should influence clients to mend their ways morally and enable them to lead a proper and moral life without relying on the generosity of society.

2. *The social justice trend* was introduced to correct the social injustice and dependence caused by an unequal and unjust distribution of social resources. In accordance with this trend, many hard social problems, such as poverty, delinquency, unemployment, and even certain forms of mental diseases are connected to the inferior social structure and capitalistic regime, and therefore society must undergo a basic change, including corrective distribution of wealth, social welfare services, various benefits, and so on.

3. *The religious trend* that was dominant in the early decades of the twentieth century in social work, and is still prevalent in various circles among social workers in many parts of the world, saw in the social mission of the profession the translation of religious commandments regarding social justice. Therefore, it developed services to ease the suffering of the poor, such as soup kitchens to provide hot meals free of charge to all in need, a supply of warm clothes in the winter, the loan of medical equipment to the disabled for home-based care, and so on. The giving of charity as a religious value and obligation symbolizes this trend even today.

4. In the 1970s *the clinical trend* became the dominant trend among social workers and psychologists. This trend concentrates mainly on the ethical behavior of the practitioner toward the client. Among the important subjects in this trend are secrecy and confidentiality regarding the information that passes between the therapist and the consumer of service, informed consent and trust in the professional relationship, ethical decision making, and solution of problems concerning professional obligations.

5. In *the defensive trend*, which has lately become more and more prevalent in the profession, emphasis is placed on the protection of the worker against accusations of malpractice and lawsuits. This trend has developed out of the growing threat of complaints being brought against social workers for negligence, breech of confidentiality, and dereliction of duty.

6. *The "immoral" trend* that deals with the place of values in social work ethics denies the existence of central values in the profession. This trend is now the favorite among workers who give

preference to psychotherapeutic techniques, assessment of projects, and cost-benefit analyses.

In 1996 the new NASW Code of Ethics for social workers went into effect in the United States of America. It comprised six major values and related principles binding all members of the profession. These are the following:

1. *Service:* The main purpose of social workers is to help people in need of their professional services and to relate to social problems from a basis of knowledge, skills, and values of the profession, while elevating the service above the personal interest of the worker.
2. *Social justice:* Social workers are committed to social change. Their efforts are aimed at the elimination of poverty; securing full employment for all who request it; the eradication of discrimination on the basis of race, religion, and gender; and benefiting the vulnerable, weak, and oppressed people. The aim is to secure access to information and to essential services and resources, to create opportunities and equality, and to gain meaningful participation in decision making.
3. *Value and dignity of the human being:* Social workers respect the value and dignity of human beings, relate to them accordingly, are cognizant with cultural differences, and promote the self-determination and self-responsibility of their clients.
4. *Importance of social relations:* Social workers realize the importance of human relations and work for their enhancement, involving the client in the process of therapy for the sake of change and the promotion and welfare of the individual, the group, and the community.
5. *Integrity:* Social workers comport themselves as trustworthy professionals. They act out of a sense of responsibility, are aware of their social and professional mission, and promote ethical practice in all services agencies and organizations in which they work.
6. *Ability:* Social workers are engaged according to their respective personal abilities and in accordance to their specializations. They wish to increase and to enlarge their professional knowledge and skills in order to make a contribution to the quality of the profession.

Beyond these basic values we can differentiate among *final values, proximal values,* and *values as means.* The first refer to some general purpose that is preferred by various groups of people. Values commonly accepted by leaders and teachers of social work ethics, for example Levy (1976) or Reamer (1999), are: the dignity of the individuals; a person's ability to change; self-determination; equal access to opportunities and self-actualization; securing social and economic resources for the needy; opposition to discrimination on the basis of gender, race, religion, or political belief; respecting confidentiality of information given by the clients and client privacy; and willingness to share professional knowledge with other. These values are cited by many authors as well.

Proximal values are usually practical in their nature. They refer to specific policies for groups of clients concerning their rights to various benefits. These values specify goals sought, for example, the right of the client to secrecy and to give consent based on knowledge about the treatment offered.

ACHIEVING COMPROMISE
BETWEEN CONFLICTING VALUES

Even if social workers were able to define the values that guide their work uniformly, the difficulty remains regarding the need to compromise between their sometimes conflicting personal and professional values. Social workers are frequently faced with situations in which tension exists between their own personal values and those of the clients, the boss, or the profession. It is impossible to prevent such conflicts a priori. The attitudes of social workers to potential conflicts in their work and their responses to them are dependent on their perception of values at work.

CASE EXAMPLE:
A REQUEST FOR HELP HAVING AN ABORTION

Sara, a social worker with a master's degree is a new worker in a social welfare agency specializing in family counseling, family planning, and adoption of children. Sara likes her work placement. She made a great effort to get this job. Among her clients is Suzan, aged seventeen, and two months pregnant. Suzan asked Sara for help to arrange an abortion. She has also asked Sara to keep the pregnancy secret, for she is afraid of her father's wrath, a man with "old-fashioned" ideas about pregnancy outside of marriage.

Sara herself grew up in a family who kept religious tradition and morals, and abortion for her stands in opposition to her personal values. She is annoyed by Suzan's request. On the one hand, Sara is aware of her professional commitment as a social worker to work for the best interest of her client. On the other hand, however, Sara is agonizing and struggling with her personal values that forbid abortion. Sara knows that she cannot escape from making a critical decision about the question of whose welfare or good comes first, her own commitment to the religious values she grew up with or the commitment to the welfare of her client?

Cases such as Sara's are rather frequent in social work. Conflicts often arise between the worker's personal values and professional obligations when the religious or cultural values of the worker and those of the client are dissimilar. Abortion is an act charged with emotions and values. The religious values of the worker can have a decisive influence on her response. Sara may think that she must reject Suzan's request in accordance with her own personal and religious values, and the client may see in the rejection of her request unwillingness of the worker to help.

Conflicting opinions exist among social workers regarding the need to share their own personal values with their clients. For a long time social workers thought that they must remain "neutral" in their approach to the values of the client and their values could influence the considerations of their clients in resolving their problems. Today the situation is different. Many social workers think that the workers should inform the client about their own values so that the client is not able to claim deception or misdirection. The worker should be permitted to honor his or her own values and opinions about what is right or wrong in relation to the actions of the client, and "accepting" the client does not necessarily mean agreement with all the failures or unethical behavior of the client. Along with this the worker must be guided in his or her decision, in order to be ethical, by the professional values and norms that are part and parcel of ethical and professional conduct.

The workers' beliefs as an expression of their personal values affect the process of treatment as a whole. They determine the workers' perception about possible changes in the behavior of their clients and the method for achieving change. Values even affect the content of the help that will be given to the client. The old conflict between self-determination and determinism in the professional literature of social work reflects the opposing attitudes to values among social work educators, researchers, and theoreticians (Ephross and Reisch, 1982).

Social work is open to political and ideological influences. The meaning of the profession in well-developed democratic societies is different from the meaning given to it in totalitarian regimes. In the former the value of client self-determination is almost taken for granted, whereas in the latter the pressure for social conformism is great.

Professional values are worthless without their implementation in practice. They serve as "a guide to the perplexed" (title of a famous book by the great philosopher, physician, and religious leader Moses Maimonides). They must serve the immediate needs of the worker in making and accepting ethical decisions, therefore they can be regarded as values only when they are followed by the appropriate action, and only then they can serve as ethical guides in practice and be of value to the social worker. For example, the nonjudgmental approach is an important value for social workers as well as for many other helping professionals. This is an abstract concept. In reality, all professionals bring with them into their practice their own values and value hierarchies. They influence their behavior toward their clients, colleagues, and society at large. Their perception of good and bad in client behavior often impedes the development of positive therapeutic relationships, and leave both parties frustrated and angry.

The principles of practice in social work are connected directly to the values of the profession. Charles Levy (1976) stated that the client's trust that he or she will receive adequate and decent treatment serves as a central ingredient in the relationship between worker and client. Levy has developed his principles for practice on this basis and has emphasized that distributive justice is a very important factor in ethical practice, for it is directed at improving the living conditions of the most vulnerable population.

One of the difficulties in the training of social workers centers on converting the abstract and conceptual values into practical guides in daily work. Only knowledge of the professional values can help the worker solve conflicts between values that create ethical dilemmas.

Knowledge of professional values is insufficient in itself for knowing how to behave ethically. A need exists to know ethical theories to which the worker may turn to receive help in solving dilemmas that happen frequently in real-life practice.

Chapter 5

Etiquette for Social Workers

THE CONCEPT OF ETIQUETTE

The origin of the concept of *etiquette* is from the French meaning, "petty ethics," a collection of rules both written and unwritten that define public appearance, including the proper clothing, habits, and behavior that is appropriate for a given social status and behavior as well as the rituals related to a certain profession or occupation. As a means to regulate the relationships among people and within the "free professions," including the helping professions, etiquette is the sum of all rules, courtesies, approaches, and expectations that should be observed by a professional worker in his or her dealings with people who come to him for service (Blasszauer, 1995).

Etiquette in professional work is aimed at maintaining the manners, forms, and ceremonies developed over long periods of time to build harmonious relationships within a given profession and with members of other professions and society. Etiquette helps to maintain a certain image in the eyes of the public about a profession and about the behavior of its practitioners. The image can be positive or negative according to the behaviors of the individuals in their professional roles toward their clients or patients.

Levy (1976) cites Pellegrino (1964), who differentiated between the etiquette and ethics pertaining to medicine and to medical practitioners in the following way:

> Ethics deals with the rightness or wrongness of a physician's activities in accordance with the principles appropriate to the nature of man. Ethics forms a 'normative guide' that directs behavior in certain situations in such a way that the rights of the sick are always kept. Professional etiquette, on the other hand,

Ethics in Social Work: A Context of Caring
© 2006 by The Haworth Press, Inc. All rights reserved.
doi:10.1300/5577_06

deals with the obligations that arise in the relationships among physicians and in keeping the dignity and respect of the profession and its mission. The public never had difficulty understanding the true ethical principles that promise high standards in service and in devotion of the physician toward the sick. Medicine, nursing and social work cannot neglect the principles in professional behavior that affect directly or indirectly the welfare of the patients. (pp. 178-179)

I consider etiquette to be an expression of a society's culture in a given historical period, or to be a set of rules and behaviors among people in general in the society or in part of it, such as various organizations within society. Etiquette is the basis for a culture of reciprocal relations among people. It changes with social and technological changes and is expressed in courtesies, punctuality, politeness, tact, and good taste, that is, it is expressed in the ways of "external" behavior that contain moral content and contribute to the creation of a certain social atmosphere.

Etiquette is important today with the great uncertainty regarding the courtesies to which one should adhere in all helping professions. The codes of ethics of these professions do not deal with this subject. The uncertainty about the desired courtesies between the practitioner and the patient or client reflects the reality of society in constant development when each subculture exhibits its own concept of etiquette and values.

It is easy to dwell on this uncertainty with the help of a questionnaire that any practitioner can use. Take for example the following few questions: Who should greet the other first, the social worker or the client? Should a social worker help the client take off his or her coat? Should a social worker answer his or her phone while talking with the client? Is getting a present from a client permissible for a social worker?

Nearly every practitioner has witnessed some ugly scenes resulting from lack of courtesy in the corridors of a hospital or in a clinic where some workers refer to patients as "numbers" and reply to their legitimate questions in rough language or with impatience. Many times clients and their family members are shrugged off and are left waiting for hours in uncertainty as to the "verdict" regarding their situation, thus heightening their fears and anxieties. Unprofessional behavior also occurs when various therapists or their assistants shout into the phone at the top of their voice so that anybody in and outside the office can hear intimate details about a client's condition, or when the client is forced to disclose private information and problems in public. The lack of compatibility between what is common today and what was common in the past should bring us to invest in an effort to change unwanted behavior radically and to bring back the good old-fashioned courtesies of past eras.

HIPPOCRATES' MEDICAL ETIQUETTE AS GUIDE

The "father of medicine," Hippocrates, who lived 460-377 BC, established classical ethics in medicine. He was born in Kos, then called island of Istankoy, a place mentioned twice in the works of Plato and once by Aristotle, and died in Larisa when he was eighty years old. The collection of works on medicine assumed to be by Hippocrates, which comprise some seventy publications, is called *Corpus Hippocraticum* and includes works of his own and of his students and followers and even of doctors before his time. This corpus contains the Hippocratic oath, which was created to establish moral rules of conduct for the physician to avoid wrongdoing and inappropriate use of his or her knowledge and authority. This oath has been accepted as the basis for moral behavior in medicine in the world, and in accordance with its tenets all later oaths in medicine were developed.

Hippocrates directed the famous school of medicine in Kos for forty years. His main achievement is related to freeing medicine from the many superstitions and prejudices prevalent in his time. Hippocrates organized and founded medicine on scientific methods. The greatest contribution he made to medicine was his system of observation regarding the natural course of an illness. Thus he became the founder of modern scientific medicine. He was also keen on the importance of detailed observation and scientific experimentation. Furthermore, he emphasized the importance of the patient's personality in diagnosis and treatment. These characteristics of his are called "the Hippocratic approach" to medicine. In his *The Judgment* he wrote that for the doctor who arrived at perfection in his profession his knowledge is a source of security and joy, whereas lack of experience and knowledge cause him fear and rashness. The fear makes him impotent, and rashness is testimony to his lack of authority (Hippocrates, 1967, p. 343).

In Hippocrates's ethics the normative, the practical, and the moral-philosophical aspects are interconnected, and ethics and etiquette are closely connected. His medical ethics is based on the principle of choice, and choice, of the practitioner and the client or of the patient, is based on values. Hippocrates saw in medicine a noble mission similar to social work today, but he insisted that such a nobility should fall on those who have acquired their training by way of deep knowledge and learning and who are equipped with a decent and stable personality. In his writings he called for love of the people and of science, for these two are closely connected. As for etiquette, it should guide those who engage in medical activities and in treating the sick. Hippocrates wrote: "It is necessary that the doctor be of good color in his skin, well fed in accordance with his bodily structure, for the people think that who is not himself completely healthy cannot change others to be healthy" (quoted in Pecz, 1902, p. 928). We should remember that in classical Greek culture much importance was given to bodily health and perfection as expressions of one's morals.

In his works Hippocrates suggested that doctors should behave politely, especially when they treat patients. They should then be calm and cheerful and speak briefly and purposively. They should also be modest in speech and action and be polite, for politeness and good habits enhance the prestige of the doctor and his or her good name. The faces of the doctors should be serious but friendly, so that they will not be thought of as proud, and they must be decent and just. The doctors should remember that they have in their hands a great treasure of sick people and therefore they must observe well-developed morals. Above all, he said, the doctors should gain the trust of the patients and their cooperation in their work, for disobedience to the doctor's instructions may lead to worsening the condition of the patients and even to their death, and in such cases the doctors would be accused of negligence.

Hippocrates was the first doctor who dealt with the delicate subject of fees for medical service. His approach to this subject is thought today to be very advanced, for he decided that in setting the fee consideration should be given to the economic situation of the patient. He also advised doctors to treat the poor without charging a fee, for the good deed and its memory are worth more than the immediate gain.

More than a hundred years ago Pecz (1902), a historian of medicine, cited a sentence associated with Hippocrates in the book called *Praecepta* which reads: "It is better to ask for money from those the doctor has saved from death, than to squeeze out money from those who stand in the gates of death" (Pecz, 1902, p. 927).

Etiquette in Practice

What advice did Hippocrates give to doctors that can be used by social workers? First of all, to respect the dignity of the patient (or the client). This respect is expressed in the physical appearance of the practitioner. A neglected appearance, such as running around in the hospital or clinic in dirty clothes or making house calls in stained dress, sloppy shoes, unkempt hair, and worn-out shirts, cannot lead to a feeling of trust on the part of the client. Without trust no social work practice is worthy of the name. The same applies to doctors who are addicted to smoking, or nutritionists who eat fast food every day. According to Hippocrates, these doctors do not represent enlightened medicine. The clothes of the doctor was a subject to which Hippocrates paid much attention. He claimed that many people judge doctors in relation to the clothing they wear, rightly or wrongly. Clothing is not a matter of money only, but more a matter of taste, and the doctor should remember this.

Punctuality in arriving at meetings or appointments as scheduled, fulfillment of a promise given voluntarily, gentleness and tact, courtesy, and good taste are basic demands made of the doctor and the social worker. They serve as models to others. One must take into consideration the social status and age of the client and approach him or her accordingly. The social worker should not demean himself or herself in meetings with the rich and powerful. Similarly, the social worker should not disregard the poor or relate to them disrespectfully just because they have no money. (For those interested in this subject, an enlightening account about doctor and patient relationships can be found in Axel Munthe's [1990] lovely book titled *The Novel of Saint Michele*).

The social worker administrators or supervisors should instruct their assistants to behave in accordance with the demands of professional etiquette and to refrain from any and all insults toward the clients. Most etiquette-related demands do not involve the spending of a large amount of money. They only require paying attention to the condition of the client.

Guiding the patient (client) toward a healthy life was another important part of Hippocrates's approach toward the sick. This guidance, called *diet,* included not only matters of healthy nutrition but instructions regarding movement and rest, sleep and awakening, physical exercises, bathing, and massages. The medicines given to the patient occupied a secondary position in Hippocrates's medicine. He emphasized that the contribution of the doctor to the welfare of the patient is not the therapeutic activity, but rather it is the giving of an opportunity by way of an appropriate "diet" to remove anything that prevents nature from fulfilling its role. Hippocrates saw medical activity as helping the power of the living defense organism to act in the best interest of the sick (*Encyclopaedia Hebraica,* p. 343).

All human beings, sick or healthy, feel ashamed when requested to bare themselves physically or mentally before another person, even before a doctor or professional helper. Therefore professionals must create an appropriate and relaxing atmosphere to defuse the fears and anxieties of the patients, and develop in the client an atmosphere of trust toward the practitioner. Without such an atmosphere of trust the patients will suffer from an abuse of their human dignity. Today, in the conditions prevalent in our hospitals and clinics, and especially in government-funded emergency rooms, many patients see in the over-crowded facility and in the lack of privacy dehumanization of the seemingly most important value in medicine and social work—human life.

The rules of etiquette encompass all practitioners in the helping professions. Adherence to them can improve the conditions of the patients in today's social work. We can even claim that treatment in accordance with the rules of etiquette is able to hasten cure.

TEN COMMANDMENTS OF MEDICAL ETIQUETTE FOR SOCIAL WORKERS

Almost twenty years ago Pasnau (1985), a professor of psychiatry, assembled "Ten Commandments" of medical etiquette for psychiatrists that can serve all social workers and other helping professionals. Pasnau was concerned about the image problem of his fellow psychiatrists, i.e., that they tend to be "holed up" in their offices, seldom answer their phones or never get back to the caller, and shy away from active involvement with hospital staff and committees. Pasnau attributed these complaints to lack of medical etiquette and offered as a remedy the following "commandments":

Love Thy Fellow Physician As Thyself

Professionals should speak in person with the referring physician about the patient in order to discover what the referring doctor really wants done for the patient.

Thou Shalt Not Procrastinate

Medical etiquette requires that the patient's records be read before consultation about the case. This reading can save a great deal of time. It can also serve as a good base for reference. A letter containing information about the patient's physical condition and prescribed medications should accompany the record. These would help the psychiatric consultant to make a reasonable assessment of the patient's situation.

Thou Shalt Not Obfuscate

A psychiatric consultation should be written promptly and succinctly. It should be short but complete and contain the needed information.

Thou Shalt Be Concrete

This recommendation is usually the most important part of psychiatric consultation. Many doctors skip all the rest and go directly to the section that contains recommendations as to management and future disposition of the patient. Thus, Pasnau (1985) said, it is essential that these recommendations should be simple and concrete. Failure to adhere to this "commandment" can result in worsening the image problem of the profession.

Honor Thy Patient's Family

Exclusive focus on the patient can result in the failure of the consultation. The family should be involved in the discussion of the problem, the recommended treatment, and the consequences of the patient's illness, especially when he or she is suffering from a chronic or serious illness. Therefore the family of the patient should be part of the recommendations in the consultation.

Thou Shalt Not Hibernate

Sometimes issues of confidentiality, of not knowing what information should be revealed to the referring physician, can lead the psychiatrist going into hibernation and forgetting the whole case. Other times records may be lost in the mail. Pasnau (1985) recommended that psychiatrists speak directly and discreetly to the referring physician after the consultation, and should not refrain from discussing the findings and recommendations with the physician in person.

Thou Shalt Persevere

Many times one-shot consultations are not enough to solve the patient's problems. Making additional calls to verify the situation and to recommend treatment and medication as well as to confirm the effects of the recommendation require perseverance on the part of the consultant. Pasnau claimed that such "perseverance is not only good etiquette, it is good medical practice" (Pasnau, 1985, p. 131).

Thou Shalt Not Preach

Physicians want consultation not preaching, from the psychiatrist. They are seldom interested in psychiatric problems and have little patience for long lectures on the psychodynamics of the patient. On the other hand, conferences on selected topics usually draw health care personnel who enjoy them. They also boost the morale of physicians and nurses.

Thou Shalt Not Steal Thy Fellow Physician's Patients

When a recommendation is made to further psychiatric consultation or treatment, whether psychotherapeutic or psychopharmacological or both discussion with the referring physician should be made prior to making a commitment to the patient. A joint decision should be made about who will be the primary physician and who will write the prescriptions for outpatient medications. Pasnau (1985) emphasizes: "Do not let the patient fall between the chairs, for such a lack of courtesy alienates our medical colleagues and confuses patients" (Pasnau, 1985, p. 132).

Thou Shalt Not Shirk Your Responsibility

Pasnau (1985) perceived the duty of psychiatrists to participate in medical organizations and staff meetings as good etiquette. He claimed that psychiatrists can play an important role in medical staff organizations in their local hospitals. Pasnau advised psychiatrists not to shirk their responsibility to participate in such organizations. Lack of participation, he said, is not only poor medical etiquette, it also fosters the image of aloofness. Psychiatrists should remember that being inactive within the medical community breeds referrals to other mental health providers besides themselves.

ETIQUETTE AND ADVERTISEMENT

Advertising in the helping professions is not a new phenomenon, and it is not regarded by many professionals as a breach in ethical conduct. Neither is advertising contradictory to the etiquette of a profession—even the Greeks in ancient times used to advertise their services in the medical profession. The Hippocratic oath does not contain any reference to advertisement in medicine, but it is possible that Hippocrates, similar to many philosophers in his times, was against this practice. Despite these objections to advertisement in medicine, many doctors continued to tell their audiences that they have great skills in treating various illnesses. One of their methods in advertisement was to exaggerate their qualifications and knowledge. The advertisement was done in public lectures in the markets and in theaters during which the lecturers would praise themselves without shame. These lectures would attract large crowds of people, and it was easy for the doctors to recruit new customers for their services.

Yet, even in those times doctors who conducted themselves in an honorable way refrained from self-advertisement and tried to influence their colleagues to do likewise and not to sink to despised levels in professional behavior. They saw in the lectures for the public a lack of professionalism and a danger to public health, and they equated the tricks used by low-level doctors with an indication of their charlatanism. They abhorred the operations performed by certain doctors in the theaters to attract new customers (Amundsen, 1978).

Advertisement is common in our modern times in many occupations, and competition for new clients and patients is fierce. Competition in medical practice was recognized in the international code of ethics for physicians as far back as 1949. Today the codes of ethics in the helping professions have special clauses, instructions, and rules regarding what is permitted or forbidden in advertisement. Despite those rules and regulations, we often witness wild competition in self-advertisement.

In 1957 the American Medical Association published rules for doctors concerning etiquette in advertising. These rules stated that a doctor is forbidden to "recruit" patients, for medicine is not a commercial activity and service cannot be equated with merchandise. Moreover, these rules explicitly stated that self-aggrandizement on the part of doctors opposes the great medical tradition and hurts the morals and ethics of its practitioners. In addition, exaggerated self-advertisement is contrary to good taste and cannot serve as an appropriate standard for the professional conduct of a doctor or a social worker. The authors of this document claimed that American citizens have a right to know the names, addresses, and days and hours of work as well as the special qualifications of those who treat them.

Advertisement in medicine is permitted. This advertisement should refrain from being sensational. A difference should exist between advertisement that aims to attract patients, to heighten consumption of various substances, and to raise expectations and illusions in the public and advertisement that aims to benefit the public.

Furthermore, the relationships between doctor and patient, or social worker and client are different from those between a supplier of a product and a buyer. The vulnerability of patients, or clients, their dependence on the professional, and their inability to evaluate the appropriateness of the service or treatment offered make this commercial transaction totally different from any other. Therefore professional etiquette requires consideration of all the restrictions that flow from those differences in relation to advertisement.

What is permitted in professional advertisement? First of all, the existence of a service and the establishment of a new service, whether by an individual practitioner or an organization, such as a clinic or hospital may be advertised. Doctors or social workers advertising their services are permitted to state their area of specialty and credentials only. Doctors and social workers are forbidden from advertising their services by personal letters, pamphlets, or leaflets. Social workers may give personal information to the public disclosing only their name, specialty, and place of work. The information supplied must be objective and accurate.

Direct advertisement for recruiting clients is prohibited. Treating clients for special benefit is not permitted. Liability for the results of a treatment is forbidden. Social workers are not permitted to advertise themselves, or to advertise activities that can be regarded as competing for or soliciting for clients.

The latest code of ethics for social workers in Israel, which was finally approved and accepted by the Israeli association of social workers in 1994, does not contain any rules concerning advertisement. The NASW Code of Ethics for social workers is more advanced in this regard. It has several binding rules pertaining to the etiquette of advertisement in social work practice (Barker, 1999).

ETIQUETTE AND CONSULTATION

Consultation in social work, as well as in other helping professions, means discussing with one or more colleagues a client's condition in order to get advice how to proceed in a given situation when the worker's knowledge is insufficient for making a decision. Consultation as a medical procedure was used in ancient times when famous doctors were invited by the rulers of ancient kingdoms to provide guidance to court physicians and to cure the sick.

Consultation is necessary when a reasonable time has elapsed and no healing has occurred, if a complication exacerbates the problem and the attending social worker is helpless, and when the problem the client presents becomes grave. Consultation is also needed in psychiatric cases and in cases of disagreement between the social worker and his client.

The need for and interest in social work consultation is culture-bound. Certain people refer to consultation as to "having a second opinion" to feel more secure. Some other people request consultation to show others their status in society. The client has right to be involved in the assessment of his or her needs and the treatment plan. This means receiving current information concerning diagnosis, treatment, and prognosis as well as all information pertinent to giving informed consent prior to the start of the treatment. When the client is not convinced of any alternative proposed, he or she may request consultation with other social workers, such as the supervisor or the administrator, or he or she refuse treatment to the extent permitted by law. This request may serve as an area of conflict. Referral for a second opinion is dependent upon agreement between client and social worker. Such requests should be handled sensitively by the client's worker. Sometimes the request reflects failure in communication between the client and the regular worker.

Chapter 6

Good and Bad
in Professional Responsibility

Any occupation and any investigation, and similarly any activity and decision seems to be directed toward something good. Therefore the good is justly defined as that to which all things aim.

Aristotle

MARTIN BUBER'S APPROACH TO GOOD AND BAD

Martin Buber, one of the greatest philosophers of the twentieth century and a foremost authority in education in his generation, summarized in his book titled *Good and Evil* (1953) his concept according to which man decides his relationship to others as either "you" or "that one." The values of man are not necessarily stable but are relative depending on time and place. Walking in the path of values is walking on a narrow path on either side of which is an abyss, and any value-based decision entails risk because no unequivocal answers to questions about life, faith, and meaning exist.

In the fifth chapter of his book, Buber refers to the concepts of good and bad as they are reflected in Chapters 1 and 25 in the book of Psalms. Both chapters are aimed at the same purpose: to teach humankind how to differentiate between the right (good) way and the wrong (bad) way. In the right way, the way of God, walk all the just and the "proven" paths; those who go their own way and refuse to go in the ways of God are called the "wicked"; and those who have lost the way, or mistake the way of God altogether, are called by Buber "sinners." The real struggle between the just and the sinners is with the wicked. God, the good and merciful, directs the sinners toward the right way and they can therefore return to God's way. The key words in both Psalms are "just," "wicked," and "sinners," and their repetition in both chapters, according to Buber (1953), means that they have poetic and hermeneutic meaning. They provide the basic explanation for the understanding of the idea of good and bad. Buber explains that the central word in both chapters is "happy" or "happiness," and this is equivalent to good.

Who then is truly the good man? According to the Psalms a happiness exists that is hidden to the eye, a secret happiness, so to speak, that is capable of overcoming all the suffering, sadness, and despair that is part and parcel of human life upon this earth. Despite that it is hidden to the eye, this is real happiness, the only true happiness. This happiness belongs to a different sphere from the customary cause of happiness for human beings, and it is included in the relationship of man with his God. This relationship is expressed in the word *way,* as it is said in Psalm 1:6 "God knows the ways of the just and the way of the wicked will be lost."

Who, then, is the just (the good)? The Bible depicts the good and the just person in Psalm 15:1-5:

> Lord, who may sojourn in your tent, who may dwell on your holy mountain? He who lives without blame; who does righteous acts; who tells the truth in his heart; whose tongue speaks no deceit.
> Who has not done harm to his fellow; or borne reproach for his acts toward his neighbor;
> For whom a contemptible person is abhorrent;
> Who honors those who fear the Lord,
> Who stands by his oath even when it is to his disadvantage.
> Who has never lent money for interest; or accepted a bribe against the innocent.

Whereas the way of the just is known only to God, meaning that the just are connected to God, the way of the wicked ends in nothing, as in a cul-de-sac, and in the realization that their life has been wasted. The emphasis in both cases is on touch. In the first instance, God touches them with a touch similar to His touch of the prophets. They are "pulled out" from a large crowd and lifted high above and far beyond ordinary and daily existence in order to be in touch with

God, who knows their way. Their way of life was created so that in each phase they feel God's touch upon them anew. In the second instance, for the wicked, lack of God's touch upon them is the source of their failure in the ways of life.

The sinners, who always comprise the majority, are different from the just and from the wicked. To be a sinner is to be in a condition, contrary to that of the wicked, of having a constant attitude of opposition to the way of God. The sinners seem to be attacked by sin time and time again, therefore they mistake the way and are lost, whereas the wicked are always bad. A real difference exists between the sinners and the wicked: the former can return to the way of God, to the main road in life, and the latter cannot because they do not want to. The sinner must make an effort to participate in the life of the community again, to return to what gives and maintains life and to what he or she aspires to within himself or herself. Sinners can choose. The wicked also are able to choose, but they do not wish to do so. They have already made their choice. Now they must pay the price.

This attitude of Buber to good and bad is basically humanitarian and religious. It is of great importance to professional workers in the helping professions. Sinners, according to this approach, are those who have lost their way but are able to return and choose a new way, the right way, to life. They only need guidance and strong support in order to carry out what deep down in their hearts they know they prefer: the good, not the bad. The just do not need help; their strong faith in God keeps them walking in the way of God, in the right way, even when this way is full of obstacles and difficulties. The wicked are beyond repair, and it makes no sense to deal with them.

MORAL AND IMMORAL CONCEPTS OF GOOD

The good, morally speaking, is not necessarily connected to aspects of life that are good in themselves, but also to objects and ideas such as cars, paintings, knowledge, freedom, etc, which are good only when they serve a good purpose or cause. Frankena (1973) emphasized the difference between two concepts of good with the following illustration:

> Sometimes we say about someone that he had a good life. And at times we say that he conducted his life in a good way. In the

first instance we are talking about good life without connecting
it to morals. [This does not mean that this man lived an immoral
life.] In the second instance we understand that the same person
lived a good life in moral terms. Therefore we may ask: What is
a good life without morals? And which values we should use as
proof of such a life? Or more to the point ethically: By which
standard we decide what is good? (p. 79)

Dictionaries define *good* in many ways: Pretty, useful, appropriate,
efficient, productive, valid, pleasant, satisfactory, able, attractive, de-
pendable, and convincing. A mixture of personal traits is included
with the descriptions, and it is hard to use such a broad definition for
the concept. The Oxford English-Hebrew Hebrew-English Dictionary (Levy, 1995) defines the same concept differently and is more to
the point. Good is a general description of praise, or agreement,
meaning existence of qualities praiseworthy in themselves or useful
for a specific purpose. According to this definition of the good—that
which is worthy of praise or can be called worthy of praise—can be
done on either a moral basis or a general (immoral) basis.

Frankena (1973) differentiated among several meanings for good,
such as something externally good, as a means that is good in itself,
good by its nature, or desired. He noted that the same thing can be
good or bad depending on one's perspective. For example, knowledge can be good or useful, but it can be also bad or cause something
bad. Physicists, for example, used knowledge to build an atomic
bomb.

What is good in itself, by its own nature, is the activity that brings
pleasure and has internal value for an individual. Similarly, what is
good is the existence of a certain level of excellence. *Bad* in itself is
the pain, lack of satisfaction, or any other calamity, especially lack of
excellence. Therefore a "good life" is a mixture of many and different
activities that give us value and harmony. This concept of a good life
varies from individual to individual and it is impossible to set rules
applicable to all, for our personal traits are by no means uniform.
They are different, similarly to our opinions about the concept of
good. What is good for one person is not necessarily good for another. The important instruction for the professional social worker is
to act justly, decently, and in moderation with an intention to help the
needy.

CASE EXAMPLE: THE STUDENT WHO FAILED TO SHOW UP FOR WORK

In one of the schools of social work the following case was brought before the committee on ethical conduct for a decision.

A student in his second year of studies for a bachelor of social work degree was assigned for fieldwork to an agency specializing in adoption of children by foster parents and other child welfare related services. At the end of the first semester the student's supervisor and field instructor evaluated the student's work and gave him a failing mark. Prior to the final evaluation were several discussions between the supervisor and the student about the quality of the student's work and particularly the problem of his irresponsible approach. After the final evaluation was done and the failing mark given, the student disappeared and did not show up for work for the next three weeks. He agreed to go back to work only after the director of the agency urged him to do so. The case was brought before the ethics committee for a decision.

The committee decided that the student breached professional responsibility expected of anyone attempting to work as a therapist and accepted the failing mark given to the student for his fieldwork performance. The committee also required that the student repeat his second-year fieldwork and to stay at the agency an additional year.

In light of this case the concepts of moral responsibility as well as professional responsibility in social work will be discussed.

MORAL RESPONSIBILITY

To be responsible ethically means to be responsible for our actions and deeds morally, said the philosopher Heller (1994). Being responsible morally includes an obligation to take an attitude toward life. It is always hard to deal with reality, especially when we must accept at times the results of our failures and negative behavior. The majority of people prefer to live with the ideas they are used to and with their self-image, even when these are far from being positive, in order to escape the need to change, for change brings with it doubts and insecurity. Coping with reality demands awareness of what is possible and what must be accepted as impossible to change. What is important morally is not what we are doing but how we are performing our obligations.

Frankl (1962) in his book titled *Man's Search for Meaning* said:

> Each man is questioned by life; and he can only answer to life by answering for his own life; to life he can only respond by being responsible. Thus, logotherapy sees in responsibility the very essence of human existence. (p. 109)

In Frankl's logotherapy a human being is human insofar as he or she is responsible not only for himself or herself, but for others as well. In his book titled *The Doctor and the Soul* (1986) is a story of a sanitation worker who received the highest honor from the German government. This man performed his duties as did any other worker in sanitation, but he also collected discarded and broken toys, which he took home to clean and repair, and then gave them to poor children as gifts (Frankl, 1986, pp. 298-299).

The Chinese philosopher Confucius said that the truly decent never preach about anything before they themselves have performed that about which they are preaching. For example, it is impossible to speak about fulfilling a promise given to the client or patient as a professional value when the practitioner does not practice the same ideology. Our obligations as professionals in the helping professions do not end with giving information and developing skills, although these are important, but in helping ourselves and others to be decent and warmhearted human beings who are not occupied only with themselves. Each individual is responsible for his or her actions, for after they have been done they cannot be changed or controlled. The action itself can strengthen or weaken others.

Another illustration of moral responsibility is taken from the world of work in industry. This illustration details the different kinds of responsibilities in order of their importance to society, and one can deduce from them what is applicable to professional responsibility. In 1943, John Seward Johnson, the son of the founder of Johnson & Johnson, wrote down his beliefs about the company, one of the oldest and most successful in America that specializes in baby food, medical supplies, and other products for health care. The values contained in his statement serve as a basis for the success of the company economically and socially to this day. The order of responsibilities, according to Johnson, is briefly stated as the following:

1. First responsibility and priority is given to doctors, nurses, patients, mothers, and fathers and to all those who use our products.

2. Second responsibility encompasses the workers in the offices and plants. Johnson emphasized that employees must feel secure in their roles and their salaries must be decent and appropriate to the effort they invest in their work.
3. Third responsibility is given to the managers of the company. Managers must be people equipped with talent, education, experience, and ability.
4. Fourth responsibility is to the community. Businesses must be good citizens and support public activities and charity.
5. Final responsibility is to shareholders. (A complete version of the company's credo can be found at http://www.jnj.comtour_company/our_credo/)

As seen, even a commercial company interested in profit as its main motivation takes into consideration its moral responsibility to all the factors connected to its survival and success. In the professional codes of ethics of the helping professions a similar approach to the concept of responsibility can be found. Accordingly, the first and most important responsibility is enhancing the welfare of clients, patients, and society at large.

A different approach to moral responsibility is offered by Heller (1994) in her well-known book on moral philosophy. The two types of responsibility included in her concept are *retrospective* and *forward looking* responsibility. The first is further divided into two parts: Responsibility attached to basic norms known by members of the community, society, and nation. Today, what is left of these norms is not much, particularly in politics in which we witness many people trying to escape taking personal responsibility for failures in their roles and/or area of responsibility. The second part of retrospective responsibility is the responsibility of an individual to act or refrain from acting in a given situation. All are responsible retrospectively for their acts, unless thy are not responsible for them in the eyes of the law or as a result of being physically (e.g., a small child) or mentally (e.g., the severely retarded) incapable of taking responsibility for their actions. Therefore, retrospective responsibility is general and encompasses almost everybody.

Forward-looking responsibility is private, personal, and self related and is a responsibility to something in the future. For example, a pilot is responsible for the passengers, the crew, and the plane; and a captain of a ship is responsible for the passengers onboard and the company of the ship. Social workers find themselves in similar roles, but are sometimes similar to the captain of the ship and at other times are similar to the passengers. That is, sometimes they are responsible retrospectively, and at other times they have forward-looking responsibility.

Professionals such as social workers receive with their roles the responsibility that stems directly from the role, meaning obligation. This obligation refers to responsibility related to actions or refraining from actions for which the professional is directly responsible. It makes no difference whether or not a person has volunteered or was elected for the role. He or she accepted the responsibility and obligations attached to the role. In the forward-looking responsibility is a promise that in critical situations the person occupying the role will behave according to what is expected by society and will even surpass the regular commitment that is commonly expected. For example, the captain of a ship has special responsibility for the ship, its cargo, and its passengers. This responsibility is a kind of ethical and moral behavior expected of him or her in the role of a captain. He or she is responsible for the regular life in the ship and also for the norms commonly connected to the role. In case of a disaster, such as the sinking of the ship, the norm is that the captain will be the last to leave the ship, and in case of an epidemic that breaks out suddenly in the ship the captain must care for the welfare of the passengers before caring for his or her own.

Heller (1994) notes that neither kind of responsibility is divided between two different groups of people; every person's life contains both retrospective and forward-looking responsibility. Every person has some obligations, and the gravity of the obligations is different from one person to another. The forward-looking responsibility of a prime minister or president is different in its gravity from the responsibility of a florist, for example, even if both have similar moral obligations in other areas of life. Consequently, both have different results in not carrying out their obligations. In both cases individuals must exhibit responsibility to society for their actions or lack thereof. In the same way that responsibility exists for the good deeds, so does it exist for the failures.

An illustration of forward-looking responsibility can be found in one of the short stories of Stendhal: A man was walking on the bridge of the river Seine and saw a woman jumping into the river on a cold winter evening. After a few seconds' hesitation the man jumped into the river and saved the woman from drowning. At night, after he had cared for the woman and was shaking from cold all over, the man suddenly heard a voice telling him that he was lucky he jumped into the river, otherwise he would have suffered from his conscience throughout his entire life.

The question of moral responsibility for others is an old one. In the first book of the Bible (Genesis 4:9) we meet it for the first time in the story about the first murder between brothers: "And God said to Cain, 'Where is your brother Abel?' and he said, 'I don't know; am I my brother's keeper?'"

This question of Cain's was in fact his attempt at escaping from responsibility. Cain knew very well that he was his brother's keeper, and we can assume that he was also aware of his forward-looking responsibility. The same kind of responsibility is repeated in the Biblical story about Joseph and his brethren who wanted to kill him in their jealousy, also in Genesis. Unlike Abel, however, Joseph was saved by his brother Reuben, who was aware of his responsibility as the firstborn toward his father Jacob. These stories are illustrations of the concept of forward-looking responsibility. Not doing what a man is supposed to do according to his obligations is, according to the Bible, a sin.

We must assume, said Frankena (1973) that human beings in general are free to do as they wish, unless they have been subjected to brainwashing, are subject to constant threat to their lives, or are mentally sick. In such cases it is impossible to influence their behaviors and even moral sanctions cannot influence them. We should also remember that reasons for the decisions of human beings always exist, and these do not happen by chance. These reasons are the moral basis of the attitude toward a person and the necessity to hold him or her responsible for his or her actions.

Social workers should know that requesting people to take responsibility for their lives is an important educational obligation and an integral part of any psychosocial treatment. It is right morally to use educational means of praise or blame in accordance with the principles of beneficence and justice, as long as people can act freely without coercion. Reamer (1999) emphasized that the purpose is to enhance people's abilities to make a change in their attitude toward their problems. Another purpose is to prevent them from escaping direct responsibility, and, by providing support and encouragement, to strengthen their will to accept responsibility for their life.

Cases exist in which refraining from carrying out civil obligations and obeying the law is actually a virtue. For example in World War II, those who helped Jews and others to escape from persecution and death from the Nazis were lawbreakers in the eyes of the Nazis but in reality were heroes in moral terms. Raoul Wallenberg, the Swedish diplomat stationed in Budapest, Hungary, in 1944 saved the lives of tens of thousands of Jews by issuing them Swedish certificates of protection. The responsibility he took upon himself far exceeded what could have been commonly regarded as responsibility for your fellow human beings. It is an example of heroic responsibility, one almost unparalleled in the history of mankind. Therefore, he is one of the thirty-six just men who, according to Jewish tradition, keep the world turning. Those few among the occupied people in Europe that accepted responsibility for the "good," said Heller (1994), when the whole world was in great darkness, those who did not let humankind sink to the bottom of the abyss and die performed a great service, one that would never fade. They are a living illustration of the existence of good upon this earth.

CASE EXAMPLE: A WORKER
WITH A DRINKING PROBLEM

For two years two social workers, Leah and Ruth, worked together in child psychiatric services, consulting each other frequently and becoming good friends. One day Leah told Ruth that she left her husband after eight years of marriage. After she was separated she would go to bars and cafés and drink "a few drinks." At first Ruth thought that Leah's drinking was due to the separation and depression that followed, but when she saw that the drinking was getting worse, and that the children might get hurt by Leah, she started to think about approaching the director of the agency and telling him about Leah's problem. One day Leah confessed to Ruth that she had a problem with drinking and was in need of help. Ruth advised Leah to turn to the director. Leah promised to make an effort and to control her drinking problem, yet at times she would come to work rather tipsy.

Ruth was torn between her commitment of friendship to Leah and her responsibility and commitment to the agency as a professional worker. She wondered whether she should tell the whole problem to the director. She also wondered about what might happen to the children in Leah's care. Ruth had several options to choose from: tell the director about Leah's condition in order to defend the children from potentially improper care, encourage Leah to turn to the director of the agency for help, or decide not to interfere in Leah's personal problems and let them take their natural course.

Where are the limits of good and bad in terms of professional responsibility in such a case and in general in social work as a profession? The questions with which the social worker is struggling are central in ethics: what is right ethically in that situation? Whose welfare comes first, the children's need for proper professional treatment or the agency that employs Leah? How should one relate to professional responsibility binding all professional workers?

In order to respond to these questions, workers in the caring professions should turn to the code of ethics of their profession, in this case to the NASW Code of Ethics. Briefly speaking, this code contains standards of behavior in three broad areas. The first refers to mistakes that social workers are liable to make, mistakes with ethical implications, such as leaving on their desks sensitive and secret information about their clients so that anybody can read it. The second area encompasses ethical dilemmas and ethical decision making in cases of secrecy and confidentiality that can cause serious harm to clients and or third parties. The third area deals with unethical behavior of the worker, such as exploitation of the client, etc.

In the case offered previously, the second area seems to be most relevant. It involves the professional responsibility of workers not to mix their personal life with their work. Mixing the two would seriously jeopardize professional work and make it impossible to do properly. Reamer (1999) claims that we should remember a simple fact: social workers are not angels. They get involved at times in personal problems that are part and parcel of daily life. Yet, the code of ethics states that it is forbidden for social workers to let their personal problems interfere with or prevent fulfillment of professional obligations, nor can the problems affect professional judgment or endanger the lives in the worker's care, those for whom they have professional obligation.

When a social worker finds that his or her personal problem interferes with carrying out his or her role as a professional worker, he or she must turn to others for professional advice or change assignment and make other appropriate steps to defend the clients. If the worker cannot do so, a fellow colleague who knows about the worker's situation must bring the information to the attention of the director.

It comes as no surprise that of the sections included in the latest NASW Code of Ethics, three are devoted to the subject of responsibility. The first refers to the responsibility of social workers to their clients. Section Two concerns workers' responsibility to their colleagues, and the fifth section details their responsibility toward their chosen profession. Professional responsibility pertains to all social workers. They should provide their services to clients without regard to religion, race, creed, gender, age, political affiliation, or social status. This responsibility requires social workers to maintain high standards in ethical behavior in any situation, to initiate activities for the welfare of society, to synchronize services delivery with other professions and professionals in harmony with the demands of each case, and to continuously develop professional knowledge.

The expression of a social worker's professional responsibility is anchored in behavior that is easy to identify, praise, or blame. The characteristics of responsible behavior include refraining from misusing information about a client's personality, health, social status, economic situation, political beliefs and opinions; refraining from misusing professional education and training; not giving out information about a client to any unauthorized person; not harming the client knowingly or unwittingly; respecting the values of the profession as expressed in the code of ethics; maintaining fiduciary relationships with clients based on trust and decency; serving as moral agent for the client and for society; and working toward enhancing welfare, social justice, and defense for the weak in society.

Levinas (1981), the French expert in phenomenology, has claimed that philosophy should begin in ethics, and ethics is none other than one's responsibility for the other. Therefore we must speak about the ethics of responsibility. This ethics does not emanate from a certain need as an obligation but from the situation that exists in itself, a situation in which the meeting face-to-face with the other causes a feeling of responsibility for him or her as a human being to arise in oneself. The essence of humanity we should seek is in our belongingness to the human race, and not necessarily in freedom, which is in any case limited and at the mercy of many factors (Levinas, 1981).

In accordance with Levinas' approach to responsibility, a need exists to ease the starvation of the other and to cover the person if he or she is cold. The other comes not as an equal but as a person in whose fate one commanded to intervene, and the responsibility means that the fate of the other depends on what one does with it.

How is Levinas' approach connected to responsibility in social work? Responsibility in social work is a complex subject in which legal, philosophical, and ethical aspects can appear together in certain situations. For example, in cases of malpractice in which the various aspects appear together, the concept of professional responsibility is hard to separate from the moral aspect. This responsibility is connected to the performance of professional obligation, together with will, freedom of choice, and such legal aspects as to what extent workers can relate to the client as one who has control of his or her actions and is responsible for those actions.

The first and foremost responsibility of social workers, for whose actions medical ethics serve as a model, is to provide, above all else, help to the needy in accordance with their abilities and specialty. The social worker is responsible for the activities that emanate from the helping process: diagnosis, giving information to the clients concerning their condition or situation, obtaining the agreement of their clients for any intervention before it is carried out by the worker or others (informed consent), deciding about the means and execution of the treatment plan, and maintaining professional relationships with the family of the patient, including explanation about the treatment the client is receiving or going to receive.

Situations exist in which the worker can fulfill all of the previously mentioned functions and roles, when for example the physical or mental condition of the client is deficient to such a degree that he or she is incapable of relating to the treatment that is needed. In such cases the worker's professional responsibility requires him or her to speak with the family of the client and receive its agreement for the necessary treatment or intervention. The worker should not under any circumstances engage in manipulations or force the client to accept the treatment offered. The worker is responsible for the curtailment of the treatment as well. In addition, the social worker must ensure that in case of emergency every effort will be made, even against the commonly accepted rules, to help the client.

Advancing social work knowledge is an integral part of the worker's professional responsibility. Therefore social workers must study and participate in scientific conferences and in continuing education to enrich their knowledge in their specialty. Their additional responsibilities are listed in the code of ethics (see Appendix A). Accordingly, workers are not permitted to discriminate against anybody on the basis of race, gender, religion, and etc., or use their professional authority contrary to the values of the social work profession.

CONSULTATION WITH COLLEAGUES

All professionals can find themselves in situations that require consultation with colleagues in cases in which personal and professional knowledge alone are not sufficient to solve a problem, or in cases that require special expertise, for example legal advice, psychiatric consultation, etc. Instances occur in which consultation with the appropriate professional authority in diagnosis, or method of treatment can save human lives.

In medicine, for example, Hippocrates wrote that many doctors shy away from consultation with colleagues due to jealousy, which attests to professional weakness. The good doctors (and the good social workers) will not hesitate to recognize the limits of their knowledge, will respect the superior knowledge of their peers, and will not refrain from asking for professional advice.

Today it seems that scientific and technological developments in social work led to many areas of specialty and expertise and these require the worker to consult frequently with colleagues. Clients and their families can request additional professional consultation in cases in which two workers present differing opinions or approaches to a certain procedure. Consultation can be misused and abused when it serves as means to escape responsibility for mistakes made in treatment.

Total rejection of consultation shows, by and large, exaggerated self-confidence or lack of security and fear of losing the respect of one's colleagues. The cultural background of the professional can influence decisions for or against consultation. Some therapists will not turn to their colleagues for help due to pride and concepts of honor specific to their cultures. Cases such as these are well documented in professional literature (Blasszauer, 1995). On the other hand, exaggerated reliance on consultation can indicate an attempt to cover for anticipated failures and mistakes or to transfer responsibility to the experts with whom one consults.

Improper consultation exists when the worker sends the client from one colleague to the next in the disguise of "let's hear another opinion." The worker who sends clients in clear conscience to a colleague for consultation to verify or reject the original diagnosis expects to get a response. Lack of response hurts collegial relationships among workers. It enlarges the danger of malpractice and leads to loss of respect for the profession in the eyes of the clients and families.

Social work does not have such a long tradition as a profession as medicine does, therefore it did not develop commonly accepted rules of consultation. The subject of consultation was mentioned in the code of ethics that preceded the present code (Barker, 1987) saying, "The social worker should seek advice and counsel of colleagues and supervisors whenever such consultation is in the best interest of clients" (p. 201).

In the recent version of the same code (National Association of Social Workers, 1996), consultation with colleagues is recommended to resolve conflicts with colleagues. Usually consultation with colleagues is informal and is conducted in an agency among same-level professionals. The consultation may be "technical," as in cases in which the question is technical, for example, how to perform a certain action the best way or how to use a specific technique to help the client. More formal consultation, still among colleagues at the same agency and same level, happens as matter of fact between the worker and supervisor. Sometimes a need exists to consult with the director of the agency or with legal advisors who do not necessarily have to be social workers. Such consultation may take place when a need occurs for a legal statement or when some administrative issue arises.

Consultation with colleagues in other helping professions takes place regularly, especially when social workers serve in multiprofessional teams. This consultation is not usually regarded as a threat to the professional standing and status of the worker. In recent years a growing tendency exists to turn to experts in ethics to help agency staff in the resolution of their ethical dilemmas.

Chapter 7

Social Justice

If society would accept the same ethical rules that truly serve its well-being and the people would act accordingly then society will be more ethical and live in far better economic conditions than today.

John C. Harsanyi
recipient of the Nobel Prize in Economics
(Harsanyi, 1978, p. 231)

The laws of humankind must conform to a higher ideal of justice, one that emanates from God but that can be understood through the concepts of equality, human improvement, and democratic participation.

Martin Luther King Jr.
(cited in Clarkin, 2000, p. 1020)

The tradition of helping the poor in the Western world is based on the Judeo-Christian heritage. A thousand years or more before the appearance of Christianity, Jewish religious attitude to the needy was already existent in the Bible. Social morals were based on the laws in the Torah. Moral demands in relation to human relationships were necessary parts of what God was demanding from the people. The moral commands not to hurt anyone and to refrain from doing bad are central to the Jewish religion. The Torah requires dealing with the slave with mercy and compassion, which, keeping in mind the time period, was an act of humanitarianism. In Deuteronomy 5 it is stated that the Sabbath holiday applies to the slave and the maid too, so that they can rest, for the Israelites must remember that they were slaves in Egypt. The commandment to free a slave after six years of work (Ex-

Ethics in Social Work: A Context of Caring
© 2006 by The Haworth Press, Inc. All rights reserved.
doi:10.1300/5577_08

odus 21:20) and give him or her the means to begin a new life as a free person (Deuteronomy 15:12) were based on a firm concept of social morals or social justice.

In the ancient Greek society, anybody who helped his or her fellow human did so to develop his or her soul. A Greek free person could help those whom he or she regarded as equals, as in Aristotle's attitude to social justice, which read: "Equals must receive equal treatment, and those who are not equals may receive less than equal treatment." Greek society, and later Roman society too, was divided into two societies, free persons, citizens of the state or city, and slaves, and the attitude to the slave was very different from what is written in the Torah.

Loewenberg (1995) emphasized in his work on social justice that in ancient Greece and Rome no philanthropy in the terms of the modern Western approach to this concept existed. Contrary to Jewish society in biblical times, Greeks and Romans in those times did not recognize their duty to support the needy. In the Jewish tradition the poor relied on laws that specified the measure of help and support, not as a matter of charity but as a duty. For the Greeks, slaves were no more than a material means and their owners could force them to work as much as they thought necessary. Therefore, the free Greek could totally disregard the condition of an entire society that lived in dire distress.

Aristotle's principle regarding social justice, which differs in its approach to the treatment of the free citizen and of the slave, is called the principle of formal equality. Sometimes it is regarded as "minimal justice," meaning justice dependent on arbitrary decisions made by the rich concerning the welfare of the poor (the slave). In social work's history the difference in treatment of the "deserving" and "undeserving" poor by workers of the charity societies in late nineteenth century is well documented. These differences were accentuated in the poor's relative right to aid.

Many principles of social and distributive justice exist. Common to all is that they are designed to allocate goods in limited supply relative to demand. They deal with questions related to the subject of distribution (such as income, wealth, or opportunities), to whom the resources should be distributed (individuals, groups, communities, etc.), or on what basis should the distribution be carried out (on equality, individual characteristics, merit, etc.).

Distributive justice may adhere to one or more of the following approaches:

- on the strict egalitarian principle
- on the difference principle
- on the resource-based principles
- on the welfare-based principles
- on the desert-based principles

Each of these approaches has their followers, critics and shortcomings. Several of these principles will be briefly presented here.

The *strict egalitarian principle* states that every person should have the same level of material goods and services. The *difference principle* is based on the idea that the most common way of producing more wealth is to have a system in which those who are more productive earn greater incomes. John Rawls' (1971) theory of distributive justice (presented later in this chapter) deals with his two main principles: That each person has an equal claim to a fully adequate scheme of equal basic rights and liberties, and that social and economic inequalities are to satisfy two conditions: (1) to positions and offices are to be open to all people under conditions of fair equality of opportunity, and (2) the greatest benefit is to be given to the least advantaged members of society (Rawls 1993, pp. 5-6).

Theorists of *resource-based principles* agree that people have unequal natural endowments and social circumstance over which they have no control, such as low levels of natural talents, ill health, or handicaps that adversely affect their earning capacities, therefore they should not be disadvantaged and should be compensated. *Desert-based principles* are based on one of three categories: on contribution to society, on the effort extended in the work activity, and on compensation.

In Aristotle's approach to social justice, virtue formed the basis for the distribution of rewards, whereas in our times a just distribution of rewards and resources is, or rather should be, done according to the different levels earned or deserved by individuals for their productive labors, efforts, or contributions. In terms of an ethical approach to social justice, what really matters, and what morally can be justified is the welfare that results to society from the different ways of the distribution.

Social justice refers to justice in the distribution of good and bad economically and socially. Social workers, for example, are duty bound to treat the needy in accordance with their professional judgment and one of the criteria listed previously. This attitude to social justice is characteristic of all modern and democratic societies. The criteria of need as the only basis for social justice were tried during the twentieth century in communistic regimes and in Israeli kibbutzim and failed.

Today it is customary to speak about giving "equal opportunity" to all the citizens as an important value in democratic countries. This concept of equality means that people should have equal access to law, education, health care, employment, etc. Behind this attitude to equality is an assumption that giving equal opportunities to all the citizens in all areas of social and economic activities, including sources of power (politics), will enhance social justice.

Martin Luther King Jr.'s concept of justice is different from both ancient and modern approaches to justice. Relying heavily on God as a higher authority than on the law of the land, he maintained a definition that is applicable to nonbelievers as well as to believers. For King, a just law was one that improves the human personality and seeks equality. Placing one group in society above another, as in ancient Greece (free persons above slaves) or in the American society until the abolishment of slavery and racial segregation, is wrong and unjust. It creates strife and tensions, conflicts and violence, and eventually degrades both groups. Therefore laws that promote unjust divisions in society must be violated and broken.

The well-known teacher of ethics, Frankena (1973), has stated that just distribution of economic and social resources should be based on the principle of justice. Justice in his approach means giving preference to the needy. We may imagine for example two families needing heat in the winter in Wisconsin, but the resources are sufficient for buying only one heater. This means that only one family can enjoy this benefit, yet social justice requires that both families should enjoy heating in the winter. Therefore the question is raised: By what criteria should it be decided which family will get the heater? Would it be the equality in need? Or would the contribution to society be the criteria? Would it be according to the value or merit of the family? It is most likely that other criteria could also serve the purpose of social justice, such as the number of people in the family, the ages of children, or elderly parents who live together with the family in the same household.

Benefit as part of morality and justice means affirmation of action that enhances the good. Justice, according to Frankena (1973) refers to distribution between good and bad. Distributive justice is relative to treatment. We can say that justice is equal treatment and injustice is unequal treatment or dissimilar treatment in similar situation, as in the previous illustration.

Justice requires action for the special needs of individuals or groups in society, for example, the disabled, the old, the widowed or orphaned, and all minorities. For only by caring for the special needs of these people will they be able to have "equal opportunity" and enjoy life in the same way as the rest of the population.

JUSTICE AND CHARITY IN JEWISH TRADITION

Conceptually speaking, justice occupies a central position in the Jewish outlook on the world. Around this concept revolve other values that are connected to religion and morals. In the Jewish religious tradition, which is accepted by Christianity as well, God commands the people of Israel and all other nations to pursue justice (Deuteronomy 16:20) by fulfilling the commandments and the law he gave.

God's justice is identical to saintliness, whereas charity is identical to the work of justice, meaning that justice must be done rather than only talked about. Justice in Jewish tradition is dissimilar to that to which the ancient Greek philosophers referred. Justice for the Jews is first of all essential, is a part of what the life of a human being should be, and is based on a value commitment to what a decent society must perceive as its duty, meaning a universal ideal. For the Greeks and even in modern Western society, justice is identical to distribution or remuneration according to principles of procedures of how to distribute or remunerate individuals and groups in society.

The Jewish approach to justice emphasizes enrichment of the social life of the community and collective responsibility for the welfare of the public by stating that the children of Israel are responsible for one another. Schwartzschield (1974) referred to two opposing approaches to justice in the Jewish tradition: The first takes Moses as representing the ideal of absolute justice, and the second, represented by his brother Aaron, is an approach of compromise. Some see in the inability to compromise (particularly in legal matters) a denial of justice, and some think that justice is the ideal that needs to be kept and aspire to a future when justice and mercy will join together in one unit at the individual and universal levels.

Two expressions frequently appearing in the Bible refer to divine and to human justice as well as to the "work of justice": charity and justice. Both are central in Jewish religious life and occupy a central position in the outlook on life of a Jewish person in general. In the Bible we may frequently encounter two words in addition to justice *Hesed* (loving-kindness) and *Mishpat Ivri* (law). The concept of charity became significant from the time of the Talmud (fourth century AD and on) and expresses the practical approach to justice, piousness, and law. Justice is equivalent to truth, belief, and uprightness.

The greatest contribution of Judaism to the world is included in the concept of charity. The Torah requires that the landlord (the well-to-do or rich) help the poor and needy. In the Passover Haggadah, this is expressed in the sentence "Anyone needy is welcome to enjoy the Passover feast" (free of charge, of course). Giving of alms or charity was regarded by the rabbis in all historical times as the greatest good deed in Judaism. Contrary to other religions, Judaism never accepted poverty as an unavoidable social phenomenon. Judaism rejected the Christian approach, which culminated in the saying that the poor should be happy for they will inherit the kingdom of heaven, and created laws and rules of conduct aimed at coping with and defeating poverty.

In the times of the Bible and the Talmud Israeli society was agrarian. Therefore charity was built around agrarian concepts, such as not harvesting the margins of the field, leaving the gleanings and overlooking the grains in these places for the poor. These were regarded as taxes or benefits for the needy. Even concepts such as *Shmita* and *Yovel, Shmita* (or sabbatical) occurring every seventh year during which fields are left fallow and *Yovel* (or jubilee) occuring every fiftieth year during which all debts are forgiven and all slaves set free, served the same purpose so that the poor could eat and not fall under the weight of their debts. Poverty was perceived as the greatest of misfortunes. In Deuteronomy it is said that the poor will not cease from the land (Deuteronomy 15:11) therefore the children of Israel were commanded to remember the poor on the holy days and festivals and care for their needs (Deuteronomy 15:7). Strangers, people who were not citizens in Israel, were regarded as poor due to their inferior economic situation, and help for them was anchored in reminding the Israelis that they themselves were slaves in Egypt and inferior to the Egyptians (Deuteronomy 10:19).

Charity was regarded as the main trait of God himself. Therefore a "woman of valor" is one who extends her hands to the poor (Proverbs 31:20). Despite that the Bible contains many references to the idea of charity, the word charity itself was never mentioned until the sages of the Talmud accepted it and used it to denote the help that should be given the poor in the shape of gifts. Since then and until today Jews use charity and *Hesed* (kindness or conpassion) for the same purpose. The word *Hesed* refers to physical help or to giving loans without interest.

Charity is not doing a "favor" to the poor. It is the obligation of the giver and the right of the receiver. This is a very important principle in modern approaches to social justice in the well-developed welfare states in which the citizens have rights to receive services and benefits and the state has rights to use taxes for the same purpose. Jewish communal leadership has developed charity as a good deed and turned it into a commonly accepted social institution and obligation. They clothed charity in religious and moral clothing and compared it to the most important religious duty that hastens the coming of the Messiah (Brick, 1999).

In rabbinical literature charity was accepted as the most important good deed (mitzvah). The rabbis explained that in fact the poor do a great favor to the giver of alms (the landlord) when they accept a gift or donation, for they are helping the giver to fulfill this commandment. Rabbis such as Rabbi Elazar saw in charity the most important commandment.

Moses Maimonides developed a most liberal approach to giving charity, one that can serve as guide for present day approaches to social justice. His approach to charity is briefly explained and presented in the following section.

MAIMONIDES'S APPROACH TO CHARITY

Maimonides ruled that the same charity that is owed to the poor should be given equally to all to whom it is due. Fulfillment of the laws and commandments in the Torah do not constitute charity. Paying paid laborers their wages properly and without delay is similarly not charity. The same applies to repayment of a loan. Correcting the distortion or fulfillment of a given promise is, however, charity. All the moral virtues of a person are charity, for they do charity to his or her soul.

Maimonides devised a "ladder of charity" in giving alms and compared the rungs of the ladder to the personal and moral effort of a human in fulfillment of this good deed. At the bottom of the ladder stands the one who gives alms, but gives them sadly. Above this person is one who gives less than he or she should. On the third rung from the bottom stands the one who gives only after he or she is asked, and above this person is the one who gives before he or she is asked. The next four rungs in the ladder of charity represent more valuable giving and morally higher levels of charity. On the fifth rung stands the one who gives so that the recipient will know his or her identity. Above this person is the one who will give and the recipient will not know the identity of the giver. On the seventh rung stands the one who gives secretly in such a way that the giver will not know to whom he or she gave, nor will the recipient know who gave to him or her. The highest rung on the ladder of charity is occupied by those who do not give alms at all but who help the poor by rehabilitating them. That is, the ones who will find work for the poor or take him or her into their business as partner or provide him or her with work. Thus the dignity and self-respect of the individual is kept intact and injury to either is avoided. It can be said without hesitation, therefore, that Maimonides preceded modern day social work by more than seven hundred years when he emphasized the importance of rehabilitation and safeguarding the dignity of the needy.

This approach to the poor, the downtrodden, the needy, and the stranger, practiced during thousands of years in all the Jewish communities in the world, has influenced and still influences social justice and social policies in Israel and elsewhere where Jewish people live, and it is relevant no less for all others.

SOCIAL WORK AND DISTRIBUTION OF RESOURCES

Distribution of a society's resources is an ethical question in essence, that is, it can be approached from various perspectives in accordance with the theories in ethics that have already been presented. Social work as a profession deals with distribution and redistribution of resources that have social values. The resources for distribution are divided into two groups: the material, such as money, work, entrance to institutions, etc. and the immaterial, such as status or stigma. The following case example is an illustration of this.

CASE EXAMPLE: DISTRIBUTION OF MONEY FOR NEW IMMIGRANTS

The committee for the absorption of new immigrants from the former Soviet Union in Israel was asked to draw up a proposition for how to deal with the money allocated to the city council for helping with the absorption of the newcomers. During the past year some four thousand new immigrants came to settle in the city. Members of the committee were the deputy mayor and the directors of the major social services, all of them social workers. The committee discussed the problem in several meetings and tried to come to a consensus. Some members suggested equal distribution among the newcomers' families. Others claimed that the money should be divided according to recognized needs, and thus a survey of needs should be conducted. Still others said that the money should be given to special groups within the newcomers, such as widows, the elderly, and families with numerous children.

The question was raised regarding by which principles the various proposals were to be examined. In order to answer this question, the commonly accepted values of social workers must be known regarding decision making for distribution of resources in particular. The code of ethics of social workers does not define the concept of social justice in practical terms, and is not helpful as a means for solving problems involved in the distribution of resources. It lacks the social component, meaning the result of professional intervention in social welfare. An old dispute has existed within the profession regarding the approach to social problems and needs since the days of the "charity organizations." On the one hand are those who favor making an effort to promote individuals, and on the other are those who favor promoting the community and the law for the welfare of society. At the same time attempts are made to define anew the functions and roles of the profession in the same code.

Leaders of the profession of social work agree that science is only one way to gain knowledge about the needs of human beings and their behavior. A need also exists for flexibility in thought to avoid falling into conservative and outdated patterns and dogmas. A professional worker needs to be equipped, beyond knowledge, skills, and values with a hefty measure of humanism and sense of justice. Only synthesis between humanism and therapy can produce a fine and excellent professional.

Members of the absorption committee agreed on the following:

Priority in resources allocation or distribution should be given to general human interests. These interests include the need to avoid hurt and damage and to ensure normal living conditions as much in accordance with the standard of living prevalent in society as possible.

Members of the committee agreed that at the basis of their decision should stand the concept of equality in social justice. That is, the need to distribute the resources equally among the families who need help. They also agreed that social workers must act according to their professional values—despite expected stress from political forces and old-country values and habits of the newcomers. The principle of self-determination is central in social work, and no deviation from this value can occur. Members of the committee should respect the rights of those who ask for help to make decisions about their own lives and destinies, including their right to receive the proposed help or to reject it.

The question can be raised regarding which theory of ethics is the best suited to advance social justice. Many social workers would point to teleology without hesitation. They would argue that resources should be distributed in such a way that they will bring good to the greatest number of people. In the previous case, many would say that equal distribution of the resources would bring the greatest good and utility. However, in this approach no differentiation exists either in status or between the needs of the rich and the poor. It is impossible to assume that all the immigrants arrived in exactly the same situation. If the distribution were made equally, many immigrants would receive benefit (money) they really did not deserve or need, such as the well-to-do or those who were fit to work but refused to do so, and those who wanted to receive benefits without making their contribution to society would eventually join the subgroup of dependent people and become a burden on society.

RAWLS'S THEORY OF SOCIAL JUSTICE

One of the most creative and influential thinkers in our times, whose works have particular relevance for social work ethics is John Rawls (born in 1921). His most significant book, *A Theory of Justice*, was published in 1971, and has changed the attitude of many thinkers, social scientists and philosophers to the concept of justice from placing the emphasis on the individual to placing it on the group, or rather, the community.

In this book Rawls opted for fair and nonenvious cooperation among free and equal citizens (a somewhat utopian quest), living in a modern constitutional democracy whose main interest would center on liberty, equality, and social justice (almost similar to the slogans of the French Revolution). Yet in Rawls's philosophy, these terms and concepts do not express mere slogans, they embody the cornerstones of an entire theory. Rawls aimed at creating a just society, one in which people would cooperate with one another fairly as free and equal citizens, endowed with a moral capacity for a sense of justice. He also was aware that people would have differences in knowledge and circumstances. Therefore they would have or develop different conceptions of the good and would make conflicting claims on the scarce resources. The "good" in Rawls's theory included that one's philosophical and religious convictions and an ethical way of life give meaning to one's existence.

The needed resources were thought by Rawls to be "primary social goods," such as rights and liberties, powers and opportunities, income and wealth, and self-respect. This latter concept, Rawls averred, was the most important. He defined it as people's sense of their own value, their secure conviction that their conception of the good, their plan of life, is worth carrying out, along with the conviction that they have the ability to carry it out (Mattison, 2000).

How to divide the scarce resources in a just way was, therefore, a philosophical and practical problem for Rawls (1971). He insisted that the division must be made by using some principles of justice. Basically, Rawls asserted, two such principles existed: First, that justice is equal and goes along with maximum feasible liberty for all, and second, that power and wealth are to be distributed equally except when inequality would work to the advantage of all. This approach to inequality in Rawls's theory of justice is called the "difference principle" (Weiss, 2000).

Rawls thought that every human being, irrespective of his or her aspirations and desires, wants "primary goods." The principles of justice thus refer to the distribution of these resources. The "primary goods" themselves were social and natural—as detailed previously. In his book, Rawls (1971) presented his idea of the principles of social justice. He also has given the rationale why these principles can be satisfied only in a liberal society. As for the redistribution of income and wealth for the benefit of the least advantaged in society, Rawls's theory stands in opposition to the utilitarianism that permits the sacrifice of the few for the good of the many. For Rawls this was considered an untenable moral theory. It is the irony of fate that Martin Luther King Jr. was dead when Rawls's book was published in 1971. Were King alive at that time, he would, no doubt, have endorsed Rawls's theory.

To recapitulate Rawls's theory and major concepts, Rawls assumed that those who think that it is possible to maintain social justice are likely to opt for equality. He differentiated between "natural obligation," such as the obligation to help someone who happens to be in great danger or need, and "noble acts," which are praiseworthy but do not necessarily obligate the worker.

An additional contribution of Rawls to the ethics of social work is connected to the ordering of priorities in values and obligations. These will be elaborated upon in Chapter 10. In accordance with his theory of social justice, one should take into consideration two leading principles in the distribution of social resources: Each individual is entitled to equal rights and maximum freedom, provided that the same principle is acknowledged for others too, social and economic inequality is permitted assuming that it is expected and regarded as beneficial for all and connected to status or position open to anybody.

For Rawls, justice is the central social value that determines (or should determine) social policy. Justice guides the entire society. Rawls endorsed the "principle of difference," meaning that all primary or basic social resources, such as electricity, water, health and welfare services, and public transportation should be distributed equally among members of society, unless unequal distribution of these resources favors the weak in society.

PART II:
APPLIED ASPECTS
OF THERAPEUTIC WORK

Chapter 8

Social Welfare
and Distributive Justice

During the 1990s the United States underwent major demographic changes. The dramatic rise in population growth resulted in an increase in people of color from 20 percent to 25 percent (National Association of Social Workers, 2001). These changes have emphasized that America is a mosaic of cultures, races, religions, languages, customs, and behaviors. The concept of multiculturalism came into vogue, expressing the diversity that confronts social workers in service delivery. The profession of social work has responded to the challenges posed by this change by stating standards for cultural competence, based on ten points and in practice binding on members of the profession. These standards were prepared by the NASW National Committee on Racial and Ethnic Diversity and adopted by the NASW Board of Directors on June 23, 2001, and endorsed by the Council on Social Work Education Board of Directors in 2003.

Behind these standards was the old quest of the profession to advance social justice in society in general and distributive justice in particular and to strive to end discrimination, oppression, poverty, and other forms of social injustice. The following two of the ten points listed in the standards are particularly relevant to this book:

> Standard 1: *Ethics and values:* "Social workers shall function in accordance with the values, ethics, and standards of the profession, recognizing how personal and professional values may conflict with or accommodate the needs of diverse clients."
> Standard 4: *Cross-cultural skills:* "Social workers shall use appropriate methodological approaches, skills, and techniques

Ethics in Social Work: A Context of Caring
© 2006 by The Haworth Press, Inc. All rights reserved.
doi:10.1300/5577_09

that reflect the workers' understanding of the role of culture in the helping process." (National Association of Social Workers, 2001, p. 4)

The standards have called for the inclusion of cultural competence in the skills, values, and knowledge used by social workers working with clients, agencies, and administrators on behalf of people of diverse cultural backgrounds. This request raises the issue of competence in social work in general and cultural competence and ethics in particular.

Competence in social work has been defined by Barker (1987) as:

> the ability to fulfill the requirement of a job or other obligation. Competence in social work includes possession of all relevant educational and experiential requirements, demonstrated ability through passing licensing and certification exams, and the ability to carry out work assignments and achieve social work goals while adhering to the values of the profession. (p. 30)

Cultural competence, and in particular *multicultural* competence were omitted from Barker's (1987) *Social Work Dictionary,* an indication that at the time this dictionary was compiled the issue of what constitutes cultural competence and multicultural competence had not yet been raised in the profession of social work.

Today many requirements are connected to and mentioned under the term cultural competence. These are elaborated upon in the standards, yet they may mean different things to different people, not only in each racial and ethnic group but also for members differently placed in various organizations. The "relevant educational and experiential requirements" listed in Barker's definition of competence can be debated. However, a basic understanding exists that in order to be effective in practice with members of so many different ethnic and racial groups living together in a multicultural society, a social worker needs to possess several characteristics beyond the requirements of the NASW Code of Ethics.

Methods to obtain these characteristics were recently listed by Marsh (2004) as consisting of the following. First, the worker must assess his or her own understanding and attitudes toward the "strangers" and take personal responsibility for his or her beliefs and approach. This process of self-scrutiny resembles the age-old teaching in ancient Greece: know yourself. Second, the worker should expose himself or herself to different cultures, languages, and social groups. Work and socialize with one who is different from you in terms of race, religion, ethnicity, gender, sexual orientation, and socioeconomic status. Try to gain rich experience, and learn through teaching and listening. Third, use your newly acquired learning to develop multicultural competencies in your daily work, and practice your commitment to social work's basic values to create more social justice in the world.

Beyond these characteristics perhaps the most important quality to possess is having an open mind. This means having a positive attitude to the differences, sensitivity, and respect for anything human and valuable as well as an interest in the world around you. The Standards for Cultural Competence in Social Work Practice (National Association of Social Workers, 2001) identified several areas in which social workers can apply their cultural-competence related skills, including in assessment of cultural norms and behaviors as strengths rather than pathologies in the provision of services and in treatment, in advocacy and planning, and in development of organizations and communities. In all these entities the differences should be seen as sources of interest and innovation. Social workers should use all opportunities for developing and participating in educational and training programs that help advance cultural competence within the profession (National Association of Social Workers, 2001, pp. 4-5).

In addition to the personal characteristics of the culturally competent social worker, social justice would also require that the staffing, management, and leadership of social work organizations and agencies reflect the diversity of the client population. This perception of social justice is perhaps the best expression of cultural competence. It shows an attitude of trust in the ability of culturally different people to manage their own affairs and to share in the allocation of power in a given agency and in the distribution of its resources, and it may ensure a fair level of equity among the services providers and their clients.

The NASW Standards for Cultural Competence include a clause about empowerment and advocacy. It "requires social workers to be aware of the effect of social policies and programs on diverse client populations, advocating for and with clients whenever appropriate" (p. 5). Translated into common language this means that a culturally competent worker will insist on reviewing agency policy with regard to the decision-making process in matters of personnel, space, and allocation of resources. Such practices would most likely generate the conflicts and power struggles inherent in the process. At the same time, however, these efforts will eventually help bring to the surface, identify, and resolve those conflicts. Progress toward social justice will emerge through struggle among members of different racial and cultural groups. The struggle would encompass clients, workers, and management. It may also mean risk-taking behavior on the part of courageous workers, clients, and managers ready to take issue with outdated practices and attitudes that perpetuate social injustice.

DISTRIBUTIVE JUSTICE

In its broadest meaning, the term *social welfare* includes the actions of organizations and institutions and the entire system of welfare aimed at providing the needs of those members in society who are unable to care for themselves. A social welfare system is an expression of a society's moral relationships between the people and between the community and society in which these people live. The moral foundation of society has deep roots in values and religion. It demands from its members that they help people in distress. This foundation was at one time connected to the commandment of personal charity and to the idea of exchange of gifts between people. In modern societies the moral foundation finds its expression in activities organized by institutions. These function to strengthen social cohesion and enhance the relationships within the community, similar to the role of charity societies in late nineteenth and early twentieth century.

Modern welfare systems work on the assumption that the aim to redistribute resources should be "one directional," that is, transferring from the well-to-do to the poor. The emphasis on a unilateral direction was given a strong impetus after World War II, following the political and social changes that swept many nations all over the world. It was a direct expression of the will of the people to have more equality in social and economic matters and their interest in a more just distribution of the resources in society.

Common to all social welfare systems is that they function with limited resources. Each one needs therefore to devise principles of distribution to regulate services provision. These principles shape the character of the welfare system.

Social Justice and Distribution of Resources

Health care in Barker's (1999) definition refers to:

> Activities designed to treat, prevent, and detect physical and mental disorders and to enhance people's physical and psychosocial well-being. The health care system includes personnel who provide the needed services (physicians, nurses, hospital attendants, medical social workers, and so on); facilities where such services are rendered (hospitals, medical centers, nursing homes, hospices, outpatient clinics); laboratories and institutions for detection, research, and planning; educational and environmental facilities that help people prevent disease; and myriad other organizations and people involved in helping people to become more healthy, return to health, or minimize the consequences of ill health. (p. 211)

The following case is borrowed from Reamer (1999). It refers to the allocation of limited resources as an ethical dilemma in "indirect" social work. Indirect social work does not deal with individuals, families, or small groups but with community organization, administration, and social policy. Resources allocation entails ethical dilemmas that social workers frequently encounter in this area of service.

CASE EXAMPLE:
ALLOCATION OF LIMITED RESOURCES

Natalie K. is the executive director of the Camden Yards Drug Treatment center. The center provides counseling and supportive services for individuals who have substance abuse problems. For years the center has depended on state contracts and fees paid by insurance companies and self-pay clients.

Natalie K. was recently informed by the director of the state's substance abuse division that state funding for the next fiscal year is to be cut by 25 percent. State revenues have been down because of a sluggish economy and, as a result, funding for most state programs must be reduced.

Natalie K. knows that it will be impossible for her staff to continue serving as many clients as they did in the past. During the past year the center's staff provided services to approximately five hundred people. Ordinarily, the agency has no waiting list or only a short one. Natalie K. estimates that with the funding cuts her staff will be able to serve only about 375 clients.

Natalie K. assembled her administrative staff and presented them with the bad news. She told the staff that together they have to decide how to determine which clients will be served, because the agency will not be able to accommodate the usual demand for its services.

The relevant theory must be considered in any ethical choice. Those who prefer the deontological theory in ethics would say that the director of this agency's duty is to provide equal opportunities to all clients who are eligible for the agency's services. This duty refers also to the need to weigh the relative difficulty in the situation of each client and to determine an agreed-upon order of priorities by which it will be determined who will be eligible to receive service from the agency.

Those who are led by the principles of teleology in solving ethical problems will not dwell on the question of duty. They will search for a mechanism that would promise the maximum good to those involved in this case, and concentrate on the need to predict which approach would provide the best results. They would therefore try to identify the neediest clients, those who would most likely positively respond to the agency's actions, and weigh the long-term results of the treatment that they would select.

Reamer (1999) claims that in many agencies, similar to the one in the case regarding the expensive patient on p. 139, the distribution of resources is determined without weighing the relevant ethical theory. Decisions made reflect the personal attitude of the director or are due to political pressures directed at the agency from different sources, despite that the decision will seriously affect the lives of the clients.

Natalie K.'s case raises a debate about the criteria that the decision makers use in their considerations regarding policy on how to distribute available resources. Frankena (1973) called these criteria *distributive justice*. This concept includes ethical use of the term and the criteria according to which the limited resources will be distributed among individuals, groups, organizations, and communities.

In the case of Natalie K., it is impossible to get help from the code of ethics in social work because the code does not contain practical instructions how to distribute limited resources among the needy. The code provides only a general statement about the need to develop appropriate methods for distribution of resources in a just, decent, and open manner, methods that will not discriminate against certain people among the clients on the basis of gender, race, religion, etc.

It seems that Natalie K., after searching for the best method for distribution of the remaining resources, will have no choice but to act in accordance with her values. In addition she could, of course, search for additional resources, organize political support for getting a larger share in state allocation of resources than at present, and engage her staff in community organization to gain monetary support from various community sources that would enable her to escape the cut in her budget.

In social work, according to Reamer (1999), four criteria are relevant for consideration in decisions about distribution of resources: equality, need, compensation, and contribution. These are discussed at times separately and at other times jointly in various combinations. Equality is very popular in social work. In situations of chronically limited resources in social services, all those who are eligible for a service or benefit should receive an equal share. In the previous case, Natalie K. could divide the time of her staff so that all five hundred of the agency's clients would get some time from her staff. This distribution of the resources would be equal but would cause an additional burden to be placed on the staff's workload and would not permit individually based intensive work with the neediest among the clients.

Another approach to equality in distribution of the resources is by emphasizing priorities. Those 375 clients out of the 500 that asked first for the services of the agency will be the ones who will actually receive them. Here the emphasis is on the procedure and not on the results. It is possible to uphold the criteria of equality in limited resources distribution by chance choice. Here the criteria of equality would be expressed by equality in opportunity for each client in the group of five hundred to be included in the 375 selected to receive the services of the agency. Still another way or method for arriving at the same end is to evaluate the need of each client among the five hundred and selecting the neediest 375.

Irrespective of the final choice, social workers must weigh their decisions according to the relative weight of each of the criteria discussed previously. It is important that the choice rely on ethical considerations that social workers are able to justify.

Resources allocation has several approaches and strategies. None of them is fully adequate for dealing with all possible problems because resources are never fully available, and it is impossible to escape from choosing among many priorities. Buchanan (1989) differentiated between two models of allocation, the efficiency and the ethical model. The former refers to issues such as utility maximization, cost benefit, or cost effectiveness as standards for judgment, whereas the ethical model relies on criteria that are necessary in making allocation-related decisions. The following case is taken from Blasszauer (1995) for illustration. Although this case refers to resource allocation in medicine, the dilemma posed for the doctor can easily be applicable to the social worker too.

CASE EXAMPLE:
THE MAN WHO CHOSE TO TRAVEL THE WORLD

A sixty-three-year-old owner of a small business decided to retire. After a short while he became sick with cancer that was diagnosed as leukemia. He was too young for old-age pension and was not eligible for Medicare. He did not have private medical insurance. His entire savings amounted to ten thousand dollars. He asked his doctor what to do and was told to put his health situation in the center of his deliberations. The doctor also told him that he would honor his decision.

The patient was not satisfied with the doctor's advice and consulted with his local priest about what to do with his savings: Should he use them to pay the expected medical bills or to go on a worldwide trip with his wife? The priest encouraged the patient to choose the latter. He told him to forego the expensive medical treatment that he found morally wrong and not binding and to go ahead and enjoy the trip. The couple accepted the priest's advice and went away for three months. Two months after their return the condition of the patient deteriorated and he died.

The ethical dilemma facing the doctor in this case was, on the one hand, the right of the patient to decide what to do with his life and to determine his own priority, such as the trip around the world, and on the other his commitment to prevent the loss of life due to the patient's improper response to his health. The doctor resolved his dilemma by accepting the right of the patient to self-determination, even if he did not agree with that decision.

Sometimes a client or patient behaves extremely irresponsibly. His or her behavior causes high monetary expenditure to the social or medical service and damage to many sick people that could have benefited from those resources in a more efficient way, as the following case illustrates.

CASE EXAMPLE: THE EXPENSIVE PATIENT

A fifty-two-year-old woman had a bypass operation. The complications developed after the operation forced her to undergo additional operations that left her in the hospital for three years. Her medical expenditures were two hundred thousand dollars. She needed a special diet, low in calories. The patient refused to cooperate with the medical staff. She expected the staff to satisfy all her needs. She was demanding and tended to accuse the staff and the doctors for all of her shortcomings. Yet, despite her behavior, she never stopped eating the foods her doctor told her not to.

The irresponsibility of this patient is an extreme case, yet it is not unique. The question can be raised whether doctors in this case should force her to change her behavior or whether they should satisfy themselves with easing her suffering and preventing further deterioration in her condition. The ethical dilemma that arises in this case is the following: What is more right, to respect the patient's right to self-determination, or to respect the right of society and the hospital to use its limited resources wisely and responsibly? This is a difficult question. Although the life of a human being takes priority in any consideration, a useful mechanism should exist to help in arriving at a decision that would be ethically correct and stand in all ethical criteria. Such a mechanism, lacking so far in social work, is, for example, available in medicine in what is called the medical order of priorities. This will be presented briefly via four cases taken from Blasszauer's (1995) book. The uniqueness of these cases is that they represent a situation in which four sick people with different kidney problems are "competing" for the only dialysis machine available for the doctors and consequently a need exists to determine who gets priority in its use and what will be the reason or the argument for the decision.

CASE EXAMPLE:
FOUR DIFFERENT KIDNEY PATIENT SITUATIONS

A married woman with two children is suffering from an infection in her urinary tract. Her kidneys are gradually losing their ability to function. She feels ill at ease for weeks, is depressed, and loses interest in living. Her medical condition requires treatment via the dialysis machine.

A fifty-five-year-old man has had insufficient functioning of his kidneys for the past four years. He had an unsuccessful kidney transplant. He receives necessary treatment in his home, has learned to operate his machine for dialysis, and lives a normal life as far as his medical condition allows him to. Lately a part in the machine broke down. This part can be fixed only by the company that manufactured the machine. The company, however, is far away and the new or fixed part could take, in the best case, two or three days to arrive, but the patient cannot wait this long without dialysis.

A fifty-eight-year-old man, very fat, alcoholic, and works occasional jobs has suffered for a long time from improper functioning of his kidneys. The opening in his vein to which the kidney machine is connected is in bad condition. He touches this place frequently and speaks about suicide. The medical team is of the opinion that he seriously means to commit suicide. This man is divorced and maintains no relationships with his two children.

A twenty-four-year-old student who ate a poisoned mushroom she thought was edible was poisoned and her kidneys stopped functioning. Due to her severe medical condition she needs immediate dialysis. If she receives it her chances for recovery will be very good.

BLASSZAUER'S DECISION-MAKING CRITERIA

According to Blasszauer (1995), eight criteria need to be taken into consideration in decision making regarding these cases. Each of these criteria is an important element in the doctor's professional deliberations to reach a decision that could be firmly anchored ethically and can be defended if needed. These will be briefly described in the following sections.

Triage

Triage is one of the oldest methods used in sorting out the wounded on the battlefield. The method is based on a clear order of priority according to which the doctor must determine whom to serve first. The method was adapted to civilian life as well and is used in cases of disasters, road accidents, and so on when many among the victims are wounded. The advantage of triage is that it causes less agony for the doctor than do other methods because it is based on considerations of utility. That is, the method gives preference to the wounded that would be able to function in the shortest period of time after the treatment and help in the rescue of others. Among the wounded to be treated first are the doctors, the firefighters, and the police.

In line with this method, the wounded are divided into three groups: Those who will most likely die shortly irrespective of the quality or quantity of the treatment they would receive, those who will most likely recuperate even if they do not receive treatment because their wounds are light and no danger to their lives exist, and the third group consists of those who can be saved if they receive immediate treatment. In case of insufficient resources, the priority given to this last group seems reasonable.

Prognosis

The medical prognosis is an important factor in the decision concerning to whom to give priority when the medical supply or skilled personnel are insufficient for all who need help and treatment. The prognosis is taken into consideration in assessing the chances of recovery for the sick. Prognosis alone cannot serve as the sole criteria, for it is not free of possible mistakes. Yet, it is the moral responsibility of the doctor or medical council to take into consideration the prognosis prior to reaching a decision.

Psychological and Environmental Factors

The first criterion is used frequently despite that the psychological condition of a sick person can change and cannot be predicted with certainty. Therefore this factor should not be taken seriously in the distribution of scarce resources, especially when the life of the sick or wounded is in direct and immediate danger. Even more difficult from among the psychological criteria is determining which of the environmental factors may help or hurt the patient. Therefore, these two factors are not given much weight in decision making, unless it can be shown concretely that they do influence the success of the treatment directly.

Randomness

This concept, known from the world of research, means that everyone has an equal chance to be included in the treatment, yet not everyone can actually obtain it. The majority of the sick can accept this criterion more easily than the decision of the doctor or the medical council, saying that it is better to leave things to chance or fate than to fall victim to the decisions of human beings.

Randomness is divided into two methods: (1) by way of lottery, which is used when not enough medications or medical equipment are available for all the sick, and (2) first come, first served, according to a list. The assumption behind this second method is that not all the sick will arrive at the same time for treatment. Here one must take into consideration additional factors, such as the distance the sick must travel in order to get to the hospital. The method is not free from manipulation, such as advancing a friend on the list, etc., and these manipulations hurt its credibility and reliability.

Immediate Danger to Life

Patients who need special equipment for saving their lives comprise two groups. The first group consists of those who will die shortly without treatment, and the second, those whose death is a matter of several days. These patients hope that they will be the first to enjoy new medicines or treatment that will save their lives. This was the basis for the doctors' decisions when insulin was first introduced in limited quantities. The same method was also used when a need arose to decide who will be the lucky one to get a heart implant.

Doctors can temporarily stop the treatment of patients whose treatment is expensive and direct the treatment resources to those who are in immediate danger of their lives. Such a decision can morally be justified if the patients whose treatment was temporarily stopped received a full explanation of the need and agreed to it, knowing that no immediate danger to their lives existed.

Age As a Criterion in Choosing

When a patient is selected for transplant of an organ or for dialysis, sometimes the decision is based on age of the candidate. In such cases a difficult problem can arise: Whose life is worth more? The life of a young person or of an old one? Morally speaking, the question is improper and wrong, for all life is equal. Therefore, decisions should not be made on the basis of age alone, for it would allow discrimination against the young and the old.

Using the Market As a Criterion

The buying of life-saving medical resources by those who can pay for it is morally wrong, for it hurts the principle of equality and respect for the life of a human being. Therefore this criterion cannot serve at all in decision making regarding the distribution of limited resources.

Social Value and Contribution to Society As Factors in the Decision

Sometimes the doctor must weigh the value of a patient to society and his or her potential future contribution as additional criteria in decision making about the use of limited resources. Many factors are for and against these criteria, and they pose a difficult choice for the decision maker. The main problem is that no social control regulates such matters. It is possible that what is regarded today as of value or as a contribution to society will be looked at differently in the future. Discriminating among patients on the basis of their value to society is dangerous and undemocratic, for it can result in grave consequences for certain groups.

These criteria can help in sorting out patients only if certain patients are willing to show altruism and forego their place on the list voluntarily for the sake of someone in greater need. Such altruism has moral and educational value and is praiseworthy. When the resources are very limited, it is permissible to favor a patient who needs a dialysis machine for a limited time, say a month, until his or her turn for kidney transplant will come, over a patient that needs the same machine until the end of his or her life.

Behind all the criteria listed previously are values and ethical theories that directly or indirectly influence critical decisions. In any choice related to the use of limited resources, no escape exists from conflicts and ethical dilemmas arising from tragic situations. The following chapters will deal with these dilemmas in detail.

Chapter 9

Trust in Client–Social Worker Relationships

FIDUCIARY RELATIONSHIPS IN SOCIAL WORK

Trust plays a crucial role in individual and social well-being. When one goes to a barber, for example, one expects the barber to execute faithfully his or her obligation as a skilled worker, meaning that he or she will not hurt another, will not cause harm, and will not ruin a person's hair. The trust vested in this case is a limited and conditional one. It is based on belief—the customer believing that the barber has both the necessary skills and the obligation entrusted in him or her by society to carry out the function of cutting hair faithfully. When a person with a difficult problem goes to the social worker, he or she submits much more than his or her hair to that person's care. And this makes a tremendous difference between the two kinds of trust. What is delivered into the hands of a social worker can change a person's entire life for good or bad. In both cases, however, the principle of reciprocity is in operation. An explicit agreement exists about the expectations of what each party has to do. Failure to maintain this reciprocity exposes the parties to various degrees of sanctions.

Trust between a social worker and a client is a condition of therapy. Without trust it is impossible to talk about successful therapy in any of the helping professions. Only in an atmosphere of trust can those who seek help disclose their secrets and express their hopes and wishes. The social worker ought to respond to the interest of the clients in a way the client perceives as beneficial for them and should base the process of treatment on this trust.

Levy (1976) has stated that the social worker–client relationship may be seen as fiduciary. This concept, based on the Latin word

Ethics in Social Work: A Context of Caring
© 2006 by The Haworth Press, Inc. All rights reserved.
doi:10.1300/5577_10

fiducia, meaning trust is the central nucleus in social worker–client relationships. Included in this concept are the autonomy and privacy of the clients and the risk they are taking. These are what clients value and risk most when they ask for help. They entrust these into the hands of the social worker knowing that the latter will not abuse this trust. Since no greater disappointment exists than to discover that this trust was abused, the social worker must act sensibly, in moderation, in wisdom, and carefully in order to keep this precious asset that was deposited in his or her hands.

Social workers must remember that their clients, similar to the clients of a lawyer, open up their intimate life to them, including information regarding their family, relatives, and friends, their economic situations and means, and their secrets—all parts of their lives that have psychological meaning for them, parts whose public discovery may cause serious harm to their family and social standing. On the basis of this trust social workers are expected to deal with the information received professionally decently, honestly, and in accordance with their professional ethics.

Social work has a value perspective that is beyond the scientific basis, the expertise, the skills, and professional values that are characteristic of a helping profession. An interesting fact is that the new code of ethics for social workers in Israel, for example, fails to relate to the trust that must exist between a worker and a client. Similarly, empathy is another concept that is omitted from the code's many paragraphs that describe the obligations of social workers toward those who comprise their professional world. Yet, trust and empathy are the "soul" of the profession. They represent the humanistic approach to people. Such an approach is possible only if a certain measure of trust exists, for trust is a matter of heart, not mind.

Fiduciary relationships are not limited to worker and client. The "third party," such as the agency that employs the worker, expects the same relationship. It expects the worker to deal honestly and in accordance with the law and the code of ethics, not only toward the client but toward the employer as well. This means that social workers will not exploit their professional standing and will not engage in forgery, deceit, or deception, or in any other ethical misbehavior that may be linked to their status. Thus the code of ethics fulfills a double function: (1) it defends the clients against the possibility of unethical behavior on the part of the worker, and (2) it defends the workers in cases in which they acted properly and yet are forced to justify their behavior in the court or in front of an ethical committee.

CASE EXAMPLE: THE RESIDENT WHO WANTED TO KEEP HIS AFFAIR SECRET

A nursing home has a clear-cut policy regarding intimate relationships among the residents: they are strictly forbidden. Miriam, who has been working in this home as a social worker for many years, takes care of Abe, a seventy-two-year-old widower. A trust relationship was formed between the two of them over the years. In one of their discussions, Abe confided in Miriam and told her in confidence that for the past two months he had been seeing Debbie, a seventy-one-year-old widow, romantically. Abe asked Miriam to keep this information secret saying that he is certain that he can trust her. He also said that he has deep respect for Miriam's decency.

Miriam faces a difficult ethical dilemma: On one hand she must be loyal to the request of her client in line with the code of ethics for social workers, which emphasizes that the worker's first responsibility is to the client and that the worker must keep secret any information the client requests, and on the other hand, in the same code it is stated that the worker must act in line with the employer organization's policy. Miriam is torn in her loyalties to her client and to the agency that employs her. She is aware that the client is transgressing a rule in the agency's policy. She identifies with the opinion of her client that it is not the business of the nursing home to interfere in what two adults are doing between themselves in full agreement. Miriam is aware of the conflicting situation between two opposing values that forces her, as a professional worker, to choose one of them. She must decide whose benefit comes first. If she decides to disregard agency policy and to keep Abe's confession secret, she will damage her loyalty to the employing agency.

Miriam can turn to the NASW Code of Ethics for guidance. Such a code is found in each and every social work–related agency. The code declares that social workers should refrain from situations of conflicting interests as much as possible. The code also states that social workers' responsibility includes sensitivity and awareness of the values involved in their decisions. The code also states that social workers should enhance the existence and welfare of their clients. This clause in the code is directly relevant for Miriam's case. The client has a right to self-determination in every area of his or her life, including help from society and from the professionals. Professionals should invest any effort possible to diminish any interference in the client's relationship with his or her environment. Thus the code permits the worker to disregard agency policy if it is justified on an ethical basis, that is, if the situation entails maintaining the life of or avoiding serious damage to the health of the client. If Miriam thinks that the agency's policy is unjust, then she must act to change it. The practical solution to her conflict is thus not to disclose the secret to the administrator of the agency, and to work for changing the policy.

Miriam's conflict is only one of many involving double loyalty. Many situations exist in which the conflict is opposite to that described in the previous case. The social worker agrees with the agency's policy, but the client asks him or her to disregard it, and thus the worker finds himself or herself in an ethical conflict (culminating in the question of what he or she "ought" to do). The following case cited by Reamer (1999) presents such a situation.

CASE EXAMPLE: THE PARENTS WHO REFUSE TO ACCEPT THE DOCTORS' ADVICE

Peggy P. is a social worker at Pawtucket General Hospital. She is assigned to the neonatal unit. In the unit is a three-day-old infant, Baby R., who was born severely impaired. Baby R. is missing most of his brain, is blind and unable to hear, and has severe heart damage.

Baby R.'s parents, who have no health care coverage, are overwhelmed with grief about their baby's medical condition. The hospital's doctors explained to the parents that their child will never lead a normal life and probably will die within a year, even with aggressive medical care. The doctors also explained that the baby would have to undergo several complicated operations on his heart to save his life.

The doctors told the parents that, in their judgment, it would be a mistake to take extraordinary measures to save the baby's life. They explained that the surgical procedures were complex and remarkably expensive. The doctors were also unsure whether their efforts would improve the quality of or prolong the baby's life.

The social worker, Peggy P., agrees with the doctors that it does not make sense to pursue aggressive medical procedures in this case. The cost would be astronomical and the likely benefit minimal. Peggy P. met with Baby R.'s parents to discuss the options described by the doctors. Baby R.'s parents said they want to insist that the hospital staff do everything possible to save and improve their child's life. They explained that they feel "bonded" with the baby and believe he has a right to as much health care as any other baby.

The ethical dilemma that the social worker is facing in this case illustrates many dilemmas in bioethics, especially in cases in which a calculation of benefit versus expenditures needs to be done. It would not be fair to accuse the doctors as being "cold-hearted professionals" just because they make economic considerations of efficiency—such calculations are relevant in situations of limited resources and therefore such calculations must be made before deciding on the best use of public moneys for the greatest number of people.

As in case of Abe and Miriam, we can relate to Peggy P.'s dilemma from many different perspectives, ethically speaking. As per the theory of deontology, society has an obligation to save the life of the baby. Another obligation in this theory is namely to prevent the baby from suffering unnecessarily. Therefore the baby should not undergo a set of extremely painful and complex operations, but should be allowed to die a "natural death."

In this case one cannot rely on the NASW Code of Ethics as the "final arbiter" of the dilemma. The clauses that would be relevant for the case are contradictory. On one hand they obligate the social worker to respect the decision of the parents, and on the other hand the social worker must also respect the policies of the hospital that employs her. Thus the social worker must explain to the parents why she is supporting the doctors' attitude to the case. This way the parents will have a chance to accept or to reject the social worker and the doctors' reasoning. The parents have other options too. They can ask the hospital administration to transfer their case to another social worker, one whose ethical attitude may be different from Peggy's. The social worker also has several options. She can ask for consultation or turn to the ethical committee in the hospital for advice and guidance before telling the parents her decision. The consultation would give the social worker the necessary support ethically and legally for the final decision she will make.

FIDUCIARY RELATIONSHIPS
IN OTHER CARING PROFESSIONS

We can speak of two kinds of trust: thick and thin (Peternelj-Taylor and Yong, 2003; Schultz, 2004; Tauber, 2006). The former refers to trust based on strong and frequent personal relations. Thin trust applies to new acquaintances. It fosters a willingness to trust people outside of our immediate circle.

Axel Munthe (1990), in his best-selling autobiography titled *The Novel of San Michele* (originally published in 1929), has candidly stated his ideas about trust and confidence in doctor-patient relationships:

> I was not a good doctor; my studies had been too rapid; my hospital training too short, but there is not the slightest doubt that I was a successful doctor. What is the secret of success: to inspire confidence. (Munthe, 1990, p. 37)

What Munthe has described so well with regard to the doctor as a fiduciary professional is equally true of the social worker. Today clients and patients expect their therapists (social worker, doctor) to place their interests ahead of their own self and/or business interests. Clients and patients still trust their workers, but this trust is conditional, no longer automatic. It is not only the client or patient who is vulnerable; the social worker or the physician too is vulnerable. Pellegrino (1991) listed the factors responsible for the vulnerability of the physicians, for examples, the malpractice crisis (of which more will be said later in this book), a legalistic atmosphere surrounding treatment, and commercialization of medical care and the specialty practice. All of these separately or in various combinations can cause the physician and/or the social worker to lose his or her most precious asset: the trust of his or her patients.

Social workers can be technicians, businessmen, or scientists. They can even be social workers—if in addition to having knowledge and training they also happen to be a "mensch." Professor Viktor Frankl, the founder of logotherapy, whose best-selling book *Man's Search for Meaning* (1962) has brought solace and help to millions of people all over the world, used this term from the Yiddish language to express those qualities that make a person a decent human being in every respect. In his remarks upon having conferred on him an honorary doctorate from the University of Haifa in 1988, he said that as a young man he wanted to become a physician—and he became one. He also wanted to be a good physician and this wish too was granted him. But above everything else, he wanted to remain a mensch, someone that could be trusted by all without reservations.

Axel Munthe (1990) has described the opposite of a mensch in medicine the following way:

> If you come across a fashionable doctor, watch him carefully at a safe distance before handing yourself over to him. He may be a good doctor, but in very many cases he is not. (Munthe, 1990, p. 38)

In recent years throughout the more developed countries of the world we have been able to detect a movement away from paternalistic traditions. Professionals are no longer seen as keepers of the "best interests" of their clients or patients. There is more and more insistence on client/patient rights, on respect of client/patient wishes, and on securing their consent to procedures and treatments. Client/patient autonomy is now viewed as a standard, and it is becoming obligatory for all health care professionals. One-sided trust relationships are no longer characteristic of modern fiduciary relationships in social work or in medicine. All those who work in health care are parties to "forward-looking responsibility." Nevertheless, clients/patients are responsible for their own life as an ethical obligation. They are obliged in this not only to themselves but also to their family and to society, for the health of the individual affects the health of the society and vice versa. The following case illustrates this point.

CASE EXAMPLE: THE WOMAN
WHO REFUSED AN OPERATION

A forty-two-year-old mother of four children had a periodical checkup during which a lump was found in one of her lungs. The doctor explained to her husband the meaning of this medical condition and advised the transfer of the woman to a hospital, but the husband refused and said that he would cure her with onion leaves. After five years the woman came back for another checkup. This time the doctor, assisted by his colleagues, prevailed on the husband to let his wife be admitted to the hospital. The woman went to the hospital but refused to undergo the operation despite the doctor saying that it was still possible to stop the illness from spreading further if the woman would agree to the operation. Although the doctor and his colleagues agreed that the woman had a right to refuse treatment, they nevertheless thought that her decision was lacking moral responsibility not only toward herself but also toward her children and husband. Aside from lack of trust in the doctors, this woman's case posed an ethical dilemma for them.

The ethical dilemma that calls for a resolution in this case concentrates on the question what it is right to do: respect the woman's will and not operate, or ignore her wishes and perform the operation to save her life? The solution to this ethical dilemma is based on the moral and professional obligation of the doctor. His mission in society is based on preserving the life and health of the sick. Here is a case in which there are plenty of scientific and verified indications that the woman's life is in grave danger. Seen in a "ladder of priorities" this means that saving a life stands above all other considerations, including the right of the patient to refuse the operation.

Trust among people is important in all known cultures in the world. Some societies exist still in which people need no written and signed papers and contracts for an agreement. To shake hands suffices. Such a handshake is as good as any written contract—if not better. Yet in our age, the general trust in doctors and other health care practitioners has diminished considerably. It is no wonder that many patients— particularly the rich—do not regard the doctor as the single authority concerning their health. Since it is the patient who delivers his or her whole life into the hand of the doctor, the trust that such a move entails must be totally necessary for the treatment. Patients sense instinctively in whom they can trust and who responds to them in earnest. This sense of the patient refers to the rest of the therapists in the helping professions. The trust in them or lack of it is not based on law or rules or regulations, it is created, or fails to be created, as a direct result of the professional's behavior toward the patient.

O'Neill (2002) emphasizes that the only trust that is well placed is given by those who understand what is proposed, and who are in a position to refuse or choose in the light of this understanding (p. 18). In the relationship between social worker and client are mutual expectations of a full trust that aims to serve the recuperation of the client. We may safely assume that the majority of social workers and the majority of the clients are interested in keeping good working relationships with one another. Therefore the time they spend together and to the dialogue they maintain is important, for these are necessary for a good relationship to occur.

The respect that the social worker is asked to give the client must be reciprocated by the latter. Clients must be sincere and open in the dialogue with the social worker in relation to their problems past and present and in disclosing their aches and pains, their habits, and the symptoms of their ailments. The patient should come to the appointment with the social worker on time, clean and well groomed, and behave courteously and patiently. The hope the client has in the improvement of his or her condition is an important ally of the social worker. If trust and hope are crumbling then the whole system may fail, and an irreversible harm can happen to the mental system of the client. The opposite of this is also true: Despair and hopelessness are major stumbling blocks to efficient social work care. A social worker who leaves his or her client with negative feelings and with destructive thoughts diminishes the chances of successful treatment. Lack of dialogue between a social worker and a client and poor communication may result in the client's isolation and even in depression.

The silence that many therapists use as a therapeutic means, especially in psychological intervention, is as an expression of respecting the client's right to keep silent can be harmful, particularly in treating the elderly. They may think that the silence of the therapist is a sign that they lack interest in them or even resent them. I know from many years of experience working with the elderly that many of them turn to clinics, emergency rooms, and doctors to be with people and to gain some attention. Many of these people do not need any medical treatment. What they do need is time, time to tell their story, time to hear that they are still all right, to feel that they are still welcome in this world.

Dialogue between the social worker and the client is an integral part of the treatment. If dialogue does not ensue, the social worker will lose his or her therapeutic influence. Many people crave the "good old days" when the "family visitor," the social worker, was not only a worker but a friend of the whole family, when he or she acted not as a detached professional but as a person, when unshaken trust was in his or her words and deeds. (I remember those days in the beginning of the 1960s when I was a student of social work. I would accompany my field instructor on visits to homes of the clients in one of the worst neighborhoods in Tel Aviv, yet every person she met on the street or at the market would grab her hand and talk to her in a friendly tone about the problems, hopes, and aspirations.) The chances for recuperation are better when the client has full trust in the social worker, and in particular in the worker who remains a decent human being. Such trust in the social worker bolsters the client's self-security and diffuses the doubts and the fears in his or her heart.

Some social workers cannot tolerate it when the client or his or her family turn to other social workers with a request for a second opinion—even when they agree that it is the right of the client and/or the client's family. They see in this a matter of distrust, or violation of the fiduciary relationship they thought existed between them and their patients.

Chapter 10

Ethical Dilemmas

ETHICAL DILEMMAS IN SOCIAL WORK

Social workers learn to see decision-making skills as an integral part of their profession. Their professional intervention encompasses work with clients to help them deal with the demands of society and life and to utilize opportunities for self-fulfillment. The help given by social workers entails more than values and skills. It is basically an art. Many times a social worker is forced to make a decision that entails an ethical dilemma. Ethical decisions are connected to conflicts between rights and values. At times the ethical principles that guide decision making conflict with one another and make prioritizing them very difficult (Callahan, 1994).

The term *dilemma* in the ancient Greek language denotes a choice between two opposing ways or a conflicting situation. Starr (1999) cites Max Weber who said that conflict pervades all aspects of our lives. Conflicts abound in the struggle for material and social control, even in our inner minds and our thinking, and it cannot be excluded from social life. It is possible to change its means, its object, and its direction, but it cannot be eliminated. In social work theory and practice conflict has two meanings. First, it is the striving of two or more parties to achieve opposing or mutually exclusive goals, and second, in psychological terms, it means the mental struggle of two or more mutually exclusive impulses, motives, drives, or social demands (Barker, 1987, p. 31).

In the regular use of this term today we tend to see in dilemma a problem. Not all problems have ethical or moral repercussions, and not every dilemma is ethical. For example, we are asked to give money to a charity organization and we are uncertain whether or not this organization is worthy of our support. If we decide not to give,

Ethics in Social Work: A Context of Caring
© 2006 by The Haworth Press, Inc. All rights reserved.
doi:10.1300/5577_11

our decision will not have serious results, except perhaps some slight pangs of conscience. A dilemma deals with choice between two unsatisfactory alternatives.

An ethical dilemma is a situation in which professional obligation and professional duties, anchored in basic values of the particular profession, are in conflict, and the worker is asked to decide which values connected to the obligations and duties of the professional are more salient than the others. Loewenberg (1992) points out that the worker may feel highly committed to both values, even when in the specific situation only one can be actualized (p. 433). Barker (1987) explains:

> Conflict resolution entails a process of eliminating or minimizing the problems that result when different parties or groups compete with one another for the same limited objectives. Social workers often engage in this process when they help clarify, educate, mediate, and propose compromises or alternative solutions to clients or client systems who are contesting some mutual objectives. (p. 31)

The following case illustrates such a conflicting situation.

CASE EXAMPLE: THE SUICIDAL CLIENT

Mr. K., a thirty-two-year-old lawyer, was living in fear over the past five years that he may develop Huntington's disease as his mother had. This disease usually appears in a person's thirties or forties and the patient suffers from facial convulsions and irreversible dementia that leads to death within approximately ten years. For about fifty percent of people with Huntington's disease it is a genetic inheritance. The lawyer disclosed to his friends that he would rather die than suffer as his mother did. His fear lead him to drink a great amount. He is depressed and anxious, but keeps his job without much difficulty. One day he discovered convulsions in his face, and in the medical checkup the doctor found that he was suffering from Huntington's disease. The lawyer turned to the social worker with whom he had worked on several cases and asked for his help to commit suicide. The social worker found himself in a serious dilemma.

In this case we witness a serious conflict between the rights of the client to self-determination and between the duties of the social worker to enhance the welfare of his client. Callahan (1994) claims that a social worker is not permitted to assist one who contemplates suicide. Such help is contradictory to the rules of professional ethics and the values that are central to social work. Several studies have verified that the judgment of people seriously depressed and wishing to commit suicide due to their vulnerability to mental stress is hampered.

Minahan (1987) divides ethical dilemmas of social workers into seven main areas. These are the following:

1. Secrecy and confidential information
2. Truth telling
3. Paternalism and self-determination
4. Laws, rules and regulations and policies
5. Whistle-blowing on a colleague
6. Distribution of limited resources
7. Personal and professional values

Loewenberg and Dolgoff (1996) noted three root causes of ethical dilemmas in social work practice: Competing values, competing loyalties, and ambiguity and uncertainty. Certain special agencies, such as schools (Garrett, 1994) and hospitals (Proctor, Morrow-Howell & Lott, 1993) create difficult choices and ethical dilemmas for the social workers working in them as professionals. For example, ethical dilemmas connected to the subject of secrecy in cases of requests for abortions, or truth telling regarding a serious and life threatening illness occur. At times other ethical dilemmas arise due to the feministic orientation of certain workers who happen to be in conflict with the prevailing values of the employing organization (Glassman, 1992).

A unique area in ethical dilemmas is in social group work. Northen (1998) has stated that so far insufficient reference to this problem exists in professional literature, although many group workers find themselves in situations of conflict regarding such issues as professional values in fiduciary relationships with members of the group, equal access to services, informed consent to the proposed intervention, confidential information, the right to self-determination, proper ending of treatment, and the professional expertise of the worker. The following cases are taken from the professional literature on ethical dilemmas in social work.

CASE EXAMPLE: A REQUEST TO KEEP
A MEDICAL DIAGNOSIS SECRET

Molly is a social worker in a large hospital. She works primarily with cancer patients and their families in the department of operations.

One of the patients, a sixty-eight-year-old man, was hospitalized in her department for an operation on his stomach. The patient was described by the doctor who treats him as weak, feeble, and unstable. One day the daughter of this patient came to Molly and asked her to keep secret the cancer the doctors found in her father's stomach. She said that her father would not be able to stand the shock if the "verdict" were to become known to him. She also asked the social worker to explain the family's request to the doctor who is in direct charge of this case.

The ethical dilemma Molly was facing centered on the question of what the right thing to do was: Honor the request of the family for secrecy, or respect the right of the patient to medical information about his condition? Which would be better for the well-being of the patient: hiding the information from him, or disclosing it? Molly tended to agree with the opinion of the medical team that supported the idea of telling the truth to the patient.

This kind of ethical dilemma is not unique to social work, says Reamer (1999). Molly's dilemma arises each time one is asked to decide whether one wishes to be paternalistic and intervene with the right of the client to self-determination for his or her own well-being. Reamer claims that paternalism happens in one of three ways: First, when the worker believes that it is justified to prevent clients from having the information for their own sake, for disclosure may cause harm to their life. Second, when the worker lies for the benefit of the client and delays giving information or gives untrue information in order to prevent the client from harming himself or herself. Third, when the worker forces the client to do something against his or her wishes, for example, transferring a battered woman into a shelter or an old man living in solitude to a home for the aged.

In politics, for example, paternalism refers to the principle and practice in which the authority takes care of people as if a father, relating to the citizens as subjects who owe gratitude to the state, thereby restricting democratic and civil life (Fencsik, 1986).

Other definitions of the term *paternalism* vary with each philosopher and philosophic attitude, but common to all of them is interference with other people's rights to basic freedom and determination about their lives, or forcing someone to do something against his or her wishes. Paternalism is always "dressed" as caring for the welfare of the one who is the subject of the interference. In general, and in all due respect and professional caution and care, paternalism is justified only in those cases, usually few and limited, when the client is unfit mentally or when a real danger exists that he or she may harm himself or herself in one way or another. In modern social work legal steps were taken to prevent as many cases of paternalism as possible. The code of ethics and the law referring to the practice of social work address this subject in earnest.

Ethical dilemmas emanating from conflicts between personal and professional values are among the most difficult ones. They happen when a worker's personal values are in conflict with the rules in the code of ethics or with the policies of the employing agency. The following case illustrates such a situation.

CASE EXAMPLE: THE GIRL WHO ASKED FOR ADVICE REGARDING ABORTION

Joseph is a social worker and devout Catholic. He works in a family service as a therapist. The bulk of his clientele are girls and boys in a nearby high school. Between the family service and the high school is a contract to provide services and consultation for clients sent to the social workers by the school administration. Recently a sixteen-year-old female student was referred to the service with problems of depression and sadness. Joseph was asked by the family service director to work with this student.

Joseph and the student met several times and spoke about many subjects, including the student's relationships with her parents and brothers and sisters, and about her difficulties in the school and with her studies. At the end of the fourth meeting, the student said to Joseph that she had something important to tell him. Joseph reminded the student about the limits of confidential information that bind him as a social worker. The student nevertheless disclosed that she was in the sixth week of pregnancy, despite the precautions she had taken with her boyfriend. She also told Joseph that she is considering an abortion and asked for his help with the decision making and with all that the decision entailed.

Joseph rejects abortion on religious grounds. He is convinced that abortion is invalid morally and religiously and cannot support it as an idea nor can he condone it in practice.

The code of ethics for social workers does not deal directly with the subject of abortion but emphasizes that social workers are requested to support their clients' right to self-determination. Another clause in the code states that the worker should respect the policies of the employing agency, and that this respect is part of his or her professional obligations. Both of the clauses present a serious ethical dilemma for the worker. In this case, Joseph is obligated to provide help to his client as part of his professional and primary duty. In addition, the employing agency's policy supports the right of the client to self-determination even in matters such as abortion. On the other hand, the religious beliefs of Joseph oppose abortion.

Joseph has several options to choose from in this case, and among them the option to refrain from direct or indirect intervention. If he chooses this option, he will be following the advice of Chilman (1987) who said:

> A professional social worker should carefully consider his values and beliefs regarding matters of sexual behavior, such as abortion, sexual relationships out of marriage, use of contraceptives to prevent pregnancy, and etc. Should a social worker find that he cannot take an objective attitude in such cases, it is then preferable not to engage in them, unless he is employed in an agency that its policies are in line with the worker's own values. (p. 5)

Social workers employed by municipalities, government agencies, and public organizations sometimes find themselves in conflict with rules, laws, and regulations that seem unjust in their eyes. They must decide whether or not to obey or oppose them. They are aware that laws are needed to prevent chaos in social relations, yet they also know that the laws do not always serve the interests of the individual and sometimes need to be "bent" a little for the benefit of the client.

The question of agreeing or not agreeing with the law is relevant not only for the individual but for the managers and directors of large agencies. Social workers protest at times against injustice and discrimination contained in some law or regulation. In such cases they find themselves in an ethical dilemma. The following case presents such a situation.

CASE EXAMPLE: WHETHER TO GIVE FINANCIAL SUPPORT BEYOND THE TIME ALLOCATED

Lauren, aged twenty-three, is supported by Social Security due to physical disability. Lauren has signed up for a seminar in computer programming, paid by Social Security. The law states that such support will be given for up to six months. Lauren was industrious in her studies and the social worker was proud of Lauren's achievement. About a month prior to the end of her studies Lauren told the social worker that the college in which she was studying had decided to add two more months to the program so that the students would be able to learn the latest developments in computer programming. Lauren was aware of the policy regarding Social Security financial support for purposes of education, yet her heart demanded that she continue studying for those two extra months with the rest of her colleagues. She asked the social worker assigned to her case to "do something" for the fulfillment of her dream to become an excellent computer programmer.

The social worker brought this case for consultation before her colleagues and told them that she is torn between her obligation to the employing agency and rules of Social Security and her wish to help her client.

This kind of ethical dilemma is rather frequent in the agencies that employ social workers. The following chapter will deal with various methods of resolving ethical dilemmas in the helping professions.

Chapter 11

Resolution of Ethical Dilemmas

As shown in the previous chapter, ethical dilemmas frequently arise in the relationship between a social worker and client in practice. To better resolve the dilemmas, those that occur most frequently in therapy will be discussed. First, we need to know what is meant by a client's "fitness to make decisions." This fitness is central in treating clients.

The principles of treating terminally ill clients, for example, can serve as important guides for all professionals in the helping professions when differentiating between what is and what is not permitted regarding such clients/patients. The principles are listed in *The Hastings Center Report* published bimonthly in New York. This center is one of the most prestigious institutes in the world. The principles were summarized by Kovacs (1998). According to the translator, the "fitness" of the patient for decision making concerning the treatment he or she is apt to receive is a very complex matter. The doctor cannot make decisions instead of the patient, unless the court has ruled otherwise, which occurs only when the patient is unable to make decisions, whether fully or partially. Thus, only patients who are able to make decisions can reject medical treatment aimed at lengthening their lives.

Fitness to make decisions is always connected to the unique situation in social work and/or medical intervention, thus it is possible that one patient is fit in one situation but not in another. Patients' fitness to make decisions is judged by three standards: (1) by the standard of result, meaning the personal reason, sense, and/or logic of the decision and its result; (2) by the standard of status, which applies to those who can't make decisions legally, based on criteria such as the age of the decision maker, for example children under fourteen years of age are included in the category of those who cannot make decisions; and

Ethics in Social Work: A Context of Caring
© 2006 by The Haworth Press, Inc. All rights reserved.
doi:10.1300/5577_12

(3) by the standard of process, meaning that the ability of the patient to make decisions will be taken into consideration during the medical process.

The patient's fitness to make decisions is assessed in two steps. In the first step, unless no other information is available, the social worker/doctor assumes that the patient is capable of making decisions and therefore he or she must provide the necessary information for decision making on the part of the client/patient. In the second step, if it happens that the client/patient is unfit to make decisions, then he or she cannot make decisions. It is preferable that such a decision be made by a psychiatrist.

Fitness for decision making represents a situation in which the client/patient is able to understand the necessary information to make a decision, is able to weigh and assess in accordance with his or her goals and values the various alternatives for action, is able to understand the possible results of his or her decision, and is able to give his decision to the social worker.

TERMINATION OF TREATMENT: PRINCIPLES OF INTERVENTION

The basic principle in decision making concerning treatment is deciding which is greater: the burden of the treatment for the client or its benefit. If the burden is greater than the benefit, then it is acceptable to postpone the treatment as an ethical act. If a certain treatment will not bring a socially accepted benefit, that is, will not reach its aim, then it should not be given to the client. If the client asks to forego some treatment and his or her request contradicts the social worker's belief and conscience, the latter should discuss it with the client, and if necessary, transfer the case to someone else with the permission of the client. Clients have a right to forbid the inclusion of their family in the decision about their therapy. If clients are fit to make decisions then it will be they who decide. In the absence of such fitness it is permitted to choose a substitute in accordance with the rules guiding substitution. This person is the legal representative of the client. In any case the decision should be documented in writing and the social worker who cares for the client must sign this document.

ETHICAL DILEMMAS AND DECISION MAKING

The method chosen in social work intervention has far-reaching consequences on the outcome and the choice must therefore be made very carefully. It is impossible to reverse the treatment at its end and try a different approach. When the obligations to the client conflict and a choice must be made between two potentially bad results, then it is an ethical dilemma. In such cases, the social worker must decide which of the two obligations is more right ethically.

It is impossible to ensure total security in a given social work decision. It is possible to learn different perspectives of treatment, such as the reasoned planning of the various steps. The ability to make ethical decisions and having sensitivity to others are gained through personal experience and by learning from wiser and more experienced colleagues. A need exists to be "armed" with moral and intellectual virtues together, as Aristotle taught. The intellectual virtues refer to understanding, to knowledge of various methods of treatment, and to professional reasoning that can be used in the search for the solution of an ethical dilemma. The moral virtues are connected to the reliability and validity of the decision and to its effect and benefit as characteristics of the social worker.

The ethicist Rozsos (2000) differentiates between conflicts emanating from differences of professional opinions, from deficiency in communication connected to treatment, or from mistaken guidelines. These, according to her, are not real ethical conflicts, for they will not disappear when the reason for the conflict does. At times problems occur in identifying ethical dilemmas for various reasons.

Sometimes a social worker cannot recognize the conflict, or does not know how to describe it and thus he or she is in stress. Sometimes the social worker tries to cloak the ethical dilemma in professional or legal terms, or sometimes the therapist is indifferent to the ethical dilemma. This state is called in social work "burnout." It is characterized as a form of depression and apathy related to on-the-job stress and frustration. The social worker becomes bored, unmotivated, and uncreative, and is often unresponsive to improved conditions (Barker, 1987, p. 18).

At times the social worker displays an unethical attitude, stating that he or she does not want to be moral when "all the rest are immoral any way." Sometimes he or she has an internal and moral objection to a professional decision of another therapist, such as a doctor, regarding what the law determined as the rights of the patient. Sometimes the requests of the family of the patient can raise the social worker's objections.

These kinds of problems and others demand from the social worker real efforts in analyzing the ethical conflict. The ethical principles and norms of behavior need to be analyzed separately in each case. The uniqueness of each case represents a unique and different situation that is composed of many factors that need to be taken into consideration in ethical decision making.

BASIC ETHICAL PRINCIPLES

The basic duty of social workers is to their clients. This duty is both a principle and a priority in the practice of social work. The duty consists of treating each client equally and respectfully, taking into consideration the psychological position of the client, charging clients as little as possible or providing services free of charge especially for poor patients, informing the client about alternative treatment methods, avoiding pessimistic and too-optimistic language about clinical diagnosis, decreasing unnecessary pain and suffering, and giving hope to the client (Erdemir, 1995).

Caring is tied to its social context. Ethical problems do not happen in a vacuum. Social workers deal with many different people. They have to relate to the individual client, or to clients in groups, to the families of clients, to colleagues, to members of other professions, to the administrators of various agencies and institutions, and to society at large. All of them have expectations and they all at times can present ethical problems and dilemmas. The dilemmas center most of the time on matters of power, equity, and just distribution of scarce resources.

Modern social work ethics is based on three essential principles: autonomy, beneficence, and justice. The principle of beneficence has a long tradition. It is based on the moral command not to cause harm. According to this principle, the social worker who respects the clients' decisions, who defends them against harm, and who makes sincere efforts to support them and acts on the basis of this principle is an ethical person and his or her behavior is ethical too.

The concept of beneficence includes four commands that form one unit (Frankena, 1973). The first states that it is forbidden to cause pain, harm, and hurt. In Latin this principle is stated as *Primum nil nocere,* meaning first and foremost do not cause harm. The second command states that one should prevent harm. Removing harm is the third command, and doing what is good and promoting the right is the fourth command. The harm in social work and in other helping professions can be sloppy therapy or intervention, immoral behavior, or unskilled treatment. The harm must be prevented along with the bad. One must remove the harm and do what is good.

The principle of beneficence is valid in all cases of professional intervention in the lives of the patients and clients, at least in the philosophical sense. For example, medical intervention is accompanied in many instances with causing pain. The use of medicines and surgery require that the physician weigh the benefits and the deficiencies of any medical action and choose the one that causes the least suffering and brings about the best results.

Autonomy is anchored in moral attitude, freedom of choice, and respect as moral/religious values, and the principle of justice is based on religious and legal traditions as presented earlier in this book. The principle of respect for the autonomy of the client as understood in today's health care ethics has its philosophical roots in the writings of Immanuel Kant and John Stuart Mill. Kant's basic idea was anchored in his humanistic attitude to ethics according to which people should be treated differently from materials, plants, or animals. They have intrinsic values, rational capacities to be self-determining, and they should be treated as ends rather than means to someone else's ends (Gauthier, 2002).

For the philosopher Mill, the "inventor" of utilitarianism and its aim of providing the greatest possible happiness for the greatest possible number of people, freedom of the individual from the tyranny of the mobs represent his principle of liberty. Accordingly, the only purpose for which power can be rightfully exercised over any member of a civilized community against his or her will is to prevent harm to others (Mill, 1962, p. 9). His concept of liberty is limited to those who are in possession of well-developed decisional faculties or who are competent and capable of making decisions. In terms of clients, they should be offered information about their condition and choice in the treatment proposed. However, such autonomy should also include the duties and obligations of the individual to take into consideration the rights and interests of others, such as the client's responsibility to family, community, and society. This responsibility is basically a moral one. It is seen by Gauthier (2002) as an overarching virtue, covering all choices and actions that have a moral dimension. This moral virtue binds social workers to see in their responsibilities the inclusion of the consequences of treatment decisions for the family and to urge clients to consider these in reaching a decision.

Autonomy in social work is the opposite of the paternalism that exists in the Hippocratic tradition and the medical ethics that followed it. Practically speaking, autonomy is the right of clients to self-determination regarding all social work interventions that touch upon their lives and fate. The choices of the client reflect his or her world of values and personality. Of course, the fitness of the client for making decisions must be assessed first, including his or her ability to understand the meaning of his or her decision.

In ethical decision making, the principles are taken into consideration along with the norms of behavior binding the social worker. The individual is seen as a free person who can choose. The social worker–client relationship is a contractual one based on respect for the autonomy of the troubled person and on the provision of reliable and sincere information regarding the client's condition and prognosis.

The process of decision making for the resolution of an ethical dilemma begins with the ethical theory on which the social worker relies, continues with the principles, rules, and norms, and ends with reaching a decision and the action that follows from it. Among the three basic principles that guide modern social work, the decisive principle is the principle of autonomy. This principle refers to the client. The principle of beneficence is central for the social worker, and the principle of justice should guide society.

The principles are frequently at conflict with one another, but all three should be taken into consideration in each concrete case analysis. For example, autonomy of the client opposes the beneficence of the social worker when the client refuses to accept the treatment that the social worker thinks is necessary for the health and welfare or survival of the client.

Before analyzing the various steps and phases in decision making, several models used in social work need to be briefly described. The first is the model that integrates virtue ethics, justice, and ethical caring (Cameron et al., 2001). It is based on three major questions: What should I value? Who should I be? What should I do? Accordingly, professionals should integrate the values that ensure their ethical position and develop their characters, and they should resolve ethical conflicts by using a subjective perspective of ethical caring based on justice, advocacy, and truth telling.

The second model is based on Frankena's (1973) mixed deontological theory of moral obligation. In the center of Frankena's theory are the principles of beneficence and justice. Beneficence requires refraining from doing harm, preventing harm, removing harm, and doing what is good. Justice means treating people as equals. The good and bad are distributed among them equally.

Adherence to universal ethical principles is another model for making ethical decisions. It is based on a set of values to which professionals in the helping professions should adhere: individual freedom, goodness or rightness, truth telling or honesty, valuing life, and justice. For example, the value of individual freedom states that one should give people freedom to choose their own ways and means of being moral. As for goodness and rightness, the emphasis is on striving to be a good person and to perform the right actions.

Social workers should be aware that no one particular model applies to all situations that require ethical decision making. Rather, several models can be applied, depending on the particulars of a given situation and case. Some models are based on philosophical positions, and some are based on the problem-solving approach used in social work. Some models combine problem solving with a theological perspective, and others have different perspectives (Benjamin and Curtis, 1992; Johnstone, 1999).

Common to all models of ethical decision making is that they provide a systematic approach in analyzing the factual and value dimensions inherent in any ethical dilemma. They also offer an approach that can be used for implementing the ethical decision one has arrived at in actual care. The values of the decision maker are decisive in the selection of the model that will be used in the process of ethical decision making and for the action that the social worker will eventually take.

One interesting model developed by Yeo and Moorhouse (1996) is called RESPECT. It is based on a business perspective, and is oriented to the "stakeholder," meaning the person who will be most affected by the decision and consequently has a stake in the outcome. RESPECT refers to the seven steps that in combination cover the entire decision-making process. These are listed in Fry and Johnstone's book (2002) as:

Recognize moral dimensions of the task or problem.
Enumerate the guiding and evaluative principles.
Specify the stakeholders and their guiding principles.
Plot various action alternatives.
Evaluate alternatives in light of principles and stakeholders.
Consult and involve stakeholders as appropriate.
Tell stakeholders the reasons for the decision. (p. 57)

PHASES IN THE ANALYSIS OF ETHICAL DILEMMAS AND DECISION MAKING

Most books and articles in professional journals dealing with ethics recommend the use of a six-step method in decision making. The first step is giving a brief description of the facts pertaining to the dilemma at hand. The second step deals with the values and principles of the involved parties—the client, the professional, and the client's family. Clarifying the conflict between the values and determining the order of priorities in decision making is the third step. The fourth consists of assessing the moral principles and deciding which action will provide the best result. Step number five includes the decision reached by the analysis, and the last step, the sixth, calls for the justification of the action taken.

Among these six steps the last, the justification of the decision reached, is the most important. The justification itself can rely on intuition, especially in the case of religious people who turn to their moral values in making ethical decisions, according to Rozsos (2000). The classical method of justification was based on the Socratic Dialogue, so named for its founder and great promulgator, the philosopher in ancient Greece. The Socratic Dialogue is essentially dialectics in which the analysis begins with a question the answer to which is followed by other questions to examine the answer rationally. The Socratic Dialogue is aimed at discovering the truth. Socrates emphasized in his method the importance of clarifying thoughts and concepts and insisted on their definitions. He thought that knowing the good and the right (ethics) would necessarily lead to the right action.

Contrary to the patient- or client-centered approach in medical and social work decision making, today more and more attention is called to the family's role in that process (Hyun, 2003). This is true in particular when the decision concerns patients in acute care. The patient who enjoys total freedom in making his or her own decisions about the terms of treatment may ignore its affect on family members. Yet, the family has legitimate financial, emotional, and rehabilitative interest in the member's care. Whether or not one agrees with the reasons cited for including the family in the decision-making process, few physicians or social workers would totally reject this idea.

Hyun (2003) presents possible conceptions along with their difficulties in his discussion of "family decision making" for the patient. The first is "collective decisions" for the benefit of the patient. Even competent patients prefer at times to place their fates in the hands of their trusted loved ones, especially at a time of serious illness. Whether or not such confidence is fully warranted is a matter that needs further verification.

The second conception of family decision for the client or patient is based on the notion of the common good of the family. The idea is that the family as a whole is targeted as a beneficiary of the treatment decision, not just the patient. This alternative too has its shortcomings, one of which is defining what is the common good for the family. Another problem concerns the financial good of the family. Many times treatment decisions could have detrimental effects on the economic situation of the entire family. The lives of the members are interdependent to such a degree that the welfare of one is closely tied to the welfare of all the others.

Still another conception tied to family decision making relates to questions such as who in the family will make the decisions and which overlapping interests will be satisfied. Hyun (2003) claims that the concept of family is ambiguous and that many different versions and definitions exist, which makes it difficult to determine the correct application of a family-centered decision-making style. Whether or not family decision will replace the current patient-centered ethics and approach to acute care remains to be seen. It will be important to raise first the philosophical question of what people ought to do in such situations (Hyun, 2003, p. 200).

ETHICAL DECISION MAKING IN SOCIAL WORK

The founding mothers and fathers of social work invested a great deal of effort in developing rules of ethics and professional conduct that could stand against even very strict social criticism. The educators and theoreticians of the profession, and especially teachers of ethics (Levy, 1976; Joseph, 1989; Reamer, 1998, 1999) and others, agree to the need to approach ethical decision making rationally as a process built on logical steps that aim to assure the decision maker that the decision will stand up to ethical criteria accepted by the profession.

This approach to ethical decision making in cases of conflict between values and obligations, each of which binds the social worker, is based on the theory of Rawls (1971). This philosopher explained in his writings that it is possible to arrange the values and ethical obligations in a logical order, for frequently the decision revolves around the question of which obligation takes precedence over another. For example, respect for the law and prevention of deceit, or the obligation to keep harm away from the client? What is the actual obligation of the social worker? The philosophers, educators, and the theoreticians of the profession of social work agreed with the ancient rule in medicine: Do not harm. Therefore, in the choice among obligations the social worker should select the one that will bring the least harm to the client.

The subject of ethical decision making in social work is discussed in works in the professional literature from various perspectives. Social work in hospitals is treated by Proctor, Morrow-Howell, and Lott (1993). Another area of interest in ethical decision making refers to professional social work in schools (Garrett, 1994). Dolgoff and Skolnik (1992) investigated the subject from the perspective of social group work. The dilemmas waiting for solution as a result of the technological developments encompassing the world found their expression in the professional literature on ethics (Cwikel and Cnaan, 1991), and the work of Congress (1992) deals with ethical decision-making by fieldwork and instructors in social work.

Before detailing the steps connected to the process of decision making we should refer to the philosophical approach behind this process. Gewirth (1978), among the important philosophers in moral philosophy in the twentieth century, in his book titled *Reason and*

Morality maintains that people have basic rights to freedom and well-being, and in order to actualize this freedom they should evaluate the following three kinds of goods:

- *Basic goods*—the aspects of well-being such as life, health, nutrition, dwelling, mental equilibrium and so on that everyone needs in order to engage in purposeful activity
- *Nonsubtractive goods*—goods that should not be subtracted, meaning that their absence or loss would diminish the ability of a person to reach his or her goals, leaving him or her to such consequences as inferior dwelling, forced or harsh labor, or loss of property as a result of stealing, being cheated or lied to, etc.
- *Additive goods*—goods that enhance and improve the ability of individuals to pursue and achieve their goals (education, self-respect, wealth, etc.)

Gewirth (1978) coined the principle of general consistency that is a deductive process based on the following steps:

1. Responsible people control their behavior by a conscious choice to fulfill some destiny or goal.
2. A responsible person values freedom and well-being as preconditions for engaging in any activity and as a necessary good.
3. A responsible person is of the opinion that freedom and well-being are general rights given to him or her as a citizen. Therefore he or she would recognize the rights of other people to freedom and well-being, and therefore feel obligated to refrain from any activity that would interfere with the rights of others to achieve freedom and well-being.

Reamer (1999) has stated that Gewirth's approach to the nature of rights and duties permits one to assess conflicts between the various obligations of social workers on the basis of value priorities and thus find solutions for them.

It is possible to use the theory of Gewirth either directly or indirectly. Direct use of his theory, the activities that permit reaching the goals of an individual, such as freedom and well-being, are moral—provided the individual recognizes the rights of others to the same goals. The basic duty is to help others get the "goods." As for the indirect use of the theory, one can justify rules and laws that direct the profession of social work and preserve the rights of the clients to freedom and well-being.

REAMER'S MODEL OF ETHICAL DECISION MAKING

Gewirth's (1978) theory, with its order of priorities of the values and the obligations emanating from them, provides moral support to the professional obligation of social workers to care for the basic necessities of those least capable in society. Reamer (1999) used Gewirth's (1978) theory as the basis for the development of his own model of ethical decision making. The model is based on six steps, which order the obligations and their priorities systematically. This model can guide social workers as to which option should be chosen when faced with conflicts among various professional obligations.

Reamer's priorities were based on the principles contained in both deontological and teleological theories of ethics. They correspond to the fundamental values of the social work profession. Reamer was cognizant of the impossibility of finding a uniform and complete solution to each and every ethical dilemma in professional work. Social workers, similar to other caring professionals, are influenced by more than just their professional roles and obligations. They are also influenced by their own personal motivations, attitudes, and preferences in making their decisions. Some of these factors influence their behavior unknowingly and affect the value choices they eventually make (Mattison, 2000). Therefore Reamer (1999) offered a model that can help social workers organize their thinking regarding how to resolve a conflict and an ethical dilemma. He found the following criteria applicable to this purpose:

> Rules against basic harms to the necessary preconditions of human action, such as life itself, health, food, etc. take precedence over rules against harms such as lying or revealing confidential information or threats to "additive goods" such as recreation, education and wealth. (Reamer, 1999, p. 72)

In accordance with this rule, transfer of a disabled old man who cannot take care of himself to a nursing home is justified and takes precedence over the transfer of another old man to the same institute who has the necessary means to survive in dignity and has family support but who just needs to be among people for recreation. The threat to the well-being of the former is more important and compelling than the need of the other man.

> An individual's right to basic well-being takes precedence over another individual's right to self-determination. (Reamer, 1999, p. 73)

An individual has a right to self-determination and to act as he or she wishes—unless his or her actions threaten the well-being of others. Therefore social work interventions need to safeguard, for example, the right to the basic well-being of a destitute old woman without shelter, even if the woman has a right to freedom and self-determination. The social worker may decide that the woman's well-being is more important than and overrides her right to remain free and open to danger. The social worker may turn to the court and request help in placing her in a shelter.

> An individual's right to self-determination takes precedence over his or her right to basic well-being. (Reamer, 1999, p. 73)

For example, a woman may prefer to return to her abusive husband rather than remain in a shelter for battered women. The social worker in such a case should respect the client's right to self-determination, but only after he or she has become convinced that the woman's decision is voluntary and she is fully informed about the potential consequences of her choice.

> The obligation to obey laws, rules, and regulations to which one has voluntarily and freely consented ordinarily overrides one's right to engage voluntarily and freely in a manner that conflicts with these laws, rules, and regulations. (Reamer, 1999, p. 74)

Here Reamer maintains that if a social worker voluntarily joins the staff of an agency that prohibits discussion of abortion with clients, it would ordinarily be unethical to violate this policy deliberately. He states that " individuals' rights to well-being may override laws, rules, and regulations, and arrangements of voluntary associations in cases of conflict" (Reamer, 1999, p. 74).

Compliance with laws, rules, and regulations should not be blindly maintained. Situations could occur in which the threat to the basic well-being of an individual justifies overriding these laws, such as in the case in which a woman in the shelter for battered women wishes to return to her abusive husband. The social worker may object to this wish in fear for the woman's life. Violation of the law may be justified in exceptional situations, but it cannot be sanctioned nor used in a systematic way.

> The obligation to prevent basic harms such as starvation and to promote public goods such as housing, education, and public assistance overrides the right to complete control over one's property. (Reamer, 1999, p. 75)

This guideline, Reamer explains, pertains specifically to the justification for taxation and other forms of coercion required to provide aid to people in need and to protect children, the poor without housing and health care, the disabled, and others from basic harm (Reamer, 1999, pp. 72-75).

The intelligent use of these five guidelines requires first a differentiation between a practical problem and an ethical dilemma. In order to differentiate between the two, the following must be weighed:

1. *The source of the problem:* Is it the client, the service, the family, or another outside factor?
2. *Professional perspective:* Is it helpful to clarify a situation, meaning that it is possible to classify the dilemma by what appears in the code of ethics for social workers?
3. *Level of action:* At what level does the ethical dilemma appear, and at what level is it possible to find a solution? Is the solution to the dilemma at the level of the service; the policy; the practice with individuals, groups, or organization; or at the level of the individual's values and beliefs?
4. *The ethical theory:* How can the theory clarify the dilemma? Which ethical theory would be applicable in this particular case for solving the dilemma?

Knowledge of the difference between a practical problem and an ethical dilemma can help social workers arrive at the appropriate solution. To prevent conflicts among the six guidelines offered by

Reamer (1999), ethical decision making needs to be approached in a systematic fashion to ensure that all the aspects of the ethical dilemma are taken into consideration.

Reamer (1999) thinks that the following steps may help social workers deal successfully with ethical dilemmas and arrive at their solutions.

Identifying the ethical issues that are controversial, including the values of social work and the obligations in conflict with one another is the first step. The second step consists of identifying the individuals, the groups, and the organizations that would be affected by the decision. The third step requires temporary identification of all the possible means of action and the characters involved in each, in both their potentially positive and negative aspects. A thorough investigation of the reasons for and against an action is the fourth step. Such an investigation requires reference to ethical theory, rules and principles, the code of ethics and legal principles, the practice-related principles of social work, and the personal values of the professional, particularly those that may conflict with each other such as religious and political values. Counseling with colleagues and with experts is the fifth step, and taking the decision and documenting the process of decision making is the sixth step. Finally, the seventh step involves follow-up and evaluation of the result.

This procedure, although very thorough and basic, is rather cumbersome and long. In real life no professional worker can and does go through all the steps that Reamer has included in his model.

OTHER MODELS FOR ETHICAL
DECISION MAKING

A more practical model than the one developed by Reamer was offered by Mary Vincentia Joseph in the late eighties (Joseph, 1985, 1989). It was based on a logical process in which the various steps were shown in a predetermined sequence. According to this model, the ethical dilemma is expressed in comparing one benefit with another competing one. The model requires that the social workers be aware not only of their own personal values but also of their personal bias in their professional practice. In using Joseph's (1989) model, one should pay attention to the background of the ethical dilemma and to the relevant facts pertaining to it, and one should weigh these for both their positive and negative aspects. When this is done, the phase of ordering the preferences follows as well as forming the justification for the final option taken.

As explained in the model, the process of decision making begins with a description of the service and with details about the situation pertaining to the conflict. Then follows the determination of the nature of the conflict: Is it related to a practical problem, or is it an ethical dilemma? If it is the latter, then the process of ethical decision-making begins. The background information refers to the various positions for and against an option or alternative put before the persons involved in the conflict. The relevant laws and the code of ethics are also taken into consideration. The value judgment in the model identifies the values in conflict and enables the workers to be conscious of their personal biases and preferences. Once the various options pertaining to the dilemma have been identified, they require of the worker to weigh each in its positive and negative aspects and to detail the reasons why one option is preferable to another. This weighing of the options, or alternative ways of action, enables the decision maker to arrive at the final choice and the decision that can be justified professionally and, if it needs to be, in court.

The last and most recent model for ethical decision making in social work is presented by Mattison (2000). The author of this model states:

> Ethical decision making in day-to-day practice must never be considered a discrete act or a task that is unremittingly logical or scientific by nature. Although theoretical and technical expertise direct professional practice, it is clear that there are aspects of social work that require thinking beyond scientific proficiency. (Goldstein, 1987, as quoted in Mattison, 2000)

Mattison, similar to Reamer and Joseph, emphasizes the importance of documenting the process and the procedures used in making ethical decisions as well as the need to be able to justify the final position taken so that it could stand not only in professional judgment but also in a court of law.

Mattison has developed a model for analyzing ethical dilemmas. In this model the social worker needs to pay attention to ethnic-based traditions, distinguish the practice aspects of the case from the ethical considerations, pay attention to value tensions, and evaluate the various obligations in the code of ethics as to which of them is most relevant for the case. In addition, matters of cost benefit should be weighed and analyzed, and the action needs to be selected. The final phase in the model includes the implementation of the decision reached and the reflection and self-awareness that should accompany the entire process.

Chapter 12

On Keeping Secrets
and Confidentiality

If you wish to keep your secret—don't tell it to anyone.

A British proverb

CONFIDENTIALITY IN SOCIAL WORK

The importance of keeping secrets has been recognized since biblical times. In Leviticus it is said "Thou shalt not go up and down as a talebearer among thy people" (Leviticus 19:16), and in Proverbs, "A talebearer revealeth secrets; but he that is of a faithful spirit concealeth the matter" (Proverbs 11:13). The gossiper was punished severely in ancient times. The Bible tells us that Miriam, Moses' sister gossiped about her brother and was punished with leprosy.

Forbidding gossip and revealing secrets in the Jewish tradition, for example, is important in social and religious ethics, for gossip can endanger a person's life. "Saving the soul," the duty to save life from mortal danger as a result of a serious illness or other dangers, is an ethical commandment in the Bible. It is based on the verse, "Thou shall not stand on thy friend's blood" (Leviticus 19:16). Therefore, whoever endangers others is similar to a murderer, and his or her identity can be disclosed to the authorities. However, before doing so, he or she must be warned not to repeat his or her actions.

Confidentiality and privacy in professional practice have long been considered major obligations of social workers. Confidentiality in social work has been defined by Biestek (1957) in his now classic work *The Casework Relationship* as "the preservation of secret information concerning the client which is disclosed in the professional relationship" (p. 121). This approach to confidentiality corresponds to what has been discussed in Chapter 9 as fiduciary relationships and the responsibility of the social worker to clients. In the "old days" of social work, prior to the new technological era and the electronic devices that are taken for granted by the new generation of social workers, confidentiality meant simply keeping the written records in a safe place. Keeping a promise, on the other hand, is an issue of ethical obligation that dates back as far as the days of Socrates, some 2,500 years ago.

Confidentiality in professional intervention has accompanied social work since its beginnings. Its anchoring in law during the past decades came as a result of the complex legal, values, and ethical aspects of the subject. The complexity is expressed in the ethical dilemmas that spring up in daily practice. The law protects social workers by giving them immunity from prosecution when they are not specifically ordered to reveal confidential information about their clients. Each new law that further protects the immunity of social workers from prosecution in cases involving confidentiality adds to the prestige of the profession.

Knowledge of the law, both federal and state, pertaining to confidentiality in social work is the professional obligation of the practitioners. Knowledge of the clauses of confidentiality in the laws is essential for successful coping with ethical dilemmas. Social workers should remember that this knowledge can act as a double-edged sword: Just as it can protect workers in relation to the information they receive from clients, so the law also states the punishment for those who do not adhere to it and who violate its language and intentions.

What then are the main values inherent in confidentiality in social work? Safeguarding confidentiality of information is an ethical expression of the contract between a social worker and a client. This is the precondition to the client's agreement to share his or her secrets with the social worker. Confidentiality is an act of prevention of harm to the client. The worker is responsible for preventing the potential implications of revealing clients' secrets concerning their personal, family, and social life against their wish.

Clients who tell their secrets to the social worker must be sure that the worker will keep them and will not disclose them without their consent to anybody or to any authority. Confidentiality is the basis for the professional connection and the precondition to its existence. Confidentiality is basic to the establishment of a trust relationship between the worker and the client. Without this trust the chances of successfully treating and helping the client are slim. This knowledge about confidentiality is what enables clients to come to the agency for help with their problems.

Social workers must keep information confidential without reference to whether or not the client does. A question can be raised, From whom does the confidential information need to be kept secret? As the professional literature in social work indicates, such information must be kept secret from almost everybody and anybody. It must be kept from the general public, from interested groups and parties, from administrative systems, from the police and the courts, from other social workers, from the family of the client, and from the client himself or herself. Almost no area of life or social factor exists from which secrets should not be kept, thus legal, moral, and religious arrangements and rules determine how to relate to secrets and to confidential information.

The following case is offered for illustration.

CASE EXAMPLE:
THE STUDENT WHO DID NOT REPORT
TO THE DIRECTOR OF THE SCHOOL

A private high school had a policy that all personnel, including social workers employed by the school, should report cases of pregnancy among the students to the director of the school. A pregnant student is summoned to the office of the director to plan the continuation of her studies, her medical treatment, the abortion or the baby's adoption, and for any other matters connected to the decision, including notification of the student's parents about the pregnancy.

Michel, a third-year social work student in fieldwork at this school thought that the student's parents should not hear about the pregnancy unless the student consented to the notification. Thus she refrained from reporting cases of pregnancy to the director of the school. She was told that her refusal would result in her losing her free tuition. She would also get a failing grade in fieldwork unless she complied with the school's policy in these matters.

What is the responsibility of the social work student in this case? What is the responsibility of the student's field instructor? How should they behave, both separately and together? What are the ethical implications of the case?

The central questions regarding confidentiality in this case include, Does Michel have the right to ignore the request of her client to keep the pregnancy secret? Under what conditions can such a request for confidentiality be maintained? Should the contents of the secret serve as criteria for its keeping? If the decision is taken to disclose the secret, how should it be disclosed? Are the client's right to self-determination and confidentiality applicable in all circumstances? Who is the client? Is it the high school student? The school's director? Is it the family of the student?

The client is the person or people with whom the social worker has a therapeutic contract that includes keeping confidential any information given by the client to the worker and that spells out the specific instances in which disclosure of the secret to another party is permitted by the client.

Keeping secrets of and preserving loyalty to the client and to the employing agency simultaneously are among the most difficult problems in the social work profession. A responsible social worker loyal to his or her profession can keep in secret information given on the condition that it will not be disclosed, unless under the force of the law. Even under such threat he or she must ensure that the client understands this necessity and agrees to it without any coercion. Therefore, in cases of conflict between loyalty to the client and loyalty to the employing agency or the state, the duty to remain loyal to the client takes precedence.

The NASW Code of Ethics, which serves as a "guide to the everyday conduct of members of the social work profession and as a basis for the adjudication of issues in ethics when the conduct of social workers is alleged to deviate from the standards expressed or implied in this code" (Barker, 1987, p. 197), has seen several revisions. Each new revision has added to the clauses pertaining to confidentiality. Thus, for example, the duty to warn and protect third parties that was established following the well-known case of *Tarasoff v. Regents of the University of California* (Kopels and Kagle, 1993) served as basis and precedent for social workers and other professionals to breach confidentiality when a risk of life-threatening harm to another person exists.

Each social work code of ethics, beginning with the first one in 1960, has specified what is meant by this term. Basically the term "confidentiality" encompasses all informations obtained in the course of professional service and their use in professional work, along with their limits. "Compelling professional reasons" for violating the rules about confidentiality in social work refer to those instances in which there are well-documented reasons that justify the violation and are able to stand up in the court if needed.

According to Reamer (1998), four conditions are necessary to permit disclosure of confidential information (1) sufficient evidence that the client presents a threat of violence to another must exist, (2) the violent act must be foreseeable, (3) the violent act is impending, and (4) the social worker must be able to identify a potential victim.

Today, the ethical responsibility and legal obligations of the social worker are closely connected. Clients have a legal right to confidentiality based on the individual's right to privacy say Rock and Congress (1999). The use of modern technology in documentation of professional work has created much needed ease in communicating, recording, classifying, and transmitting written and audio materials, yet it has also created new ethical dilemmas in confidentiality. Rock and Congress (1999) cite telephone reviews, facsimile transmissions, voice-mail reports, and computerized databases used by managed care companies, for example, as seriously compromising the guarantee of confidentiality (p. 257). This can be avoided, however, if social workers use the necessary security and ethical safeguards recommended by various social work ethicists and educators. The proposed framework for matching security and sensitivity of data along the guidelines offered by Rock and Congress (1999) to promote and protect confidentiality in the technological age are valuable to all social workers. They are invaluable especially to teachers of ethics, fieldwork supervisors, and agency administrators.

Despite modern electronic devices now available to almost everybody in the caring professions, no substitute exists for the human touch. Social workers still need to go through the process of ethical decision making without shortcuts in order to arrive at and justify an ethical decision they take in cases of conflict among competing values and subsequent ethical dilemmas. The following case presents the problems that social workers may face in their use of confidentiality.

CASE EXAMPLE:
A REQUEST TO KEEP A FRAUD SECRET

Rebecca was staying with her two small children in a shelter for battered women where Miranda, a social worker, was caring for her family. Miranda is struggling with an ethical dilemma. Rebecca has told her in secret that for some time she has been receiving money from the welfare department to which she is not entitled, meaning that she is engaged in fraud. She also told Miranda that she wishes to return to her husband, even if it means the possibility of being abused once again.

Miranda is contemplating the right thing to do, whether to respect her client's right to secrecy and self-determination or to disclose her fraud and take legal measures against Rebecca. Miranda is worried that Rebecca's husband may harm her if she returns home, and she is worried about what will happen if the fraud is discovered.

Based on the models for ethical decision making discussed in the previous chapter, this case will be analyzed using Reamer's (1999) model. The case will provide an opportunity to encompass the whole process of ethical decision making that can be used in social work, nursing, and even in medicine.

As per Reamer, the first step in this process consists of identifying the ethical issues and professional values that are in conflict with one another. In this case the conflict is between basic professional values and various obligations emanating from those values, such as the right of the client to the information given to her therapist being kept confidential, the right of the client to self-determination, the duty of the social worker to defend and protect the client from harm, and the duty of the worker to refrain from any connection to acts of fraud, dishonesty, and breaking the law. Miranda may use her experience and professional knowledge and try to influence Rebecca in order to prevent her from further fraud. Yet, it is doubtful whether she will be able to do so given Rebecca's poor economic situation and unwillingness to refrain from committing fraud.

The second step concentrates on identifying the various factors that would be affected by the ethical decision. These include, in addition to Rebecca and Miranda, the children and Rebecca's husband, the taxpayers whose money is not directed to where it should be, and the needy citizens whom the fraud prevents receiving the help they need. If the fraud is discovered then the shelter for battered women will be affected in its image in the eyes of the public.

Identifying the relevant avenues or options for action is the third step. One such avenue in this case is to keep the information given confidential, as the client has requested. The advantage in this option is that it permits Rebecca to live separately from her husband and not appear in court. The shortcoming of this option, the continuation of the fraudulent behavior, is related to the danger of embroiling the social worker and the agency in complex legal procedures. Another option is to ask Rebecca to stop the fraud immediately and report it to the director of the agency that provides the money. If Miranda chooses this option, then she will have to explain to Rebecca that as a professional worker she cannot condone her behavior. The advantage in taking this option would be that the fraud would be stopped, whereas the disadvantage is the danger that the client would need to return to her abusive husband. Rebecca may also appear in court for the crime committed, and, if found guilty, would be separated from her children. Another disadvantage in selecting this option would be that the social worker would lose her client.

The fourth step requires finding the relevant ethical theory, instructions in the code of ethics, and legal implications in this case. The code of ethics for social workers contains professional values that need to be considered in the analysis. The most important among them are the commitment to the welfare and well-being of the client, the client's right to self-determination, the client's voluntary acceptance of the treatment offered, and keeping the information given in confidentiality. Other values included in the code refer to the subject of fraud and to the requirement to safeguard the integrity and good name of the profession, the social worker, and the agency.

The ethical theories could help the social worker assess the conflict from different perspectives and construct an ethical standpoint. Miranda could choose the deontological perspective, for example, according to which the first obligation and duty of the social worker is to respect the right of the client to self-determination and confidentiality. It is possible to use the same theory to justify another standpoint, that the duty of the worker is to respect the law and to defend the good reputation of the agency. Here we can witness the potential conflict between two different uses of the same theory.

Miranda may turn to the utility theory that aims to do good for the largest number of people as her theoretical anchor in this case. Accordingly, it is possible to argue that keeping the secret and preserving her client's right to self-determination will advance her well-being. In that way Rebecca would be able to live independently and would not suffer from the abuse of her husband. This advantage is preferable, despite the fraud. One can also argue that the welfare of the public comes first, and thus the fraud must be avoided. Rebecca's abuse of the law should not become standard for others, for it could cause irreparable harm if practiced by other welfare recipients.

The differing attitudes in ethical theories toward the same case, and the differences in the consequences that can be derived from them, lead us to turn toward some of the criteria that Reamer (1999) has developed for ethical decision making. The first rule states that securing the necessities for survival (such as being alive, health, food, etc.) overrides the rules against other harms, such as lying, disclosing confidential information, etc. It is possible on this basis to justify the fraud claiming that the harm it causes is smaller than the harm that could happen if Rebecca returned to her abusive environment. Yet, before agreeing with this explanation of the first rule in Reamer's model, we must ensure that Miranda weighed the other alternatives and found that she must prevent the return of Rebecca to her husband, even at a price.

The second rule states that the right of the individual to basic well-being takes precedence over the right of another individual to self-determination. This rule too is not unequivocal. It is possible to claim that Rebecca's basic well-being is preferable to the right of her husband's abusive behavior. Yet, it is possible to explain this rule in a different way, namely that the rights of all other welfare recipients take precedence over the right of Rebecca to engage in fraudulent activity.

The third rule, that states that the right of the individual to freedom takes precedence over the right to basic well-being, demands that Miranda respect Rebecca's right to self-determination of her life and destiny, but that means conflict with the fourth rule, which refers to the social worker's obligation to respect the law of the state and of the employing agency. These do not permit fraudulent receipt of money.

Rule number four states that the right to basic well-being takes precedence over the rules, laws, and regulations in cases of conflict, meaning that in certain situations it is permissible to violate some specific law to save a life. In this case we may argue that the return of Rebecca to her husband may jeopardize her life and thus it is preferable to enable her to live independently and agree to the fraud. Carlson

(1991) found that this solution of the conflict would be in line with the professional literature on battered women.

Those wishing to use this rule to justify Rebecca's behavior should bring convincing evidence for such a decision. This means that Mirnada should prove that Rebecca has no other option except violation of the law. It is possible that Miranda is prejudiced against abusive men in general and she supports the idea of battered women living independently. Such an attitude would bring Miranda to accept Rebecca's fraud as the latter's only chance to escape from her predicament.

The fifth step in Reamer's (1999) model for ethical decision making refers to the subject of consultation with colleagues. This consultation is valuable, especially in cases in which there is a need to include legal aspects pertaining to the case that will help the worker to arrive at the ethically right decision.

Another means that should be utilized by Miranda in her decision-making process is turning to the ethical committee in her agency. The committee can provide valuable advice on how to proceed in this case. Ethical committees are composed of members of various professions. They provide consultation services that are not binding on the worker but permit him or her to look at the ethical dilemma from many perspectives. These committees also help the worker learn from the experience of those well versed in ethical matters.

Reamer (1999) offers two reasons, why it is useful to consult with ethical committees. First, in the consultation new aspects not previously brought up by the worker could emerge. The second reason is that the consultation protects the worker in case of a court case. It provides evidence that the worker weighed all aspects pertaining to the case seriously, along with the potential implications on those involved in it, and did not act hastily or without considering the consequences of his or her action.

The sixth step obligates the worker to reach a decision and to document his or her entire process of ethical decision making. The more complicated and controversial a case is, the more difficult it is to arrive at a decision. Therefore, the reasoning behind the decision will be more difficult, too. In this case Miranda will have to document her agonizing about the fraud committed by Rebecca and her own obligation as a social worker to the employing agency. She will have to tell Rebecca that she cannot agree to the fraud, but she is willing to help Rebecca find an alternative to the present situation and problem. This approach is necessary professionally. It will require of Rebecca to make important decisions about her future. It is possible, of course, that Miranda will have to pay a price for being honest and straightforward and may lose her client. Miranda will have to take this possibility into consideration. It is important that the decision reflect the process she employed in arriving at the decision. It is equally important that the social worker as a responsible professional base her decision on a well-reasoned basis that reflect her values in thinking, emotion, and action.

Kopels (1993) has stated that in many cases the social worker is obligated under the law and the code of ethics to disclose confidential information given by the client. She cited cases in which children threaten to commit self-aggression or threats were directed toward another person, or child neglect was involved. Even in these cases the worker is obligated to keep the information given by the client confidential. Disclosure of confidential information without the consent of the client is permitted only in extreme cases when a professional necessity exists for so doing. The information given by the client is considered confidential and protected by law and by the code of ethics as a right of the client, and its violation can be justified only in extreme situations.

The documentation of the decision-making process is the last step in making an ethical decision. This step is necessary to protect the worker. A tendency exists today to go to the judicial system with malpractice claims. Therefore the social worker needs to be protected against such practices of certain clients. A full documentation of the steps taken to arrive at an ethical decision will attest to and show that her reasoning and considerations were in line with the values of the profession and the requirements of the law. The documentation will be particularly useful if the client accuses the worker of negligence, improper behavior, and/or malpractice. The following section dealing with the subject of confidentiality in medicine is offered as both an historical account of the concept and as additional knowledge for social workers.

CONFIDENTIALITY IN MEDICINE

The principle of confidentiality in medicine has existed since the times of Hippocrates and is included in his oath. It is possible that this principle has an even longer tradition. It is likely that before Hippocrates physicians in ancient Greece and in other parts of the world used to keep in secret and privacy information revealed to them by leaders of the state and by other dignitaries during medical treatment. The function of the confidentiality principle has not significantly changed over the centuries; it has remained being the protection of doctor-patient relationship.

This principle has been restated in the various medical codes, both in the West and in the East, including the International Code of Medical Ethics. According to this code, a doctor must preserve absolute confidentiality on all he or she knows about the patient even after the patient's death (World Medical Association, 1949). Confidentiality as a general principle in medicine pertains to doctors, too, who are ill. They are entitled to benefit from the same strict rules as other patients. In some circumstances a breach of confidentiality may be justified as a result of the treating doctor's overriding duty to society similar to the principle of confidentiality applied to all nonphysician members of society.

In the American Medical Association's Code of Medical Ethics, which are intended "to aid physicians individually and collectively in maintaining a high level of ethical conduct" (as declared in the preamble), we read in Principle 9 the following:

> A physician may not reveal the confidences entrusted to him in the course of medical attendance, or the deficiencies he may observe in the character of patients, unless he is required to do so by law or unless it becomes necessary in order to protect the welfare of the individual or of the community. (American Medical Association, 2006)

In part of the Hippocratic oath, which will be discussed in the following chapter, it is stated that what the doctor sees or hears in or outside of the course of his or her treatment about which he or she should not gossip, will be kept as a medical secret. Communication between the doctor and the patient is not shielded by legal privilege as is communication between a lawyer and a client or between a social worker and a client in the state of Israel, for example. The issues of medical confidentiality are beset by contradictions. These are associated with changing patterns of health care and commercial demands for health-related information.

Blasszauer (1995) emphasized that the Hippocratic oath was revolutionary in those days. At the basis of that oath was the recognition that patients will give the doctor true details about their condition and illness only after they are convinced that their disclosures will be kept in secret. These confidential details made a significant contribution toward the curing of the ailment. Hippocrates's approach to medicine is utilitarian in its essence. It concentrates on the utility of medicine for the patient.

The obligation of doctors to keep in secret information given them by the patient is based on mutual trust. The stronger and more absolute this trust is, the more useful it is to the doctor in making the diagnosis and prescribing the method of treatment that will have the best chances of leading to success and the best results. Thus confidentiality is both an ethical principle and a practical requirement of doctor-patient relationships. Doctors should keep in mind the best interests of the patient. Release of a patient's personal health information to others is permitted only with the patient's consent and only for the purpose stated previously. Loss of confidentiality is a threat to good medical care, maintains Munson (2000). Confidentiality is supposed to protect a patient in a vulnerable situation, such as when being treated in a hospital. However, such protection is highly questionable given the access that so many health care professionals and members of the health care team in modern high technology health care have to the patient's records. Thus patients are often torn between a wish to maintain their privacy and confidentiality and between the need to sacrifice it to receiving the best possible care.

Munson (2000) offers one way to reduce the possibility of confidential records getting into the wrong hands. He thinks that access to these records should be given only to those who must know. Therefore it is advisable to divide the records into a health or medical section and a financial section. In the first instance, he claims, health care professionals would have access only to the medical information. Care should also be exercised by the hospital's administration to avoid discussion of patient records or conditions in public places such as the cafeteria, elevators, etc., in front of strangers.

TRUST AND CONFIDENTIALITY

Respecting the client's rights is a moral duty, a kind of "categorical imperative" in accordance with the deontological theory of ethics. This respect of the client's rights includes the safeguarding of the client's privacy as an integral part of the social worker's morality so that the client will not live in constant fear, suspicion, and insecurity.

In the professional relationships between the social worker and the client, breach of confidentiality usually results in the cessation of further contact between them, and in some cases even to litigation. Disclosure of secrets that can endanger the life of another person is at times morally necessary. In 1993 some 450 physicians, lawyers, social workers, and others attended an international medical conference in Jerusalem. One of the decisions reached by the participants stated that patients who were sick with AIDS prior to their marriage and who did not report it to their spouse are not recognized by the halacha, the Jewish religious code of laws and that doctors must regard it as their duty and obligation to notify the spouse about the patient's sickness, even if he or she strenuously objects to the disclosure of his secret (Vincent, 1993).

A medical secret is any fact whose keeping in confidence is thought absolutely necessary by its owner. This definition includes personal secrets, too. Those who refer to confidentiality in medicine in a strict sense include as secrets even the gender of the patient, the number of his or her room in the hospital, details about the patient's family constellation, and even the seriousness of the patient's wounds or illness.

A very difficult question in all caring and helping professions is Whose welfare or "good" comes first? This question has serious implications for the livelihood of the client or patient. For example, should the doctor report to the Department of Transportation that a certain driver suffers from epilepsy? Is a doctor who believes that the answer is yes and acts on this belief, thus causing the invalidation of the sick person's driver's license, acting ethically?

Social workers frequently witness serious breaches of confidentiality on the part of the authorities. Many official forms and questionnaires contain many details about the health condition of the citizen that are supposed to be confidential.

Age As a Criterion in Confidentiality

Another problem related to confidentiality in social work and in medicine is the age of the client or patient. Today a great deal of ignoring of young persons' (under age eighteen) requests not to disclose their medical diagnosis to the parent still occurs. Reference to rules of confidentiality employed by a given agency or organization, such as the high school in a previous case study, that impedes the right of young persons to keep their condition in secret, is a sign of continued paternalism. Today many youngsters are capable of analyzing their own medical situation and arriving at intelligent decisions. Blasszauer (1995) emphasizes that in many cases of adolescent suicide, disclosure of the confidential information to another party, such as the youngster's parent, by the school authorities was the trigger that pushed the young person to commit suicide.

Many young people refrain from turning to doctors with problems related to sexually transmitted diseases, drug addiction, and especially with request for the contraceptive pill or abortion when they know that the doctor will inform their parents. The percentage of young people applying for help would be far greater if they could disclose their secrets to the doctors without fear of being reported to the authorities or to the parents.

Scally (1993) in his article titled "Confidentiality, Contraception, and Young People" has shown that in Holland only one-seventh of the girls in their teens get pregnant as compared to a far higher proportion in England and Wales. The main difference between the girls in Holland and the girls in the United Kingdom is the ease of getting the contraceptive pill and other preventive measures against pregnancy in Holland, and in their secret being kept from the parents. Getting to the doctor in time is another preventive factor in such situations when a girl gets pregnant. Girls who know that the information they give to the doctor will remain confidential are helped far more than girls who are afraid their secret will be disclosed.

The right of minors (under age 18) to privacy and confidentiality is justified when the social worker or doctor tries to motivate them to share their medical situation and the decision about the appropriate treatment with the parents. When this sharing is impossible, then the doctor must respect confidentiality for the sake of the young person.

In any case, the doctor should refrain from discriminating against an individual because of age.

Giving Information to the Family and Confidentiality in Social Work

Giving information to the family of the client is a moral responsibility, provided that it serves the client's interest. Many details about the client's condition usually appear during the treatment that can be given to the family only with the client's full consent. Many times families use the information to abuse the client. Cases of blackmail have occurred based on the information received, for example, a family interested in placing a sick elderly man in a nursing home against his wish threaten to spread a rumor that he is mentally sick. Therefore, the social worker must know the client's family rather well and find out for what purpose they need the medical information. Only after verifying that no harm will be caused to the client by revealing the information should the social worker proceed.

Relatives of the client should receive only information that benefits the client. For example, if the client needs a special diet it is important that the person closest to him or her should know about it, but if the relatives are interested in receiving details about the illness that can cause harm to the client or to his or her image and social status, such as the severity of the illness, then it is vitally important not to give the information to the family, particularly not to members in the family who are in bad relations with the client.

This attitude to information giving is valid even in cases in which such materials are needed for purposes of the instruction or guidance of students studying social work using electronic devices. The social worker is not permitted to use the information for "scientific purposes" unless the client was fully informed and consented to the request. Any use of the information that was not authorized by the client is not only immoral but also violates the dignity and autonomy of the client. Maintaining confidentiality in social work is a complex matter, especially when dealing with children, the mentally retarded, the very old and feeble, or in cases in which the client is unable to make his or her own decisions due to temporary or permanent disability.

Chapter 13

Oaths and Codes of Ethics

THE HIPPOCRATIC OATH

Intended to be affirmed by each doctor upon entry to the medical profession, the Hippocratic oath in English translation reads as follows:

I swear by Apollo the physician, and Aesculapius and Health, and All-healer, and all the gods and goddesses, that, according to my ability and judgment, I will keep this Oath and this stipulation—to reckon him who taught me this Art equally dear as my parents, to share my substance with him, and relieve his necessities if required; to look upon his offspring on the same footing as my own brothers, and to teach them this Art, if they shall wish to learn it, without fee or stipulation; and that by precept, lecture and every other mode of instruction, I will impart a knowledge of the Art to my own sons, and those of my teachers, and to disciples bound by a stipulation and oath according to the law of medicine, but to none other. I will follow that system of regimen which, according to my ability and judgment, I consider for the benefit of my patients, and abstain from whatever is deleterious and mischievous.

I will give no deadly medicine to anyone if asked, nor suggest any such counsel; and in like manner I will not give to a woman a pessary to produce abortion. With purity and with holiness I will pass my life and practice my Art. I will not cut persons laboring under the stone, but will leave this to be done by men who are practitioners of this work. Into whatever houses I enter, I will go into them for the benefit of the sick, and will abstain from every voluntary act of mischief and corruption; and, further, from the seduction of females, or males, of freemen or slaves. Whatever, in connection with my professional practice, not in connection with it, I see or hear, in the life of men, which ought not to be spoken of abroad, I will not divulge, as reckoning that all such should be kept secret.

While I continue to keep this Oath non-violated, may it be granted to me to enjoy life and the practice of the Art, respected by all men, in all times; But should I trespass and violate this Oath, may the reverse be my lot. (British Medical Association, 1993, p. 326)

The Hippocratic oath is regarded in medicine as the "mother of all oaths," and all later oaths relied on it. Its source, most likely, was in the writings associated with Hippocrates's medical treatises. This oath is the most controversial among those writings.

The oath is a contract, an ethical code, and determines the ethical conduct of the physicians. It is important in its many meanings for today's practice of medicine. The oath can serve a model for the profession of social work that lacks, for the time being, such an oath. Today the oath has mainly historical importance because, in terms of the content and the emphasis, medical ethics passed through great changes, and these changes have had a major impact on the relevance of the Hippocratic oath in its original text. The oath accompanies the social and professional changes that happened during the years of practice, and is considered to be the value basis for the science of medicine.

This oath is written in the literary structure that was common in the ancient Greek culture: That is, it begins with an introduction, continues with the main text and central issue, and ends with the reward or the punishment meted out to those who do not keep it. The oath is a contract with the gods and with people. It relies on the gods as higher authorities and rulers of people's destinies. The oath is an agreement with the teachers of medicine and their offspring to preserve the obtained knowledge from generation to generation. Even today priority is given to the children of physicians in entrance to medical schools, as people continuing the family and professional traditions through the ages.

The historians who investigated the origin of the Hippocratic oath are divided as to the identity of its author. They claim that the authentic style and language is not the one used in the historical times of Hippocrates. Two acts in the oath are forbidden to the physician: assistance to commit suicide by giving deadly drugs and giving medicine to prevent pregnancy. These two prohibitions aim at safeguarding life rather than serving the interest of women and patients. Both strengthen life, the first by preventing escape from life and the second by preserving life in its beginning and development, whereas the rest of the oath deals with protecting the life of the patients and the sick in need of help. This contradiction in the oath can bring one to the conclusion that the Hippocratic oath was created later than the days of Hippocrates, perhaps during the early era of Christianity with its values and approach to the sanctity of life and its objection to abortion and euthanasia.

According to Loudon (1994), currently 98 percent of the medical schools in Canada and the United States use some form of a medical oath. Out of 126 medical schools surveyed in the study, 119 replied. More than one half (sixty-seven) of the respondents stated that they use a modified Hippocratic oath, but only three schools reported using the classic oath. In the United Kingdom's twenty-seven clinical medical schools only two use the Hippocratic oath, and twelve use no oath of any sort. The rest of these schools use the modified version contained in the Declaration of Geneva.

The Hippocratic oath in its old and modern version is one of the oldest binding documents in history. Its major principle of treating the sick to the best of one's ability is held sacred by doctors. Yet the tremendous advances in modern day medical science and technology, and the corresponding economic, political, and social changes in a world that legalizes abortion, physician-assisted suicide, and the "use of knife" to conduct surgical procedures forbidden in the original oath make the classic Hippocratic oath somewhat of a relic whose ingredients are simply out of place in the modern world. Moreover, most modern oaths are contrary to Hippocrates's aim in making doctors fully responsible for their actions. In our times transgressors of the oath rarely, if ever, lose their licenses for malpractice or even face medical ethical boards.

What Is Included and What Is Missing in the Hippocratic Oath?

The oath contains the following:

> keeping the oath according to personal ability and judgment;
> giving respect and material assistance (if needed) to the teacher who taught this profession;

teaching the profession of medicine to the children of the one
who served as original teacher, if those children wish it;

providing the right nutrition for the sick;

safeguarding life and the prestige of the profession;

visiting the sick in their homes solely for the sake of healing
them;

keeping in secret any information that comes to the attention of
the physician in the course of his or her treatment of the sick;

reward for keeping and punishment for not keeping the Oath.

The oath does not cover the following:

the needs of potential patients,

the rights of the patients beyond the right to confidentiality, or

the distribution of medical resources that promote the health of
the public.

The style of the oath attests to a one-sided and paternalistic approach to sickness and patients in which the physician is omnipotent, omniscient, and all-powerful, and the patient has no right of choice.

The question of whether a need for an oath even exists in medical practice was raised by Gaizler (1994). He asked why it should not suffice for physicians to act in accordance with their conscience. The answer to his question was given at the World Congress of the World Psychiatrist Association in 1977 in Honolulu, Hawaii. There it was stated that a strict conscience and a personal ability to judge are necessary for the ethical conduct of physicians, but that written rules are also needed to clarify the ethical obligations and ethical principles that guide the work of the physicians to help them shape their consciences.

The Hippocratic oath serves as a compass in cases of ethical dilemmas. It helps the physician escape the need to survey all the possibilities in each problem or ethical dilemma that arise in medical treatment. The oath can ease the problems of a physician vacillating in his or her insecurity and help him or her gain the right measure of self-confidence in his or her professional behavior.

Analysis of the Hippocratic oath reveals the following main ingredients:

To whom the physician pays loyalty: The physician must decide in whose name he or she makes the oath in the introduction. Of God, the king, the state, humanity, society, or the university from which one has obtained one's medical education and degree?

The characteristics included in medical ethics: The general readiness to help the sick, saving lives, and economic arrangements.

The most important command: Do not harm. Included in this concept is enhancement of the health of the patient and prohibiting assistance to commit suicide and abortion.

Respect for the patient: Refraining from engaging in sexual relations with the patient and keeping confidentiality—except when ordered not to by the court.

Professional expectations: Respect for teachers, colleagues, demand for and participation in consultations, and development of medical science and methodology.

Moral conduct of the physician: Prohibition of accepting bribery and giving false documents.

Some theoreticians in medicine perceive the term *oath* as an offense to the right of physicians to decide whether or not they wish to swear an oath or to make a commitment. The Hippocratic oath is problematic for many physicians because it forbids killing a fetus (abortion) or giving assistance to a sick person to commit suicide. Controversial decisions must be made in difficult situations when life and its meanings for the individual are at stake, such as in cases of endless suffering from an incurable disease, total limitation of mobility, loss of self-respect or a great love, and economic or moral bankruptcy. Should the command to save life be valid in these cases too? What is the attitude of the oath to new concepts in modern societies such as quality of life, life in dignity, or a dignified death?

Each doctor must answer such questions in his or her own way in accordance with his or her conscience if unwilling to accept the traditional text of the Hippocratic oath. When we compare the Hippocratic oath with the Declaration of Geneva of 1948 (The World Medical Association [WMA] Declaration of Geneva Declaration Guidelines for Medical Doctors, adopted by the Second General Assembly in Geneva, Switzerland, September 1948; and amended by the Twenty-Second World Medical Assembly in Sydney, Australia, August 1968; and the Thirty-Fifth World Medical Assembly in Venice, Italy, October 1983; and the Forty-Sixth WMA General Assembly in Stockholm, Sweden, September 1994), which serves as a modern version of the traditional Hippocratic oath, we see some differences in the content. In both oaths emphasis is placed on health of the patient as the main focus in the physician's work. In the Declaration of Geneva's oath the concept of health expands to include all ingredients of health in the holistic sense and encompasses all people, and not only the sick. However, the respect one owes to one's teachers is different. In the traditional Hippocratic oath the teacher is compared to a parent, whereas in the Declaration of Geneva one should give to one's teachers "the respect and gratitude which is their due."

Additional differences in the two versions exist. The traditional oath does not refer to the social, economic, or religious situation of the patient, except for free men and slaves, and in the Geneva version it is said: "I will not permit consideration of religion, nationality, race, party politics or social standing to intervene between my duty and my patient." This addition is made to defend the work of the physician against all threats due to religious, economic, cultural, and political differences.

Another difference between the two oaths relates to the concept of human life. Abortion in the Hippocratic oath is forbidden, whereas in the Geneva Convention it is said: "I will maintain the utmost respect for human life from the time of its conception, even under threat, I will not use my knowledge contrary to the laws of humanity" (Thompson et al., 2000).

The Hippocratic oath has been shortened at the University of Sheffield's School of Medicine to four clauses. This oath resembles the Hippocratic oath and emphasizes its main declarations. These are the following:

1. I will remain loyal to the tradition and responsibility emanating from my mission.
2. The welfare of my patients and their health will be my first priorities. I will do everything for them and will refrain from causing harm.

3. I will try to gain the full trust of my colleagues. I will refrain from any wrongdoing, harmful or shameful acts.
4. Whatever I will hear or see in my work I will keep in secret and will not divulge to others. (Thompson et al., 2000)

These four statements are equally valid for the social work profession as well.

The medical oath in all its versions and with the detailing of punishment in case of its violation has kept the social mission of the physicians alive for thousands of years. The oath is even more significant today than in the past when the debates about the questions relating to the beginning and ending of life caused controversies among cultures and within religions and affect medicine's attitude to them. It is indeed possible to refer to the Hippocratic oath to justify a certain position in medical practice for good and bad, but one cannot avoid the central message contained in each of the recent versions of this oath—*primum, nil nocere,* that is, before all else, do not harm.

OTHER CODES OF ETHICS IN MEDICINE

The development of codes of ethics in medicine was not limited to the people living in Europe and to the Western cultures. The ancient Asian and the Middle Eastern cultures too had their share in the same enterprise. Medical and philosophical writings in ancient India, for example, the Vedas, the four holy Sanskrit books of the Hindus, contain information on medicine and ethics. They were written around 1500 before the Christian era. These refer to ethics that encompasses reality as lifestyle. Accordingly, only a person who lives a moral life can recognize the truth embedded in life as a whole as based on "divine morals." Such a person fulfills a spiritual quest. In order to achieve this goal a person must follow four specific tasks, and these will lead him to the main goal. These four tasks are: Gaining the material resources (wealth), satisfying the desires, fulfilling the moral duties, and attaining psychological wholeness. When one achieves these tasks they create the virtues of decency, modesty, and lack of aggression.

The ethical codex of the Hindus, which most likely was developed during the first century AD, presents three principles that contradict the Hippocratic oath. These are integral to the unique culture of India and reflect its tradition. The first principle provides equal defense for humans and animals. The Hippocratic oath makes no mention of animals. The sanctity of life as the second principle states that life begins the instant a seed pierces the ovum in the body of a woman, that is, before a fetus is created. The third principle states that it is forbidden to treat the enemy, a woman who comes alone to a doctor, a dying man, or an immoral person.

In ancient China two philosophers attained fame beyond their countries that reached the West: Lao Tzu, who lived and taught during the sixth century BC, and Confucius, who lived about a hundred years after the former. The Tao, or "right way," teaches people about the world and the laws of life. Lao Tzu emphasized in his teaching modesty, cleanliness, decency, sincerity, refraining from aggression and violence, and deliberation. In the year 600 before the Christian era he wrote that the attitude of the Tao to insult is kindness (Veatch, 1989). Confucius advocated respect for the ancient traditions. The noble person is courteous, generous, tries to act in justice, and his or her passions do not exceed the limits of his social status. Some people in China contribute the proverb "What you don't want to be done to you—don't do to others" to Confucius. A similar statement is attributed in the Jewish tradition to Rabbi Hillel.

Several common themes exist between the ancient Hindu and Chinese codes of ethics, such as the prohibition of treating a woman who comes alone to the doctor without a witness being present during the medical examination. The Chinese code of ethics from the sixth century AD states that the treatment of the sick must be done according to the principle of equality, discrimination between sick people is prohibited, remuneration for the doctor's work must be modest, and the poor should be treated free of charge.

The Chinese code of ethics, contrary to the Hindu, is based on the teachings of Confucius, Buddha, and the Tao, and has no religious or sacred foundation.

Jewish traditional (i.e., religious) approaches to medicine and doctors are no different than the general ethical standards of society. Doctors do not have monopoly of the sources of morals and thus they could not claim a separate ethics for medicine. In the Jewish religion it is God who heals the sick. Doctors are only his instruments. Doctors are not supermen and superwomen. They have no superiority to others in morals or in judgment. Doctors are supposed to give advice and information to the sick. They should explain to the patient and the patient's family what medicine can and cannot do in a given situation. Doctors should refrain from making decisions for the patient. In their work they should rely on the moral and religious precepts and refrain from controlling the lives of the sick. They are the servants of society, not its rulers.

Since biblical times and during the ages many prayers and oaths were created by Jewish doctors and their patients. They refer to God's infinite power to heal and restore health. These oaths and prayers differ from one another in their moral and religious intensity. The codex of Jewish religious laws, the halachah, and many other religious literary sources contain prayers that doctors were supposed to say before entering the house of the sick. Patients, too, were asked to pray and to say poems for healing and recuperation. The oaths and prayers of doctors express what is considered ethically appropriate behavior in relation to the sick. The proverb that says "the best of doctors to hell" refers to doctors who are too proud and commit sins against their patients, for doctors are supposed to be modest, pious, and full of fear of God. They were expected to study, consult with their colleagues, and rely on God's mercy and help in their work.

Contrary to other nations, such as the ancient Greeks, Hindus, and the Chinese, and even the Christians and Muslims, whose men meticulously refrained from treating women, Jewish religion does not include the same prohibition. It was aware, however, that male doctors were human beings who could be seduced by women. Therefore, doctors prayed to God to keep their thoughts in purity and to concentrate only on their work and on the welfare of the sick (Steinberg, 1976).

The most famous prayer of Jewish doctors is generally known as the daily prayer of Rabbi Moses Maimonides, the great doctor. This prayer, however, was not written by him, for it was first published in German in 1738, some six hundred years after his birth. The prayer itself was written by Marcus Hertz (1747-1803) and was translated into Hebrew by Professor Yeshayahu Leibowits from the German original.

This prayer has direct implications on social work ethics. It is reproduced here (translated by the author of this book):

I prepare myself to engage in my art. Help me, oh God, in my work to succeed. Give in my heart love toward your creatures and my art. Don't let greediness and pursuit of fame intervene in my work, for these measures are the opposites of loving truth and justice. Therefore I ask you not to let me go astray in my work for the benefit of your creation. Strengthen my physical powers and my soul to be ready always to help the rich and the poor, the good and the bad, the loving and the hating, and that I will always see my patients as human beings. Enter trust in me and in my knowledge into the hearts of the sick so that they will listen to my advice and follow my directions and commands. Let my heart listen to the voices of the truly wise in my art who wish to teach me understanding—for the field of wisdom is wide and great. (Friedenwald, 2003)

ON CODES OF ETHICS
IN THE CARING PROFESSIONS

Since the Hippocratic oath laid the foundation of modern medical ethics, it is appropriate to cite the work of Edelstein (1967), one of the most famous scholars of the writings of Hippocrates. Edelstein considered the establishment of the principles of medical ethics by Hippocrates to be his greatest achievement. This feat did not dim with age. The Hippocratic oath has become the cornerstone of all medical codes in the world, with the exception of the Hindu and Chinese. Even today the principles in the oath serve as guides for medical ethics. The oath reflects the norms of ethical behavior in the use of the power and professional knowledge of physicians. The humanistic attitude to the sick, keeping confidentiality, maintaining equality in treating patients, and honoring the teachers who taught this profession contained in the Hippocratic oath are worthy of praise.

One of the deficiencies in all medical codes of ethics is their simplicity. They refer to ethical requirements with lightness, and an importance is assigned to them that is far from being proportional to their values. Therefore, it is hard to rely on any code of ethics in medicine as the final authority, and no doctor should use the code to justify breaching confidentiality, violating the rights of the patient, disclosing the patient's secrets, or transgressing ethical and moral principles.

The International Code of Medical Ethics (World Medical Association, 1949, 1968, 1983), which lists the duties and expected behaviors of physicians, including their obligations to their patients and colleagues, was accepted by the World Medical Association in the third conference of that body in London in 1949.

The International Code of Medical Ethics lists three major duties of physicians:

1. Duties of the physicians in general;
2. Duties of the physicians to the sick; and
3. Duties of the physicians to each other.

The medical codes of ethics developed after World War II reflect the most important values of this historical era. They were expressed in the declarations accepted by the participants in many international conferences around the world. For example, the codes contained rules pertaining to medical experimentation with live human beings. These rules were adopted after the horrors of the Nazi doctors were revealed in the war crimes trials of Nuremberg in 1947. In the Declaration of Helsinki in 1964, the World Medical Association drew up a code of ethics on human experimentation. This code was amended by the twenty-ninth world medical assembly in Tokyo in 1975 and by the assembly in Venice, Italy, in 1983, and it laid down the basic principles of biomedical research.

The Declaration of Helsinki of the WMA (1964, 1975, 1983, 1989, 1996) contains

1. Basic principles;
2. Medical research combined with professional care (clinical research); and
3. Nontherapeutic biomedical research involving human subjects (nonclinical biomedical research). (Cited in Thompson et al., 2000, pp. 340-342)

An additional development of medical ethics was contained in the Declaration of Tokyo, which regulates physician conduct in relation to torture and other cruel, inhuman, or degrading treatment or punishment. Its preamble states:

It is the privilege of the medical doctor to practice medicine in the service of humanity, to preserve and restore bodily and mental health without distinction as to persons, to comfort and to ease the suffering of his or her patients. The utmost respect for human life is to be maintained even under threat, and no use made of any medical knowledge contrary to the laws of humanity.

For the purpose of this Declaration, torture is defined as the deliberate, systematic or wanton infliction of physical or mental suffering by one or more persons acting alone or on the orders of any authority, to force another person to yield information, to make a confession, or for any other reason. (British Medical Association, 1993, p. 334)

In 1968 in Sydney, Australia, a declaration was accepted by those assembled regarding determining the time of death, and in Oslo, Norway, in 1970 the main subject was abortion and therapy. In 1977 the ethical principles of psychiatric treatment for the mentally sick were affirmed in Honolulu. All these declarations and decisions found their way into the codes of ethics in modern medicine.

Codes of ethics in the caring professions are mixtures of commands and beliefs. As beliefs they strengthen a profession's esteem by the ideals that serve their bases. They also demand that each practitioner respect these ideals, similarly to the requirement contained in the Hippocratic oath. As commands these codes contain a row of prohibitions that determine professional behavior in specific situations, such as the prohibition against breaching confidentiality.

When one analyzes the various chapters in the codes, their limitations and shortcomings become more visible. For example, the Declaration of Oslo states that if a doctor cannot perform an abortion or give medical advice on that matter due to religious belief, he or she should excuse himself or herself from the duty to help and turn the case over to another doctor willing to accept it. This clause, on its surface, permits doctors to refrain from professional intervention in cases of abortion based on their conscience and religious beliefs. However, fulfilling this clause may be difficult. What happens if no other doctor is available to turn to, or if all other doctors reject abortion? Who, then, will provide this service for the pregnant woman?

All ethical codes of behavior lack the ability to give unequivocal answers to all the ethical dilemmas that arise during the course of daily work in the caring professions. Nevertheless, they can determine the rights and duties of the practitioners in a given caring profession as well as the appropriate methods that practitioners are permitted to use in services provision. The public rightly expects these from each practitioner. Another contribution of the codes of ethics to the caring professions is that they serve as "guides for the perplexed," that is, they provide guidance how to proceed in cases of conflict.

CODES OF ETHICS IN SOCIAL WORK

The social work profession came into being for the most part in the twentieth century. Its first code of ethics was published in 1960 in the United States and in 1976 in Great Britain. Earlier attempts to develop codes of ethics were made (Johnson, 1955, Pumphrey, 1959), but they did not succeed. The development of a code of ethics signified a certain status attained by the profession. Today social work stands on its own feet among the major caring professions. The most recent code of ethics was approved by the 1996 National Association of Social Workers Delegate Assembly and revised by the 1999 NASW Delegate Assembly. The NASW Code of Ethics is an explicit statement of the values, principles, and rules of the profession. Its function is to regulate the conduct of professional social workers.

The code of ethics published in 1960 contained declarations on the obligations of social workers regarding services provision and knowledge development in social work. The introduction to this code included references to the responsibility of the social worker to society and to social service. Seven years after its publication, as a result of the civil-rights struggle's achievement, a clause was added to the code prohibiting discrimination against people based on their color, creed, gender, and political beliefs.

The most recent code of ethics in the United States is a product of the changes that have been introduced to the original document since 1960. It reflects the great development the profession has enjoyed since the technological and scientific achievements that happened during the second half of the twentieth century. It testifies to the long way the profession has come to become a truly caring profession for all people. To illustrate these changes, the code of ethics contained in the *Social Work Dictionary* lists sixty-nine rules binding on social workers (Barker, 1987), whereas the 1999 NASW Code of Ethics lists 155 rules along with a well-detailed preamble that includes the purpose of this code and the ethical principles and standards upon which the code is based.

The principles and standards that serve as a basis for the NASW Code of Ethics attest to the liberal, humanitarian, and democratic attitude of this profession to people in need and to the commitment to serve the general welfare of society. They detail the rules that guide social work intervention in the lives of its clients, including rules for resolution of ethical conflicts and dilemmas.

Professional social work in general can be characterized by work based on respect for clients as human beings in need of help. This includes safeguarding clients autonomy, welfare, rights, and responsibility; refraining from discriminatory attitudes toward them; enabling them to use their potential abilities and talents; giving priority to professional responsibility and interest over the personal; being accountable for one's work to the client, the employing agency, and to society at large; and engaging in cooperative activities with other professional colleagues for the benefit of the client.

The NASW Code of Ethics entails all the guidelines just listed. It reveals the lofty ideals and wishes of the profession to serve all segments of society. This code of ethics contains no practical ideas or realistic guidance to deal with conflicting situations between opposing professional values; it provides a basis for judging the various activities social workers undertake before they actually happen and then afterward. In making ethical decisions one should rely on the principles of the entire code in its letters and spirit.

Declarations in the Code of Ethics for Social Workers

The code is divided into four major sections. The first includes the introduction, the basic values, and the statement about the social mission of the profession of social work. Emphasis is placed on the commitment to enhance the lives and welfare of the clients and on the obligation to respond to their needs. The needs of clients were the subject of a social work classic, *Common Human Needs*, by one of the great educators in social work, Charlotte Towle (1965).

Empowerment is another term in this section of the code. It means helping clients to make their own decisions in as many areas of life as possible. Helping people living in poverty and under oppression and injustice is an important social work function (Gil, 1998).

Caring for the poor and the downtrodden has always been among the most important social work activities. In our days these functions no longer encompass only the lower classes of society. Today people from the middle classes turn to social work services, mainly for problems with mental health. The popularity of private practice or clinical orientation and psychotherapy reflects the change in the value base of the profession in the past two or three decades (Reamer, 1992). The social mission of the profession has become a subject of great debate among educators, philosophers, and other leaders of the profession. The main question centers on priority in social work services delivery. Should priority be retained for the traditional clientele, namely the poor and the vulnerable to the vicissitudes of life, or for people with better resources who need family therapy and counseling in mental health?

The NASW Code of Ethics emphasizes the commitment of social work to the poor as an integral part of its social mission. This mission is one of the major characteristic of this profession that differentiates it from the other caring and helping professions. The code also stresses individual well-being of the clients in the social context. This attitude reflects the importance assigned by social workers to the ecological perspective in professional work (Hartman, 1994).

Promulgation of social justice and social change have always been social work priorities. The profession is committed to a just distribution of the resources for the benefit of the poor and needy, for those who really need social services. Yet, this commitment remains more a quest than a reality (Gil, 1998). Nevertheless, that these issues are included in the code of ethics is significant in itself, and the future generation of social workers will hopefully be able to succeed in this mission better than the present one.

Sensitivity to matters of cultural and ethnic diversity is another subject addressed in the code. Social workers today are more aware that they are practicing in a multicultural society. They are obligated to refrain from any form of discrimination in service delivery to people of different racial and ethnic compositions. The code contains a large number of standards relating to the need to be sensitive to people's cultural and ethnic backgrounds. It guides social workers on how to avoid discrimination and on what is permitted and forbidden in professional work with ethnic clients. The actualization of a certain standard is dependent on the workers, especially on those who develop and enforce policies. Their professional judgment makes the difference between what is ethically right or wrong in real-life practice.

Culturally competent practice may mean different things to different people, but it entails sensitivity to the value of difference and willingness to learn and change. Translated in terms of daily work, this maxim requires social workers to invest themselves in learning, understanding, and taking responsibility for their personal and professional beliefs and practices. This learning corresponds to what the ancient Greeks advised those who came to seek knowledge: Learn about yourself. Learn what is considered in each culture effective, valuable, respectful, and helpful to people. Learn to be authentic and open to new ideas and to new approaches in the performance of your professional activities.

The Code of Ethics for Black Social Workers

In May 1968 the *Code of Ethics of Black Social Workers* was published in San Francisco by the National Association of Black Social Workers (NABSW). The founding statement of this organization is the following:

> This organization was formed in response to issues related to providing human services in the Black community, educating social workers for effective service in the Black community, and providing opportunities for participation of Black social workers in the social welfare arena. (NABSW Code of Ethics Preamble)

Among other activities, this organization has prepared a code of ethics for the black social worker that is reprinted here, and its ramifications and importance for the practice of social work in American society are discussed.

Declarations in the Code of Ethics for Black Social Workers

> In America today, no Black person, except the selfish or irrational, can claim neutrality in the quest for Black liberation nor fail

to consider the implications of events taking place in our society. Given the necessity for committing ourselves to the struggle for freedom, we as Black Americans practicing in the field of social welfare set forth this statement of ideals and guiding principles.

If a sense of community awareness is a precondition to humanitarian acts, then we as Black social workers must use our knowledge of the Black community, our communities to its self-determination and our helping skills for the benefit of Black people as we marshal our expertise to improve the quality of life of Black people. Our activities will be guided by our Black consciousness, our determination to protect the security of the Black community and to serve as advocates to relieve suffering of Black people by any means necessary.

Therefore, as Black social workers we commit ourselves, collectively, to the interests of our Black brethren and as individuals subscribe to the following statements:

I regard as my primary obligation the welfare of the Black individuals, Black family and Black community and will engage in action for improving social conditions.

I give preference to this mission over my personal interests.

I adopt the concept of a Black extended family and embrace all Black people as my brothers and sisters, making no distinction between their destiny and my own.

I hold myself responsible for the quality and extent of service performed by the agency or organization in which I am employed, as it relates to the Black community.

I accept the responsibility to protect the Black community against unethical and hypocritical practice by any individuals or organizations engaged in social welfare activities.

I stand ready to supplement my paid or professional advocacy with voluntary service in the Black public interest.

I will consciously use my skills, and my whole being, as an instrument for social change, with particular attention directed to the establishment of Black social institutions.

Ethical Implications of the Code of Ethics
for Black Social Workers

Social workers, irrespective of their racial and ethnic backgrounds, need to understand that the helping tradition upon which many black social workers base their work is deeply rooted in spirituality. Professional helpers wishing to work within the black community must learn about black spirituality and the guiding principles that set the standards for thinking about social work practice with black people.

Spirituality as a concept may be defined as a sense of the sacred and divine. It is strongly connected to religiosity. Black caregivers throughout the ages relied on the spirituality of the black people to lift their spirit; to motivate them to endure all hardships, ills, misfortunes, catastrophes, and calamities without losing faith and to live their lives as God intended for them. Spirituality in the black helping tradition was seen as motivating force to attain decency and to treat people properly and with dignity.

Early caregivers in the black community were mindful of spirituality's power over the fate of the individual. They were aware of its power to enhance concern and commitment to the collective well-being. They were aware of the debt they owed the black community for gaining education and for achieving economic and social status. They were able to translate these achievements into serving the community in the spirit of W. E. B. Du Bois who said: "The best of us should give of our means, our time and ourselves to leaven the whole" (Du Bois, 1908, p. 99).

Spirituality and religion are two closely connected forces in the minds of many black people. Both are concerned with matters of the sacred, eternal, and divine, and with issues of justice and injustice, good and bad, and right and wrong in human conduct. Spirituality draws on a person's inner resources. It is concerned primarily with thoughts and feelings. It nourishes one's identity and helps one develop wisdom. Spirituality enables one to come to terms with the inevitable, to make peace with oneself and others, and to accept responsibility for the events that happened in a person's life.

Spirituality has important ethical implications for caregiving and for caregivers. Students and practitioners need to be educated to integrate in their professional values and knowledge that human beings are "three dimensional": biological, psychological, and spiritual, and all three dimensions must be considered in any treatment. Students and practitioners need to reaffirm their spiritual resources and develop genuine feeling for others. The divine spark is hidden in the hearts of us all. We are oysters that harbor the precious pearls. Similar to the pearl in the oyster, our hearts are covered by massive layers of hard material that shield the divine spark. It is therefore the task of every human being to peel away those protective layers, to open our hearts, and to let the divine spark ignite a fire in our souls to go forth in its light.

Martin and Martin (2002) in their excellent work on spirituality and the black helping tradition have stated that this spirituality is integrated with religiosity, communal solidarity, and racial uplift, so much so that at times it is difficult to distinguish between them (p. 193). This spirituality dates back to the times when in Africa the helping person was steeped in its people's history, tradition, values, religious practices, and spiritual outlook on life. These attitudes were carried over to the New World and kept alive during all the hardships, pain, and suffering inflicted by slave owners on black people, and they exert an influence on the professional work of black "mainstream" social workers sanctioned and legitimized by the status quo.

"Although contemporary social work practice tends to be primarily a secular profession," Martin and Martin (2002) wrote, "this can be said categorically; there can be no social work based on the Black experience that does not consider both the secular and the sacred world of Black people" (p. 243).

The major objective of black experience-based social work is to help black people rediscover their lost historical selves by use of the spirituals in their work. These spirituals are songs that can be traced back to African cultures. They were used to telling stories and celebrating events of importance in the lives of the communities, and the songs expressed yearnings, gave inspiration, hope, and faith in the redemption of the people from slavery and oppression.

Martin and Martin (2002) have emphasized that "Black experience-based social work seeks to inspire, motivate, and encourage Black people to realize their unique gifts, strengths, potential, and promise to create the sense of community that is necessary for them to work through the difficulties of their current circumstance" (p. 248). The historical past must be connected to the personal past and circumstance and to the future prospect in micro-, mezzo-, and macro-level intervention. Martin and Martin (2000) have listed five principles that social workers should adopt in their work with black clients:

1. The first principle is *internal locus of control.* This means the black people accepting responsibility for their own moral, intellectual, cultural, and spiritual development, irrespective of how circumscribed they are economically and politically.
2. The second principle, *personal responsibility and collective reciprocity,* perceives caring as a spiritual act and demands of the black people to do all in their power to "look out for one another."
3. The third principle, *social debt,* requires black social workers to remember the debt they owe to their ancestors. This debt was elaborated in the works of Du Bois and Martin Luther King Jr. as well as many other outstanding black leaders, and it indicates the need to help other black people live and grow in decency, dignity, and self-respect.
4. The principle of *sanctification of human life,* the fourth principle, is similar to and corresponds with social work's basic value of respect for each human life, irrespective of its condition. This principle requires the worker to give his or her utmost to helping others as a sacred enterprise and ultimate ethical good.
5. The principle of a *holistic approach,* the last of the five principles, proposes that spirituality in its nonreligious sense is as much a social worker's domain as that of the clergy in all religions. Because spirituality in its broadest sense, including religion, is an integral part of a client's life, it should not be neglected, ignored, or downplayed by the social worker.

These principles are incorporated in the code of ethics for black social workers. They can be useful for all social workers practicing with other ethnic and/or racial groups. The black helping tradition goes back to early historical times in Africa and continues through the days of slavery until the present day social work.

During the Progressive Era, for example, that lasted from 1890 to 1920, black social workers were in the forefront of the struggle for enlightenment, liberation from oppression and discrimination, and for justice for the black people. These pioneer social workers were among the "talented tenth," the educated elite of the African-American community, as termed by Du Bois. They subscribed to the values and principles of the emerging social work profession, such as self-help, mutual aid, and a holistic approach to caregiving. They also tried to imbue their clients with race pride, race consciousness, and worked diligently for racial uplift. Progressive Era black social workers took pride in their efforts to educate the masses. "Their legacy," LaNey (1999) said, "is a strength-based practice model on which contemporary scholars and practitioners can build" (p. 311).

In accordance with the third principle listed previously, social workers need to be extremely mindful and sensitive of their clients' spiritual and religious outlooks on life. These can often differ from their own and cause conflicts and ethical dilemmas. The ethical implication of this principle means that social workers should never impose their own values and beliefs on their clients and that they should work diligently and faithfully for the well-being of their clients, irrespective of their religious and cultural backgrounds.

Black people often turn to their spiritual leaders, and especially to their religious leaders, for guidance in the problems they face in their daily lives before they seek help from professional helpers such as social workers. The same applies to many Jewish people, and not only to the "common folk" in their midst. It is customary for religious Jews to turn to the rabbi in personal, economic, and even political matters. Social workers can form collaborative relationships with the spiritual and religious leaders in the community to solve their clients' problems.

When clients and workers are not of the same religious denomination, an ecumenical approach needs to be employed. Such an approach strengthens the principle of respect for cultural and religious differences of the clients. Caring requires an unbiased approach toward the client. An ethical social worker is one who provides his or her services equally to people, irrespective of their religious and social circumstances.

"Social workers must not only fully see the importance of spirituality in Black life and explore it as a possible resource for meeting needs, but must also include religious and spiritual matters in the assessment process" (Martin and Martin, 2002, p. 211). At the same time, these authors warn that social workers cannot assume that all black people are religious, or that the religious among them all belong to the same denomination. Yet, all black people have some sort of spirituality whose roots may go far in the family and cultural heritage of their bearers.

Spirituality in the black helping tradition refers to many concepts. These are beautifully described by Martin and Martin (2002). It involves reaching one's God-given talents and gifts and feeling a strong kinship relationship with the ancestors and a sense of oneness with one's history and culture. It is inseparable from racial and communal connections. At times it may be weak or hidden deep inside one's soul, but a person cannot be viewed as a spiritless or soulless being (Martin and Martin, 2002, p. 213). Therefore, modern day social workers need to see the spirituality of black people as a strength rather than a weakness in the lives of their clients. The caring professional must relate to spirituality as an important resource for coping, healing, and change. Being sensitive to the cultural heritage of black people has important ethical value for the profession of social work. It requires social workers to use their power and influence in society to eliminate oppression and to promote tolerance.

LaNey (1999) claims that many social workers are unaware of the cultural and historical traditions of self-help, mutual aid, and communal responsibility in black society, and many fail to understand the importance of these elements in their practice with black clients. Many are still embroiled in paternalistic approaches to clients, forgetting the need for reciprocity in worker-client relationships and forgetting the ethical obligation of empowering the client to achieve self-determination.

Social workers working with black clientele must educate themselves about the significance of the prominent and influential community institutions in the lives of black epople. These include first and foremost the black family that remains, in Billingsley's (1992) words "a resilient and adaptive institution reflecting the most basic values, hopes, and aspirations" (p. 17).

Another major source of support for the African-American community is the church. These institutions wield powers that should not be overlooked by the practitioner. Creative social workers are aware of the significant services the church provides in the African-American community that can be utilized to enhance social functioning. They should seek avenues to collaborative activities that can benefit the entire community. Social workers need to remember that the black community in the United States is very heterogeneous and should be familiar with African-American culture, lifestyle, and help-seeking behavior to be effective practitioners with this population.

The same social problems that plagued the black community in previous generations are still around. The models of practice used by the pioneer black social workers are still valid today. Social workers, irrespective of their ethnic backgrounds, are urged to examine these models and to assess their applicability in modern day practice.

The Revised National Black American Social Workers Code of Ethics

The original code of ethics of black social workers issued in 1968 was revised during the past two decades. States have made revisions in this document and included them in their examination materials for social work licensing. For example, the Texas State Board of Social Worker Examiners has published the following:

781.401. Code of Conduct

(a) A social worker must observe and comply with the code of ethics set forth in this subchapter. Any violation of the code of ethics or standards of practice will constitute unethical conduct or conduct that discredits or tends to discredit the profession of social work and is grounds for disciplinary action.

(1) A social worker shall not refuse to do or refuse to perform any act of service for which the person is licensed solely on the basis of a client's age, gender, race, color, religion, national origin, disability, sexual orientation, or political affiliation.

(2) A social worker shall truthfully report or present her or his services, professional credentials and qualifications to clients or potential clients.

(3) A social worker shall only offer those services that are within his or her professional competency.

(4) A social worker shall strive to maintain and improve her or his professional knowledge, skills, and abilities.

(5) A social worker shall base all services on an assessment, evaluation, or diagnosis of the client.

(6) A social worker shall provide the client with a clear description of services, schedules, fees, and billing at the initiation of services.

(7) A social worker shall safeguard the client's rights to confidentiality within the limits of the law.

(8) A social worker shall be responsible for setting and maintaining professional boundaries.

(9) A social worker shall not have sexual contact with a client or a person who has been a client.

(10) A social worker shall refrain from providing service while impaired due to the social worker's physical or mental health or medication, drugs or alcohol.

(11) A social worker shall not exploit his or her position of trust with a client or former client.

(12) A social worker shall evaluate a client's progress on a continuing basis to guide service delivery and will make use of supervision and consultation as indicated by the client's needs.

(13) A social worker shall refer a client for those services that the social worker is unable to meet and terminate service to a client when continued services are no longer in the client's best interest.

The Need for a Separate Code of Ethics for Black Social Workers

The NABSW Code of Ethics in its revised version is a succinct statement of rules of conduct binding on black social workers. It is written in a commanding language and provides sanctions for those who violate its letter and spirit.

A legitimate question may be raised with respect to the NABSW Code of Ethics: Why do black social workers need a separate code of ethics when today all social workers, irrespective of their cultural, racial, and religious backgrounds are aware that discrimination against clients on any ground, such as gender, national origin, political affiliation, etc. is strictly prohibited by the NASW Code of Ethics? The answer is that many social workers consider the NASW Code of Ethics as an ineffective guide for all practitioners (Kopels, 1997). Social workers are not a homogeneous group. Despite a common belief and commitment to the guiding principles of the profession's code of ethics, social workers are first of all members of cultural and ethnic groups. As such, they are not free from the specific cultural values that affect their personal and professional behavior. Similar to any other ethnic group, black social workers are interested in protecting their community and advancing and improving its social, economic, and political condition. Moreover, many black social workers feel that needs peculiar to African Americans are best dealt with their own code of ethics. The issue, then, is how to reconcile possible conflicts between personal, cultural, and professional values in a responsible manner.

Few comparative studies on the ethical behavior of practitioners in the main cultural/ethnic groups in American social work exist. One is a recent work by Jayaratne, Croxton, and Mattison (2002). These researchers have theorized that "personal identities would strongly influence a social worker's acceptance or rejection of given practice behaviors" (p. 70). They have also hypothesized that differences on some practice behaviors would exist between white, black, Asian, and Hispanic social workers who belong to the National Association of Social Workers and are in direct practice. They focused their study on the question of whether or not the acceptance of a given behavior was considered professionally appropriate rather than the actual practice of behavior. The findings of the study indicated an agreement by the vast majority of the respondents with respect to filing ethical complaints against co-workers. They also agreed that it is highly inappropriate to give gifts and loans to clients. At the same time it was noted that more than 20 percent of the respondents were uncertain about the appropriateness of this behavior—despite the requirement by the NASW Code of Ethics (National Association of Social Workers, 1996, p. 78).

The researchers also found a number of statistically important differences between the various racial groups. For example, African-American respondents were found to be significantly more likely to consider social relations with former clients and provision of concrete assistance to be more appropriate than did their white or Hispanic colleagues. Of the practice behaviors that could raise potential conflicts between personal and professional cultures, body-focused interventions, bartering for services, and billing practices were correlated primarily with race. In all these instances white workers considered these behaviors more appropriate than did their minority colleagues. The researchers admitted that the reasons for these findings are a matter of speculation (p. 82).

A major ethical problem facing the profession of social work at present is compliance with the NASW Code of Ethics by all social workers. It is well-known that about two-thirds of individuals classified as social workers in America have only bachelor's degrees and consequently do not belong to the National Association of Social Workers. The question of whether or not these practitioners are or are not free of the obligations implied in the code of ethics of the NASW is thus very important. So far, studies dealing with the ethical practices of social workers relied on members of the NASW (Jayaratne, Croxton, and Mattison, 2002; Reamer, 1995; Strom-Gottfried, 1999). This question has not yet been tested by a court of law.

Another outstanding issue in social work ethics refers to the problem of implementing culturally sensitive practice. Will the code of ethics for black social workers serve as guide for all other racial/ethnic groups of social workers, or will it remain binding only on those practitioners that belong to that group? Will that Code advance unity and integration in its spirit, or will it create new segregations? Finally, will a universal code of ethics for social workers emerge, replace all existing codes, and be enforced in the profession on all who claim to be social workers?

Still another outstanding ethical problem in working with African-American clients is related to the method of social work intervention. The presently dominant psychodynamic theory-based intervention was found by Solomon (1986), for example, to be ineffective and counterproductive. Black individuals and families need more concrete services and empowerment than psychotherapeutic approaches to solving their problems. The question is, How do social workers see the African-American families? Are they seen as sources of strength and support, or are they perceived as sources of dysfunctional behavior? The same applies to the role of the church within the black community. Is it looked upon as a natural support system for people in trouble, or is it regarded as an obstacle to "professional" intervention?

An ethically appropriate professional approach to the problems presented by clients should be based on real respect for their values and beliefs. African Americans, as with any other ethnic group, expect social workers to base their relationships with the clients on a personalized approach; to be sensitive to their personal, communal, and religious values; and to be able to establish peer relationships. Peer relationships in social work with a black client means basing the relationship on mutual trust and on mutual sharing of information. In such a relationship each party brings its own knowledge and expertise to solving the problem at hand. As Solomon (1986) has so well pointed out:

> It is not enough for the social worker to have an appreciation for cultural diversity; he or she must have basic knowledge regarding the lifestyles, communication patterns, and characteristic problems encountered by Black individuals and families. This knowledge is required for accurate assessment of the client's strengths, resources, support network and potential for collaborating in a problem-solving process. (p. 519)

Chapter 14

Professional Misconduct and Malpractice

The physical hurts can be detected by x-rays, and it is possible to tell how many days will be needed to recuperate from them. But who can tell from one word, from an accentuation of the voice, from a movement of the shoulder, or from a wild laughter how long one can remain alive afterward and from what internal bleeding a man died in such cases?

Eva Ancsel (1988)

CASE EXAMPLE:
"THE GOOD SISTERS FROM VIENNA"

In 1987 the world was shaken by a series of murders committed by four nurses in a hospital in Vienna, Austria. In the criminal investigation that followed the revelation of the murders it was found that the four nurses, Gertrud, aged thirty; Irene, aged twenty-seven; Maria, aged twenty-six and Stephanie, aged forty-nine, murdered in cold blood forty-eight old and helpless patients during their seven years of service in this hospital. The chief nurse and leader of the group confessed that she alone was responsible for murdering thirty-nine patients by giving them an overdose of insulin and by suffocation. The colleagues of the four nurses could not digest the news and failed to believe the confessions and evidence published in the papers. They claimed that the four were known as good people and good nurses and they simply could not believe that such a horrible thing could have been done by these nurses. The accused said in their own defense that they did "those things" out of pity, to ease the suffering of the poor old folks in the hospital.

This case shows the power of life and death in the hands of nurses and illustrates the broad concept of malpractice and unethical behav-

Ethics in Social Work: A Context of Caring
© 2006 by The Haworth Press, Inc. All rights reserved.
doi:10.1300/5577_15

ior in a caring professional. When this power is abused, or used immorally and inhumanly, the results can be catastrophic. Although not a common occurrence, the potential for such abuse always exists, and not only in nursing but in other helping professions, too. It is always possible to find lurking among the many good and decent professionals some people who resemble the "good sisters" in Vienna. A similar case was reported by Rozsos (2003) involving a nurse who killed seriously ill elderly patients in Hungary in 2001. These cases are important for other reasons, among them the subject of responsibility in therapy and attitude to euthanasia or merciful death.

The four nurses tried to hide behind the claim of euthanasia. Professional therapists must respect the laws of the state just as any other citizen. Furthermore, they must respect and act according to the rules of their profession and to the standards of practice. Some situations may arise in which knowledge of the law is insufficient for making and accepting a moral decision, as with euthanasia. Sometimes the patient's request to end his or her life may sound reasonable because the patient is lucid, has control of his or her mental powers, understands the meaning of the request and capable of self-determination. The patient's sufferings are beyond endurance and he or she wishes to be rid of them. He wants to die in dignity, by a death of his own choice. Even when such a request sounds reasonable, the nurse and other therapist must reject it, because laws against euthanasia are almost universal.

As for the subject of professional responsibility that was discussed in Chapter 7, we have to differentiate among three kinds of responsibility that are binding on the professional social worker and on other workers in health care:

- *Ethical responsibility,* which binds therapists to take into consideration the right of patients or clients to self-determination as long as the decision they make will not break the prevailing law or endanger their own life and the lives of other people.
- *Legal responsibility,* which concerns damage caused to the patient or the client due to improper therapy or negligence and/or deficiency in keeping professional standards. Here we can cite cases of giving the wrong medication to the patient, or therapists' inability to foresee the future results of their actions. Even actions done in good faith and in the belief that the result will not

damage the patient and will not be discovered are matters of un-professional behavior and a violation of legal responsibility that can end in malpractice suits. It is true that anybody can make a mistake. Yet, it is the duty of the caregiver to recognize the mistake and to inform the supervisor immediately to prevent further and more severe damage.

- *Criminal responsibility,* which concerns deliberate damage to the life of the patient or to his or her body or soul and ignoring the professional responsibility and rules of conduct written in the law and in the code of ethics. Such conduct entails punishment if sufficient evidence proves it occurred.

DEFINITION OF MALPRACTICE

The definition of the term *malpractice* is different in each caring profession. In medicine it is defined as criminal negligence or professional negligence, and in social work as worthless behavior. In the nursing profession it is customary to consider malpractice as negligent or irresponsible behavior (Hauck and Louisell, 1978) or incompetent and/or unethical healthcare (Morreim, 1993, p. 19).

Morreim (1993) differentiates between incompetent and unethical healthcare on the part of nurses that can be applied in social work too. Incompetent care refers to professionals that provide inadequate care due to their own impairment (physical or emotional) or from ignorance of standards of care. Unethical caregivers, on the other hand, knowingly and willingly violate fundamental norms of conduct toward others, especially toward their own patients. They resemble in their behavior what Martin Buber (1953), the philosopher defined as the "wicked," those who know the right way yet knowingly and willingly refuses to follow it.

According to Morreim (1993) five levels of adverse patient outcome indicate incompetent health care by nurses. The first is an accident that happens, such as an equipment failure. The second level concerns a well-justified decision that turns out badly for the patient, even though no indication exists that the nurse is incompetent. On the third level professionals disagree on what to do to or with the patient, and when a decision is made it turns out badly and harms the patient. Exercising poor judgment or skill is the fourth level. For example, a nurse fails to observe signs of physical abuse in a pediatric patient. When such failure is repeated over time it is a sign of incompetence. Finally, true violation of expected quality of care is the fifth level, such as leaving a confused elderly patient unattended in bed with the bedrails down.

CASE EXAMPLE: THE INCOMPETENT SURGEON

An incompetent surgeon and head of the surgical department in a cardiology center volunteered to operate on a patient aged forty-three who needed an operation to replace the valves in his heart. The entire medical team knew that the operation would not succeed because this doctor was known as an incompetent surgeon. Some members of the team predicted that the patient would not survive the operation, but they kept silent for fear of hurting their chances for advancement in their position and work. The surgeon made several serious mistakes and the patient died forty hours after the operation, by which time the surgeon was in Honolulu at a medical convention. Many doctors in the cardiology center in which this incident happened felt that they had not acted ethically. They should have warned the patient and advised him to find a better surgeon for the operation (Morowitz, 1993).

CASE EXAMPLE: CRIMINAL NEGLIGENCE IN MEDICINE

A lawyer aged fifty-three received routine examination of her lungs by X-ray during her annual medical checkups. She began having pains in her chest, and when she started to lose a great amount of weight she turned to a doctor, a specialist in lungs and he found in the X-ray picture a large swelling in the lawyer's right lung that looked "unfriendly" to him. The doctor requested all the X-rays of the patient's lungs previously taken by her family doctor and saw the appearance of the swelling and its development over the years.

The family doctor wrote on each photo that there were no pathological findings in the heart and lungs of the patient. The woman lived during those years in the security of knowing that she was healthy. The specialist had to decide what to tell this woman and what to tell her family doctor. He asked himself, Is it worth wasting so many hours in court over a malpractice suit against the family doctor? The family of this woman lawyer was well-to-do and did not need the money that could be got by a successful malpractice suit. It was too late for medical intervention. So, why cause problems? In any case it was impossible to reverse the situation (Morowitz, 1993).

These cases illustrate malpractice in medicine. They show but the tip of the iceberg. On the Internet one can find hundreds of cases referring to malpractice. As far back as 1986 the *Press Telegram* presented a hypothesis according to which ten percent of American doctors are incompetent for medical work. The conclusion was that more than fifty thousand doctors endanger the lives of their patients and cause serious damage or death to two hundred thousand people in a year. The newspaper reported that most cases of malpractice and criminal medical negligence are not reported to the courts and are not discovered. Nevertheless, a growing trend of malpractice suits against health care workers, especially doctors, has occurred in recent years. Among the reasons cited for the malpractice of doctors are drug addiction, alcoholism, depression, and Alzheimer's disease.

The *Bantam Medical Dictionary* presents two definitions of the term medical malpractice: Medical intervention or treatment not according to the standards in professional level and medical care which are expected from a doctor licensed to engage in medical services; insufficient treatment due to negligence or lack of knowledge, wrong medical diagnosis, and improper treatment or mistake in operation, as a result of which there was a serious worsening in the condition of the patient and/or he died (Peternelj-Taylor and Yong, 2003; Schultz, 2004; Tauber, 2006).

AREAS OF MALPRACTICE IN MEDICINE

The concept of malpractice in medicine has broadened considerably during the past decade and includes many cases that were not previously covered by law or by the code of medical ethics. It is presented here to show social workers where the public is heading with respect to unethical conduct on the part of a professional in health care. Social workers need only to replace the word *medicine* with *social work* to see what the future holds for them, too, in this regard.

Malpractice in medicine today includes and encompasses the following cases in which the physician can be brought to court for medical negligence:

- Leaving the patient without treatment
- Ongoing negligence of the patient in medical treatment

- Medical treatment or intervention without the consent of the patient
- Accusing the patient of wrongdoing and physically hurting him or her
- Forced treatment of the patient and ignoring what was agreed upon (in the "medical contract")
- Lack of the result the physician promised and committed to
- Misleading of the patient by the physician when he conceals facts that could verify the suspicion of negligence
- Presentation of false and misleading facts to the patient
- Misconduct and improper behavior of the physician, such as being drunk during the performance of an operation
- Violation of the patient's rights as a sick person, such as keeping him or her in a department or facility against his or her wishes (when no court order permits it)
- Damaging and hurting the patient's personal life by revealing his or her secrets
- Damage to a third party, such as the physician failing to inform a third party of a potential threat or danger to his or her life
- Any either professionally or morally improper act in the relationship between physician and patient

Three main reasons exist for turning to the courts in malpractice suits:

1. To enable quality control of the work of the physician
2. To give monetary compensation to the damaged
3. To give opportunities to patients to express their reservations and dissatisfaction with the treatment they received. (Hauck and Louisell, 1978; Annas, 1989)

Malpractice cases are present in all the helping and caring professions, albeit to different degrees of severity. The professional contract between the social worker and the client or between the physician and the patient verifies that the social worker or physician has the knowledge and expertise expected by the client or patient to be utilized for his or her benefit. This contract has broadened over the ages and today it encompasses care for the well-being of the client. When negligence is proven in the court the entire social work establishment suffers, beyond what the client and his or her worker have suffered and beyond the economic and moral punishment of the worker when he or she is found guilty. Medical negligence, for example, can result in death of the patient. If it is proven in the court, it results in lowering the profession of medicine's esteem in society and the prestige of doctors in general.

MALPRACTICE IN SOCIAL WORK

It is interesting to note that the revision of the 1960 code of ethics for social workers in the United States in 1996 contains only four clauses dealing directly with unethical conduct: clause 2.10 deals with incompetence of colleagues and clause 2.11 with the unethical conduct of colleagues. The private conduct in the code (4.03) states that "social workers should not permit their private conduct to interfere with their ability to fulfill their professional responsibilities," and clause 4.04 is concerned with dishonesty, fraud, and deception, saying, "social workers should not participate in, condone, or be associated with dishonesty, fraud, or deception" (Barker, 1999, p. 570).

These clauses are rather vague and general and lack examples of what is considered unethical behavior. Even the rule against using professional connections for personal benefit does not add to the clarification of the concept of malpractice in social work. In the law of social work in Israel (Goldstein and Rosner, 2000), for example, an offense against the discipline of the profession is defined in the following way:

> A social worker has committed a disciplinary offence against his profession if he behaved in a manner that is inappropriate for his profession; has transgressed the rules of professional ethics that the Secretary of Welfare has instituted in consultation with the national council of social workers; gained his enrollment in the registry of social workers fraudulently; exhibited irresponsibility and severe negligence in fulfilling his role; was found by the court guilty in a criminal offense that indicates his being unfitted for engaging in social work; transgressed any of the clauses regarding confidentiality and secrecy of information.

The law, concerning social workers in Israel, specifies what is considered as disciplinary offense and authorizes the Secretary of Welfare to develop regulations to ensure the proper professional behavior of all social workers included in the law. Social workers may transgress the rules of professional ethics unintentionally or purposely.

When transgression happens on purpose it is always unethical. Cases occur in which workers finds themselves in ethical dilemmas that raise questions of a general character. These cases may be related to the just distribution of scarce resources or to truth telling about a client's medical condition and prognosis. These are dilemmas that social workers find themselves embroiled in and that demand careful consideration, but other cases may raise the issue of proper ethical conduct. Reamer (1999) refers to behaviors and actions that may bring in their wake civil or criminal claims.

Sometimes a social worker may forget to obtain the client's permission to provide confidential data to a third party, or causes some damage to the employing agency by unintentionally not reporting cases of fraud to the finances of an organization. In these cases the social worker may find him or herself trapped and may be sued by the client or by a third party. In other cases the worker may be accused of serious and purposeful transgression of the rules in the code of ethics. Social workers may face charges when a complaint is brought against them to the professional organization or government agency that issues social work practice permits or to the ethical committee that supervises professional workers, or when a malpractice claim is raised against them.

In the latest code of ethics for social workers (National Association of Social Workers, 1996) one can find 155 clauses or rules and these provide lawyers with plenty of "ammunition" in claims of malpractice. The majority of malpractice suits brought against social workers who are insured by the insurance company of the National Association of Social Workers deal with charges of improper behavior or with failure in carrying out a professional obligation expected of the social worker. Not all such claims are supported by facts that can prove a social worker's guilt. Nevertheless, social workers must know what is considered malpractice in the eyes of the law or in the eyes of the various authorities that supervise the professional behavior and performance of the social worker.

Definition of Malpractice in Social Work

A decade ago Reamer (1994) defined malpractice in social work as a result of the worker's action that is not in line with the expected standard of care. A case of malpractice is brought before the courts when at the time of the incident a legal connection existed between the worker and client that was binding on the worker and he or she did not keep the information given in secret; when the worker neglected his or her duty to the client on purpose or by mistake; when the client suffered damage, such as loss of livelihood, as a result of the social worker disclosing his or her secret to his or her employer; and when damage to the client was the direct result of the social worker's negligent behavior.

Reamer (1999) cites six broad categories of cases connected to malpractice in social work: unprofessional and unethical behavior; trust and confidentiality; services provision and delivery; professional supervision of clients and colleagues; fraud and deceit; and ending the treatment. Most of these categories were discussed in previous chapters.

MALPRACTICE IN SERVING THE CLIENT

The following six components need to be present for service delivery to be valid legally and professionally, that is, in accordance with the rules of ethics:

1. The consent of the client to the service offered must be acquired without force or undue influence.
2. The client must be mentally competent to give consent.
3. The client must agree to the specific procedures or actions.
4. The documents and forms of the procedure must be valid.
5. The client has full rights to refuse treatment and to withdraw consent.
6. The consent of the client to treatment must be obtained on the basis of sufficient information. (Rozovsky, 1984; Reamer, 1994)

Another area of discontent in services delivery is found in the assessment. Charges of malpractice in this area may encompass many actions, such as accusing the worker of failure in the assessment of the problem; failure in providing the service agreed upon; failure of the service given to meet the expected professional standard, causing damage to the client; failure of the social worker to ask the questions relevant to the problem; use of improper techniques; or unfitness or lack of authorization to use a certain therapeutic technique, such as hypnosis.

According to Reamer (1999), American courts in general do not expect social workers to be perfect. They understand that it is impossible to get complete precision in diagnosis, for the nature of problems brought to the worker have many facets, yet they do expect the worker's actions to be in line with the requirements of the laws and codes. A mistake in treatment is not necessarily negligence. For example, in a case involving a hospital, a family claimed that the hospital failed to recognize the threats of a patient to commit suicide and neglected its duty. The judge ruled that diagnosis is not exact science and that getting a precise diagnosis in an absolute way is impossible.

In recent years accusations of sexual exploitation of clients by social workers has become more prevalent in the profession. Many articles and research studies published in the United States deal with this subject (Reamer, 1994; Pope, 1988; Brodsky, 1986). Brodsky found that those workers who exploit their clients sexually are usually male and in their middle years of life. Many of these workers are in divorce proceedings and lack satisfaction in their private lives. The victims are usually women who hear about the loneliness of the therapist and his need for help. He in turn usually convinces these women that sexual relationship with him is "okay" therapeutically.

The phenomenon of professional misconduct, such as sexual exploitation of clients, is not unique to social work. It happens in all the therapeutic professions. Several clauses in the code of ethics for social workers refer to the prohibition to engage in sexual relationships with the clients. Social workers are prohibited from sexual contact not only with the clients but also with the relatives and acquaintances of the client. The same prohibition applies to sexual relationships of social workers with their supervisor, students, educators, fieldwork instructors, and colleagues.

MALPRACTICE IN PROFESSIONAL SUPERVISION

Other areas that may be problematic in social work are professional supervision of workers in social service agencies, students in schools of social work, directors in government services, and in places where social work is not the primary service, such as hospitals, schools, public institutions, and nursing homes. In all of these is potential for misconduct and/or improper behavior as per the NASW Code of Ethics (Congress, 1992).

Supervisors and fieldwork instructors may find themselves embroiled in various charges due to their professional roles. We all know cases of students in fieldwork training requested by the ethics committee in the school of social work to appear along with their fieldwork instructors and directors of the employing agency to air a complaint. Usually the complaint refers to the unethical behavior of the student, as in the earlier case example of the student who failed to show up for work.

Fieldwork instructors and supervisors are legally responsible for the workers and students in their charge. They are responsible directly and indirectly for the actions and failures of their agencies. Supervisors in social work must provide precise information to their employees or students on how to obtain the client's consent to the necessary action on his or her behalf, they must identify potential mistakes in treatment, they must stop malpractice, and they must annul misuse of professional authority and discover cases of negligence or exploitation. They must carefully read each report, contract, and written agreement between client and worker. In each of the instances described is potential for transgressing the law or the code. Above all, supervisors must remember the clauses in the Code that refer to proper practice in professional supervision.

Among the most important clauses that deal with ethical behavior of supervisors are the following:

1. Social workers who provide supervision or consultation should have the necessary knowledge and skill to supervise or consult appropriately and should do so only within their areas of knowledge and competence.
2. Social workers who provide supervision or consultation are responsible for setting clear, appropriate, and culturally sensitive boundaries.
3. Social workers should not engage in any dual or multiple relationships with supervisees in cases in which there is a risk of exploitation of or potential harm to the supervisee.
4. Social workers who provide supervision should evaluate supervisees' performance in a manner that is fair and respectful. (Barker, 1999, p. 567)

Social workers may find themselves subjects of malpractice charges when they fail to consult with colleagues more knowledgeable than themselves and when they fail to transfer a difficult case to a specialist for diagnosis, evaluation, or treatment. Reamer (1999) cited a case of a social worker who treated a client complaining of headaches and suspected of having symptoms of depression. The worker is supposed to send such a client to a physician to rule out an organic reason for the complaint. If the worker ignores the headaches, thinking no organic reason exists for the client's behavior, then he or she may be charged with negligence and malpractice. Reamer (1999) therefore advises social workers to be careful and to consult with specialists. The workers should turn only to well-known specialists, otherwise they may be charged with negligence in transferring responsibility to others less competent. The worker should keep records of any such transaction with the specialist to verify that he or she has taken the necessary steps to ensure the well-being of the client.

Fraud and deceit in the relationship with the clients were strangers to social work up to recent times. It can be said that social workers by and large are decent professionals and maintain honest working relationships connected to their professional work. In the hundred years of its existence as a profession, few social workers have been brought before the courts for deceit or fraud. Today this positive picture of the profession has somewhat changed. We hear at times about cases in which social workers are charged with defrauding insurance companies or with deceiving government offices and even voluntary agencies.

Kirk and Kutchins (1988) have documented in their study, which encompassed a national sample of clinical social workers, that many of them were involved in various cases of fraud and deceit. Seventy-two percent of the subjects questioned stated that they were aware of cases in which they presented diagnoses that were worse than in reality in order to gain money from the insurance company, and one quarter of the respondents admitted to doing so frequently. Another fraud characteristic of clinical social workers described by 86 percent of the respondents in the sample was the presentation of diagnosis for an individual when the treatment actually was given to the family because the insurance companies did not cover family therapy.

Kirk and Kutchins (1988) concluded that sometimes the fraud hides behind the false diagnosis needed to ensure that the client would get the treatment needed, whereas in reality the fraud is aimed at making personal gains. At other times the service agency itself is interested in maintaining the fraud out of a desire to make money even by illegal and unethical ways.

More than twenty years ago Schutz (1982) characterized fraud in social work as falsification and distortion of the truth in order to influence someone to renounce either something important to him or her or a legal right. If a social worker gives false information about the risks of the treatment or its benefit so that the client will be influenced to receive treatment and to pay for it, this is fraud and deceit. When a social worker tells the client that sexual relations with the therapist are treatment, he or she distorts the truth and forces the client to renounce something dear to him her. Therefore, this is fraud (Schutz, 1982, p. 12).

Cases of fraud, distortion of the truth, and deceit happened in the past and are happening at present in growing numbers despite the rules in the code of ethics that call for decent practice and fairness in professional relationship between worker and client. The code of ethics for social workers in the United States expressly prohibits social workers to engage in fraud, deceit, and distortion of the truth and require the worker to report honestly the service given the client.

Another form of unethical behavior relates to fraud by writing letters of recommendation for a colleague or student that exaggerate the personal traits and abilities of the candidate for a job or a stipend. These kinds of exaggerations may result in the suing of social workers for misleading information when the sought-after stipend or job does not materialize. Therefore it is wise to remember: the truth is the best lie.

PROFESSIONAL MISCONDUCT
AND WHISTLE-BLOWING

A difficult dilemma social workers and other helping professionals may face is related to the question of whether or not one should report to the supervisor or agency director cases of misconduct in the personal and professional behavior of a colleague. This dilemma was illustrated in the case in Chapter 6 in which a social worker abused alcohol and as a result neglected her professional duties to her clients.

Malpractice can happen in any place of employment in which social workers are employed as well as in private practice. Any social
work educator, teacher, fieldwork instructor, supervisor, or director
of a social service experiences cases in which a colleague trans-
gresses the rules of ethics and gets embroiled in malpractice. Yet, not
all such cases come before the committee of ethics, and far less come
before the courts.

In medicine is a long-standing tradition according to which cases
of malpractice are covered up within the profession. Changes in this
tradition have happened only during the past few decades. Today it is
customary to see the existence of ethics committees in the helping
professions. Thus more and more cases of malpractice are known
to the public (Teasdale and Kent, 1995). Blasszauer (1995, p. 247)
stated a proverb attributed to the philosopher Schopenhauer which
says that every innovation goes through three phases: In the first
phase people are laughing at it, in the second they fight over it, and in
the third they treat it as a matter of fact. The same may apply to "whistle-blowing" on a colleague who was caught in malpractice, as the
following case illustrates.

CASE EXAMPLE:
THE DIRECTOR WHO MISBEHAVED

Mark, a social worker who worked in a family therapy agency for many
years was recently appointed supervisor by his friend the director of the
agency. One day a female colleague turned to Mark and wanted to talk about
some disturbing news that bothered her. She said that one of her clients told
her during treatment that she knows the director of the agency "closely." He
paid her for sex in a hotel and they even used cocaine together five or six
times.

Mark is torn by the dilemma of to whom his loyalty should be given: to the
values of the profession or to his friend? Should he inform his friend about
the information he has received?

Whistle-blowing in general, and in particular for a friend or colleague, has been a serious problem. The tradition in many cultures in
the world has regarded telling on someone as an abomination. In the
Jewish tradition, for example, it is said that informers should have no
hope and all evil should pass immediately from the face of the earth.
According to Maimonides, the prohibition against informing refers to

three forms of speech: The gossiper who speaks the truth without maligning others; the slanderer who disdains the value of the other, even if the slanderer speaks the truth; and the one who spreads a libel or defamation in which the lie is intended only to give the other a bad name.

In the Torah we find reference only to the first of the three forms of informing on others: "Thou shall not gossip about your people and shall not stand on the blood of your friend" (Leviticus 19:16). The other two were forbidden by the sages of the Talmud, who related to this verse very strictly. The prohibition of gossip is included in the commandment to love thy neighbor and to speak only good about him or her.

Situations occur in which one cannot escape from informing on someone. The majority of the ethicists in the profession of social work agree that such action is necessary when a colleague suffers from a mental disturbance that damages his or her functioning as a professional worker; a colleague has a physical ailment that may affect his or her functioning; a colleague has a problem of addiction to alcohol or drugs; a colleague committed a serious transgression, such as theft from a client or from the employing agency; a colleague has exploited sexually or has blackmailed a client; and a colleague worked without license or presented false documents about his or her academic degrees or work experience.

In the most recent code of ethics for social workers (Barker, 1999) are eleven secondary clauses that refer to social workers' ethical responsibilities to colleagues. Three of these deal specifically with the subject of reporting the colleague in case of impairment in fulfilling his or her professional function due to mental health and personality problems or difficulties in behavior. In such cases the social worker is requested to consult with the impaired colleague and to help him or her rectify the situation. If the social worker is convinced that the problem of the colleague impairs his or her ability to function competently, and this colleague did not take the necessary steps to correct the problem, then the social worker should take the initiative and turn to the proper channel in the service or to the professional association.

Whistle-blowing may destroy not only the professional career of a colleague but his social and family life. Therefore, whistle-blowers are hated everywhere, yet therapists must understand that sometimes they have a duty to inform the authorities in certain cases (Lewis,

1985). The worker must weigh the reasons for and against whistle-blowing. In each case of misconduct or malpractice that comes to the attention of a colleague in the service or outside of it the question of divided loyalty arises anew, and the process of decision making is never easy.

Pope, Tabachnik, and Keith-Spiegel (1987) have investigated the behaviors and beliefs of psychologists as therapists in a study that encompassed one thousand such respondents. They found that these people had difficulty answering the twelve questions related to ethical behavior included in the study. The researchers found that the law, the results of studies published in the professional literature, and the local ethical committees were the least efficient as sources of guidance for ethical behavior. The most efficient way to impart ethics and values to students so that they internalize them was by exposing the students to positive models of ethical behavior, such as educators, instructors, agency directors, etc., with whom students come into contact during their professional training.

Sometimes it is possible to resolve an ethical dilemma of double loyalty by a face-to-face meeting of the parties, as in the case of Mark and his friend the director of the family therapy service. Such a meeting can be useful only if afterward the misconduct or malpractice stops and a sincere effort is made to compensate the wronged party. Sometimes, however, whistle-blowing cannot be escaped.

Several perspectives can be applied to whistle-blowing. Those who accept the deontological theory in ethics would most likely say that certain forms of malpractice, which are forbidden for professionals, are basically bad and it is the duty of the worker to discover and report them without thinking about what the reporting would entail. These professionals would compel Mark to blow the whistle on his friend. Those professionals who adhere to the teleological theory of ethics would most likely examine the results of whistle-blowing before acting. They would do so according to the evidence that the result is better than the damage. Therefore, if it is shown that the damage to the career of the director and to the agency will be greater than the benefit accrued from the whistle-blowing, then these people would arrive at the conclusion that no justification for whistle-blowing exists.

Before deciding for or against whistle-blowing, it is wise to check the attitude and the rules in the NASW Code of Ethics first. Clause

2.11(a) states "social workers should take adequate measures to discourage, prevent, expose, and correct the unethical conduct of colleagues." Furthermore, clause 2.11(c) states "social workers who believe that a colleague has acted unethically should seek resolution by discussing their concerns with the colleague when feasible and when such discussion is likely to be productive." Finally, clause 2.11(d) states "when necessary, social workers who believe that a colleague has acted unethically should take action through appropriate formal channels (such as contacting a state licensing board or regulatory body, an NASW committee on inquiry, or other professional ethics committees)" (Barker, 1999, pp. 566-567).

Thus, Mark has several alternatives, but how will he act and which alternative will he select? This depends on his judgment of the severity of the case, the evidence, and the reaction of the director. In any case, Mark should proceed carefully and tactfully to prevent harm to the service and should not reveal the information to other workers. He should also demand from the social worker who brought this problem to him that she do the same.

This case of misconduct is difficult for decision making. Malpractice of a colleague and whistle-blowing can be harmful to all involved in the case. Social workers need to remember their duties and obligations to the profession and conduct themselves in ethically correct ways and in line with the norms and professional standards of social work. They must carefully weigh the price of loyalty to a friend against the loyalty to the service agency and society.

MALPRACTICE IN SOCIAL WORK ADVERTISEMENT

In clause four in the NASW Code of Ethics, which refers to the ethical responsibility of the worker, are two subclauses about misrepresentation and solicitation. The first of these two emphasizes the need for social workers to present themselves in accordance with the facts. Social workers are prohibited to represent themselves before their clients, their institutions, colleagues, and before colleagues from other professions, in a way not in line with their actual education, professional training, specialty, membership in professional organizations, etc. They must also clearly differentiate between being a representative of their profession or their employer. They are prohibited to present misleading opinions about and attitudes toward the professional organizations they represent.

As for the subject of solicitation, this term is not used here in the popular sense but it refers to what is and what is not permitted in advertisement as per the code of ethics. A strict prohibition is in place against solicitation of potential clients who, due to their disabilities or circumstances, are vulnerable to influence, manipulation, or forced persuasion. Similarly, social workers are prohibited to solicit clients to testify for or give certification or recommendations to potential clients or any organization or institution that the social worker wishes to impress.

As for other forms of self-advertisement in social work, the law, the regulations, and the code of ethics do not provide clear boundaries, and this lacuna may complicate the life of a covetous worker in ethical conflicts.

Epilogue

In September 2000 a civil suit of great importance to all the caring and helping professions was brought to Court in London. The court was asked to rule on the fate of conjoined twins born with their spines attached, occasioning the need to conduct an extremely dangerous and complicated operation to separate them. The problem, however, was that the twins were born with only one lung and heart system and a shared bladder, and if they were to be separated only one of them would survive. However, if left unseparated then both of them would die in a matter of months. The doctors wanted to perform the operation but the parents refused to sign the authorization forms, thus the hospital brought the issue before the court. The parents of the twins were devout Catholics, and they objected to the separation of the babies via medical intervention. They claimed that such a separation would be contrary to their religious belief that life is in the hands of God and therefore humans have no right to decide who will stay alive and who will die. The doctors, on the other hand, were interested in trying to save the life of the baby that was born with heart and lungs intact and whose brain and blood flow kept the other twin alive.

The court faced an ethical dilemma: Whose good comes first? The good of the parents, which means the death of both infants, or the good of the infant that has the best chances for survival? The court finally ruled that the doctors could perform the operation. The judges argued that only in extremely rare and extraordinary cases is the court permitted to decide about the life or death of an infant without the permission of the parents. They also added that this case could not serve as legal precedent due to its uniqueness.

The parents appealed against the decision to a higher court. The heads of the Catholic Church came to the help of the parents and strengthened their resolve to refuse to sign the documents that would permit the operation. The representatives of the doctors and various pro-life organizations called attention to the time that quickly flies away and to the immediate danger to the life the baby whose life it

Ethics in Social Work: A Context of Caring
© 2006 by The Haworth Press, Inc. All rights reserved.
doi:10.1300/5577_16

was still possible to save by the operation. The judges were aware of the implications of the final decision about the rights of the parents and the duties of the doctors, but after penetrating discussions ruled in favor of the doctors, who in turn succeeded in saving the life of one of the babies.

This case represents in a dramatic way the complexity of resolving ethical dilemmas and conflicts between opposing values. The dilemmas the judges faced were ethical. They were based on the choice between life and death and between the legitimate rights of both parties when either choice would hurt one of the parties.

Problems less dramatic in nature yet no less important have been presented in this book. The purpose was to convey the important topics professionals face in their daily work, conceptually and practically. Discussion of these topics represented the value base upon which a caring profession stands, the values that serve as ethical guides to professionals in carrying out their social mission, and the ethical behavior expected of them.

Discussion centered on raising ethical dilemmas and their resolution according to various models, on problems connected to malpractice in a caring profession, and on the need to cope with the problems to prevent the conviction of professional workers by the courts. Recent increase in the number of malpractice suits against caring professionals raises serious concern for social workers. Thus a need exists to deal with this problem openly in the classroom and in the workplace.

This book emphasizes the importance of moral virtues and values for practitioners in the hope that they will acquire them as part of their professional training and education. The code of ethics in social work not only provides a moral guide but also serves as a spiritual anchor for all practitioners. Without this code the caring profession of social work will be relegated to a bunch of technical rules and models.

It is important to note that the values guiding professional social workers are not static. They change with scientific and technological changes, cultural developments, social fashions, and with attitudes to and perspectives on the role of the caring professional. The changes demand leaders of the social work profession to not only respond to them positively but also to try to foresee other potential developments in the short and long run and to organize the profession's response accordingly.

A major change in social conditions requires a great amount of effort conceptually, theoretically, and practically to cope successfully with the new challenges it brings in its wake. For example, the dramatic increase in the number of social workers flocking to clinical and private practice—as attested by the aspirations of the majority of students in schools of social work—requires careful assessment of the impact of this new trend on the social mission of the profession: Will it help or hinder the situation of the needy in society?

The same holds true for ethical dilemmas and decision making. Social work professionals were torn in the past and are torn in the present by the ethical dilemmas that the dynamics of life and their relationships with their clients bring. Ethical dilemmas will always require the professional to stop, listen, and ponder the meaning of his or her decision before carrying it out.

Professional literature in ethics has been growing steadily in the past three decades. This growth expresses the newly found interest in the development of knowledge about ethics. Of course, no literature or course in ethics can solve the ethical dilemmas with which professionals struggle. What they can do, however, is introduce fruitful ideas, attitudes, and intellectual investment in trying to solve them. Ethics always leaves the door open for new questions for which there are no unequivocal answers. This is the strength and the weakness of ethics. The more studies done on ethics the more important ethics becomes. The beneficiaries will be the recipients of social services.

The decision-making process is long and laborious, but its contribution to ethical resolution of conflicts is immense. It helps to consider an ethical dilemma from many different perspectives. It enriches discussion about the various alternatives available for making an ethically correct decision and forces the practitioner to see the world as it is rather than as it should be, and it helps professionals to arrive at a consensus based on knowledge rather than on intuition alone.

We may argue about theories, methods of intervention, explanations, and interpretations of various laws, rules, and regulations. It is important to note that not all problems have reasonable solutions. It is also important to remember that the examination of the motives, values, and goals of professional intervention in the lives of the clients is a professional duty for each practitioner. Yet, the primary duty in caring is fulfillment of the commandment for doctors, and social workers: *Primum nil nocere.* Do not harm.

Appendix A

Code of Ethics of the National Association of Social Workers

Approved by the 1996 NASW Delegate Assembly and revised by the 1999 NASW Delegate Assembly

PREAMBLE

The primary mission of the social work profession is to enhance human well-being and help meet the basic human needs of all people, with particular attention to the needs and empowerment of people who are vulnerable, oppressed, and living in poverty. A historic and defining feature of social work is the profession's focus on individual well-being in a social context and the well-being of society. Fundamental to social work is attention to the environmental forces that create, contribute to, and address problems in living.

Social workers promote social justice and social change with and on behalf of clients. "Clients" is used inclusively to refer to individuals, families, groups, organizations, and communities. Social workers are sensitive to cultural and ethnic diversity and strive to end discrimination, oppression, poverty, and other forms of social injustice. These activities may be in the form of direct practice, community organizing, supervision, consultation, administration, advocacy, social and political action, policy development and implementation, education, and research and evaluation. Social workers seek to enhance the capacity of people to address their own needs. Social workers also seek to promote the responsiveness of organizations, communities, and other social institutions to individuals' needs and social problems.

The mission of the social work profession is rooted in a set of core values. These core values, embraced by social workers throughout the profession's history, are the foundation of social work's unique purpose and perspective:

Ethics in Social Work: A Context of Caring
© 2006 by The Haworth Press, Inc. All rights reserved.
doi:10.1300/5577_17

- service
- social justice
- dignity and worth of the person
- importance of human relationships
- integrity
- competence

This constellation of core values reflects what is unique to the social work profession. Core values, and the principles that flow from them, must be balanced within the context and complexity of the human experience.

PURPOSE OF THE NASW CODE OF ETHICS

Professional ethics are at the core of social work. The profession has an obligation to articulate its basic values, ethical principles, and ethical standards. The *NASW Code of Ethics* sets forth these values, principles, and standards to guide social workers' conduct. The *Code* is relevant to all social workers and social work students, regardless of their professional functions, the settings in which they work, or the populations they serve.

The *NASW Code of Ethics* serves six purposes:

1. The *Code* identifies core values on which social work's mission is based.
2. The *Code* summarizes broad ethical principles that reflect the profession's core values and establishes a set of specific ethical standards that should be used to guide social work practice.
3. The *Code* is designed to help social workers identify relevant considerations when professional obligations conflict or ethical uncertainties arise.
4. The *Code* provides ethical standards to which the general public can hold the social work profession accountable.
5. The *Code* socializes practitioners new to the field to social work's mission, values, ethical principles, and ethical standards.
6. The *Code* articulates standards that the social work profession itself can use to assess whether social workers have engaged in unethical conduct. NASW has formal procedures to adjudicate ethics complaints filed against its members.* In subscribing to this *Code*, social workers are required to cooperate in its implementation, participate in

---

*For information on NASW adjudication procedures, see *NASW Procedures for the Adjudication of Grievances.*

NASW adjudication proceedings, and abide by any NASW disciplinary rulings or sanctions based on it.

The *Code* offers a set of values, principles, and standards to guide decision making and conduct when ethical issues arise. It does not provide a set of rules that prescribe how social workers should act in all situations. Specific applications of the *Code* must take into account the context in which it is being considered and the possibility of conflicts among the *Code*'s values, principles, and standards. Ethical responsibilities flow from all human relationships, from the personal and familial to the social and professional.

Further, the *NASW Code of Ethics* does not specify which values, principles, and standards are most important and ought to outweigh others in instances when they conflict. Reasonable differences of opinion can and do exist among social workers with respect to the ways in which values, ethical principles, and ethical standards should be rank ordered when they conflict. Ethical decision making in a given situation must apply the informed judgment of the individual social worker and should also consider how the issues would be judged in a peer review process where the ethical standards of the profession would be applied.

Ethical decision making is a process. There are many instances in social work where simple answers are not available to resolve complex ethical issues. Social workers should take into consideration all the values, principles, and standards in this *Code* that are relevant to any situation in which ethical judgment is warranted. Social workers' decisions and actions should be consistent with the spirit as well as the letter of this *Code*.

In addition to this *Code,* there are many other sources of information about ethical thinking that may be useful. Social workers should consider ethical theory and principles generally, social work theory and research, laws, regulations, agency policies, and other relevant codes of ethics, recognizing that among codes of ethics social workers should consider the *NASW Code of Ethics* as their primary source. Social workers also should be aware of the impact on ethical decision making of their clients' and their own personal values and cultural and religious beliefs and practices. They should be aware of any conflicts between personal and professional values and deal with them responsibly. For additional guidance social workers should consult the relevant literature on professional ethics and ethical decision making and seek appropriate consultation when faced with ethical dilemmas. This may involve consultation with an agency-based or social work organization's ethics committee, a regulatory body, knowledgeable colleagues, supervisors, or legal counsel.

Instances may arise when social workers' ethical obligations conflict with agency policies or relevant laws or regulations. When such conflicts occur, social workers must make a responsible effort to resolve the conflict in a manner that is consistent with the values, principles, and standards expressed in this *Code*. If a reasonable resolution of the conflict does not appear possible, social workers should seek proper consultation before making a decision.

The *NASW Code of Ethics* is to be used by NASW and by individuals, agencies, organizations, and bodies (such as licensing and regulatory boards, professional liability insurance providers, courts of law, agency boards of directors, government agencies, and other professional groups) that choose to adopt it or use it as a frame of reference. Violation of standards in this *Code* does not automatically imply legal liability or violation of the law. Such determination can only be made in the context of legal and judicial proceedings. Alleged violations of the *Code* would be subject to a peer review process. Such processes are generally separate from legal or administrative procedures and insulated from legal review or proceedings to allow the profession to counsel and discipline its own members.

A code of ethics cannot guarantee ethical behavior. Moreover, a code of ethics cannot resolve all ethical issues or disputes or capture the richness and complexity involved in striving to make responsible choices within a moral community. Rather, a code of ethics sets forth values, ethical principles, and ethical standards to which professionals aspire and by which their actions can be judged. Social workers' ethical behavior should result from their personal commitment to engage in ethical practice. The *NASW Code of Ethics* reflects the commitment of all social workers to uphold the profession's values and to act ethically. Principles and standards must be applied by individuals of good character who discern moral questions and, in good faith, seek to make reliable ethical judgments.

ETHICAL PRINCIPLES

The following broad ethical principles are based on social work's core values of service, social justice, dignity and worth of the person, importance of human relationships, integrity, and competence. These principles set forth ideals to which all social workers should aspire.

Value: *Service*

Ethical Principle: *Social workers' primary goal is to help people in need and to address social problems.*

Social workers elevate service to others above self-interest. Social workers draw on their knowledge, values, and skills to help people in need and to address social problems. Social workers are encouraged to volunteer some portion of their professional skills with no expectation of significant financial return (pro bono service).

Value: *Social Justice*

Ethical Principle: *Social workers challenge social injustice.*

Social workers pursue social change, particularly with and on behalf of vulnerable and oppressed individuals and groups of people. Social workers' social change efforts are focused primarily on issues of poverty, unemployment, discrimination, and other forms of social injustice. These activities seek to promote sensitivity to and knowledge about oppression and cultural and ethnic diversity. Social workers strive to ensure access to needed information, services, and resources; equality of opportunity; and meaningful participation in decision making for all people.

Value: *Dignity and Worth of the Person*

Ethical Principle: *Social workers respect the inherent dignity and worth of the person.*

Social workers treat each person in a caring and respectful fashion, mindful of individual differences and cultural and ethnic diversity. Social workers promote clients' socially responsible self-determination. Social workers seek to enhance clients' capacity and opportunity to change and to address their own needs. Social workers are cognizant of their dual responsibility to clients and to the broader society. They seek to resolve conflicts between clients' interests and the broader society's interests in a socially responsible manner consistent with the values, ethical principles, and ethical standards of the profession.

Value: *Importance of Human Relationships*

Ethical Principle: *Social workers recognize the central importance of human relationships.*

Social workers understand that relationships between and among people are an important vehicle for change. Social workers engage people as partners in the helping process. Social workers seek to strengthen relationships among people in a purposeful effort to promote, restore, maintain, and enhance the well-being of individuals, families, social groups, organizations, and communities.

Value: *Integrity*

Ethical Principle: *Social workers behave in a trustworthy manner.*

Social workers are continually aware of the profession's mission, values, ethical principles, and ethical standards and practice in a manner consistent with them. Social workers act honestly and responsibly and promote ethical practices on the part of the organizations with which they are affiliated.

Value: *Competence*

Ethical Principle: *Social workers practice within their areas of competence and develop and enhance their professional expertise.*

Social workers continually strive to increase their professional knowledge and skills and to apply them in practice. Social workers should aspire to contribute to the knowledge base of the profession.

ETHICAL STANDARDS

The following ethical standards are relevant to the professional activities of all social workers. These standards concern (1) social workers' ethical responsibilities to clients, (2) social workers' ethical responsibilities to colleagues, (3) social workers' ethical responsibilities in practice settings, (4) social workers' ethical responsibilities as professionals, (5) social workers' ethical responsibilities to the social work profession, and (6) social workers' ethical responsibilities to the broader society.

Some of the standards that follow are enforceable guidelines for professional conduct, and some are aspirational. The extent to which each standard is enforceable is a matter of professional judgment to be exercised by those responsible for reviewing alleged violations of ethical standards.

1. SOCIAL WORKERS' ETHICAL RESPONSIBILITIES TO CLIENTS

1.01 Commitment to Clients

Social workers' primary responsibility is to promote the well-being of clients. In general, clients' interests are primary. However, social workers' responsibility to the larger society or specific legal obligations may on limited occasions supersede the loyalty owed clients, and clients should be so advised. (Examples include when a social worker is required by law to report that a client has abused a child or has threatened to harm self or others.)

1.02 Self-Determination

Social workers respect and promote the right of clients to self-determination and assist clients in their efforts to identify and clarify their goals. Social workers may limit clients' right to self-determination when, in the social workers' professional judgment, clients' actions or potential actions pose a serious, foreseeable, and imminent risk to themselves or others.

1.03 Informed Consent

(a) Social workers should provide services to clients only in the context of a professional relationship based, when appropriate, on valid informed consent. Social workers should use clear and understandable language to inform clients of the purpose of the services, risks related to the services, limits to services because of the requirements of a third-party payer, relevant costs, reasonable alternatives, clients' right to refuse or withdraw consent, and the time frame covered by the consent. Social workers should provide clients with an opportunity to ask questions.

(b) In instances when clients are not literate or have difficulty understanding the primary language used in the practice setting, social workers should take steps to ensure clients' comprehension. This may include providing clients with a detailed verbal explanation or arranging for a qualified interpreter or translator whenever possible.

(c) In instances when clients lack the capacity to provide informed consent, social workers should protect clients' interests by seeking permission from an appropriate third party, informing clients consistent with the clients' level of understanding. In such instances social workers should seek to ensure that the third party acts in a manner consistent with clients' wishes and interests. Social workers should take reasonable steps to enhance such clients' ability to give informed consent.

(d) In instances when clients are receiving services involuntarily, social workers should provide information about the nature and extent of services and about the extent of clients' right to refuse service.

(e) Social workers who provide services via electronic media (such as computer, telephone, radio, and television) should inform recipients of the limitations and risks associated with such services.

(f) Social workers should obtain clients' informed consent before audiotaping or videotaping clients or permitting observation of services to clients by a third party.

1.04 Competence

(a) Social workers should provide services and represent themselves as competent only within the boundaries of their education, training, license, certification, consultation received, supervised experience, or other relevant professional experience.

(b) Social workers should provide services in substantive areas or use intervention techniques or approaches that are new to them only after engaging in appropriate study, training, consultation, and supervision from people who are competent in those interventions or techniques.

(c) When generally recognized standards do not exist with respect to an emerging area of practice, social workers should exercise careful judgment and take responsible steps (including appropriate education, research, training, consultation, and supervision) to ensure the competence of their work and to protect clients from harm.

1.05 Cultural Competence and Social Diversity

(a) Social workers should understand culture and its function in human behavior and society, recognizing the strengths that exist in all cultures.

(b) Social workers should have a knowledge base of their clients' cultures and be able to demonstrate competence in the provision of services that are sensitive to clients' cultures and to differences among people and cultural groups.

(c) Social workers should obtain education about and seek to understand the nature of social diversity and oppression with respect to race, ethnicity, national origin, color, sex, sexual orientation, age, marital status, political belief, religion, and mental or physical disability.

1.06 Conflicts of Interest

(a) Social workers should be alert to and avoid conflicts of interest that interfere with the exercise of professional discretion and impartial judgment. Social workers should inform clients when a real or potential conflict of interest arises and take reasonable steps to resolve the issue in a manner that makes the clients' interests primary and protects clients' interests to the greatest extent possible. In some cases, protecting clients' interests may require termination of the professional relationship with proper referral of the client.

(b) Social workers should not take unfair advantage of any professional relationship or exploit others to further their personal, religious, political, or business interests.

(c) Social workers should not engage in dual or multiple relationships with clients or former clients in which there is a risk of exploitation or potential harm to the client. In instances when dual or multiple relationships are unavoidable, social workers should take steps to protect clients and are responsible for setting clear, appropriate, and culturally sensitive boundaries. (Dual or multiple relationships occur when social workers relate to clients in more than one relationship, whether professional, social, or business. Dual or multiple relationships can occur simultaneously or consecutively.)

(d) When social workers provide services to two or more people who have a relationship with each other (for example, couples, family members), social workers should clarify with all parties which individuals will be considered clients and the nature of social workers' professional obligations to the various individuals who are receiving services. Social workers who anticipate a conflict of interest among the individuals receiving services or who anticipate having to perform in potentially conflicting roles (for example, when a social worker is asked to testify in a child custody dispute or divorce proceedings involving clients) should clarify their role with the parties involved and take appropriate action to minimize any conflict of interest.

1.07 Privacy and Confidentiality

(a) Social workers should respect clients' right to privacy. Social workers should not solicit private information from clients unless it is essential to providing services or conducting social work evaluation or research. Once private information is shared, standards of confidentiality apply.

(b) Social workers may disclose confidential information when appropriate with valid consent from a client or a person legally authorized to consent on behalf of a client.

(c) Social workers should protect the confidentiality of all information obtained in the course of professional service, except for compelling professional reasons. The general expectation that social workers will keep information confidential does not apply when disclosure is necessary to prevent serious, foreseeable, and imminent harm to a client or other identifiable person. In all instances, social workers should disclose the least amount of confidential information necessary to achieve the desired purpose; only information that is directly relevant to the purpose for which the disclosure is made should be revealed.

(d) Social workers should inform clients, to the extent possible, about the disclosure of confidential information and the potential consequences, when feasible before the disclosure is made. This applies whether social workers disclose confidential information on the basis of a legal requirement or client consent.

(e) Social workers should discuss with clients and other interested parties the nature of confidentiality and limitations of clients' right to confidentiality. Social workers should review with clients circumstances where confidential information may be requested and where disclosure of confidential information may be legally required. This discussion should occur as soon as possible in the social worker-client relationship and as needed throughout the course of the relationship.

(f) When social workers provide counseling services to families, couples, or groups, social workers should seek agreement among the parties involved concerning each individual's right to confidentiality and obligation to preserve the confidentiality of information shared by others. Social workers should inform participants in family, couples, or group counseling that social workers cannot guarantee that all participants will honor such agreements.

(g) Social workers should inform clients involved in family, couples, marital, or group counseling of the social worker's, employer's, and agency's policy concerning the social worker's disclosure of confidential information among the parties involved in the counseling.

(h) Social workers should not disclose confidential information to third-party payers unless clients have authorized such disclosure.

(i) Social workers should not discuss confidential information in any setting unless privacy can be ensured. Social workers should not discuss confidential information in public or semipublic areas such as hallways, waiting rooms, elevators, and restaurants.

(j) Social workers should protect the confidentiality of clients during legal proceedings to the extent permitted by law. When a court of law or other legally authorized body orders social workers to disclose confidential or privileged information without a client's consent and such disclosure could cause harm to the client, social workers should request that the court withdraw the order or limit the order as narrowly as possible or maintain the records under seal, unavailable for public inspection.

(k) Social workers should protect the confidentiality of clients when responding to requests from members of the media.

(l) Social workers should protect the confidentiality of clients' written and electronic records and other sensitive information. Social workers should take reasonable steps to ensure that clients' records are stored in a secure location and that clients' records are not available to others who are not authorized to have access.

(m) Social workers should take precautions to ensure and maintain the confidentiality of information transmitted to other parties through the use of computers, electronic mail, facsimile machines, telephones and telephone answering machines, and other electronic or computer technology. Disclosure of identifying information should be avoided whenever possible.

(n) Social workers should transfer or dispose of clients' records in a manner that protects clients' confidentiality and is consistent with state statutes governing records and social work licensure.

(o) Social workers should take reasonable precautions to protect client confidentiality in the event of the social worker's termination of practice, incapacitation, or death.

(p) Social workers should not disclose identifying information when discussing clients for teaching or training purposes unless the client has consented to disclosure of confidential information.

(q) Social workers should not disclose identifying information when discussing clients with consultants unless the client has consented to disclosure of confidential information or there is a compelling need for such disclosure.

(r) Social workers should protect the confidentiality of deceased clients consistent with the preceding standards.

1.08 Access to Records

(a) Social workers should provide clients with reasonable access to records concerning the clients. Social workers who are concerned that clients' access to their records could cause serious misunderstanding or harm to the client should provide assistance in interpreting the records and consultation with the client regarding the records. Social workers should limit clients' access to their records, or portions of their records, only in exceptional circumstances when there is compelling evidence that such access would cause serious harm to the client. Both clients' requests and the rationale for withholding some or all of the record should be documented in clients' files.

(b) When providing clients with access to their records, social workers should take steps to protect the confidentiality of other individuals identified or discussed in such records.

1.09 Sexual Relationships

(a) Social workers should under no circumstances engage in sexual activities or sexual contact with current clients, whether such contact is consensual or forced.

(b) Social workers should not engage in sexual activities or sexual contact with clients' relatives or other individuals with whom clients maintain a close personal relationship when there is a risk of exploitation or potential harm to the client. Sexual activity or sexual contact with clients' relatives or other individuals with whom clients maintain a personal relationship has the potential to be harmful to the client and may make it difficult for the social worker and client to maintain appropriate professional boundaries. Social workers—not their clients, their clients' relatives, or other individuals with whom the client maintains a personal relationship—assume the full burden for setting clear, appropriate, and culturally sensitive boundaries.

(c) Social workers should not engage in sexual activities or sexual contact with former clients because of the potential for harm to the client. If social workers engage in conduct contrary to this prohibition or claim that an exception to this prohibition is warranted because of extraordinary circumstances, it is social workers—not their clients—who assume the full burden of demonstrating that the former client has not been exploited, coerced, or manipulated, intentionally or unintentionally.

(d) Social workers should not provide clinical services to individuals with whom they have had a prior sexual relationship. Providing clinical services to a former sexual partner has the potential to be harmful to the individual and is likely to make it difficult for the social worker and individual to maintain appropriate professional boundaries.

1.10 Physical Contact

Social workers should not engage in physical contact with clients when there is a possibility of psychological harm to the client as a result of the contact (such as cradling or caressing clients). Social workers who engage in appropriate physical contact with clients are responsible for setting clear, appropriate, and culturally sensitive boundaries that govern such physical contact.

1.11 Sexual Harassment

Social workers should not sexually harass clients. Sexual harassment includes sexual advances, sexual solicitation, requests for sexual favors, and other verbal or physical conduct of a sexual nature.

1.12 Derogatory Language

Social workers should not use derogatory language in their written or verbal communications to or about clients. Social workers should use accurate and respectful language in all communications to and about clients.

1.13 Payment for Services

(a) When setting fees, social workers should ensure that the fees are fair, reasonable, and commensurate with the services performed. Consideration should be given to clients' ability to pay.

(b) Social workers should avoid accepting goods or services from clients as payment for professional services. Bartering arrangements, particularly involving services, create the potential for conflicts of interest, exploitation, and inappropriate boundaries in social workers' relationships with clients. Social workers should explore and may participate in bartering only in very limited circumstances when it can be demonstrated that such arrangements are an accepted practice among professionals in the local community, considered to be essential for the provision of services, negotiated without coercion, and entered into at the client's initiative and with the client's informed consent. Social workers who accept goods or services from clients as payment for professional services assume the full burden of demonstrating that this arrangement will not be detrimental to the client or the professional relationship.

(c) Social workers should not solicit a private fee or other remuneration for providing services to clients who are entitled to such available services through the social workers' employer or agency.

1.14 Clients Who Lack Decision-Making Capacity

When social workers act on behalf of clients who lack the capacity to make informed decisions, social workers should take reasonable steps to safeguard the interests and rights of those clients.

1.15 Interruption of Services

Social workers should make reasonable efforts to ensure continuity of services in the event that services are interrupted by factors such as unavailability, relocation, illness, disability, or death.

1.16 Termination of Services

(a) Social workers should terminate services to clients and professional relationships with them when such services and relationships are no longer required or no longer serve the clients' needs or interests.

(b) Social workers should take reasonable steps to avoid abandoning clients who are still in need of services. Social workers should withdraw services precipitously only under unusual circumstances, giving careful consideration to all factors in the situation and taking care to minimize possible adverse effects. Social workers should assist in making appropriate arrangements for continuation of services when necessary.

(c) Social workers in fee-for-service settings may terminate services to clients who are not paying an overdue balance if the financial contractual arrangements have been made clear to the client, if the client does not pose an imminent danger to self or others, and if the clinical and other consequences of the current nonpayment have been addressed and discussed with the client.

(d) Social workers should not terminate services to pursue a social, financial, or sexual relationship with a client.

(e) Social workers who anticipate the termination or interruption of services to clients should notify clients promptly and seek the transfer, referral, or continuation of services in relation to the clients' needs and preferences.

(f) Social workers who are leaving an employment setting should inform clients of appropriate options for the continuation of services and of the benefits and risks of the options.

2. SOCIAL WORKERS' ETHICAL RESPONSIBILITIES TO COLLEAGUES

2.01 Respect

(a) Social workers should treat colleagues with respect and should represent accurately and fairly the qualifications, views, and obligations of colleagues.

(b) Social workers should avoid unwarranted negative criticism of colleagues in communications with clients or with other professionals. Unwarranted negative criticism may include demeaning comments that refer to colleagues' level of competence or to individuals' attributes such as race, ethnicity, national origin, color, sex, sexual orientation, age, marital status, political belief, religion, and mental or physical disability.

(c) Social workers should cooperate with social work colleagues and with colleagues of other professions when such cooperation serves the well-being of clients.

2.02 Confidentiality

Social workers should respect confidential information shared by colleagues in the course of their professional relationships and transactions. Social workers should ensure that such colleagues understand social workers' obligation to respect confidentiality and any exceptions related to it.

2.03 Interdisciplinary Collaboration

(a) Social workers who are members of an interdisciplinary team should participate in and contribute to decisions that affect the well-being of clients by drawing on the perspectives, values, and experiences of the social work profession. Professional and ethical obligations of the interdisciplinary team as a whole and of its individual members should be clearly established.

(b) Social workers for whom a team decision raises ethical concerns should attempt to resolve the disagreement through appropriate channels. If the disagreement cannot be resolved, social workers should pursue other avenues to address their concerns consistent with client well-being.

2.04 Disputes Involving Colleagues

(a) Social workers should not take advantage of a dispute between a colleague and an employer to obtain a position or otherwise advance the social workers' own interests.

(b) Social workers should not exploit clients in disputes with colleagues or engage clients in any inappropriate discussion of conflicts between social workers and their colleagues.

2.05 Consultation

(a) Social workers should seek the advice and counsel of colleagues whenever such consultation is in the best interests of clients.

(b) Social workers should keep themselves informed about colleagues' areas of expertise and competencies. Social workers should seek consultation only from colleagues who have demonstrated knowledge, expertise, and competence related to the subject of the consultation.

(c) When consulting with colleagues about clients, social workers should disclose the least amount of information necessary to achieve the purposes of the consultation.

2.06 Referral for Services

(a) Social workers should refer clients to other professionals when the other professionals' specialized knowledge or expertise is needed to serve clients fully or when social workers believe that they are not being effective or making reasonable progress with clients and that additional service is required.

(b) Social workers who refer clients to other professionals should take appropriate steps to facilitate an orderly transfer of responsibility. Social workers who refer clients to other professionals should disclose, with clients' consent, all pertinent information to the new service providers.

(c) Social workers are prohibited from giving or receiving payment for a referral when no professional service is provided by the referring social worker.

2.07 Sexual Relationships

(a) Social workers who function as supervisors or educators should not engage in sexual activities or contact with supervisees, students, trainees, or other colleagues over whom they exercise professional authority.

(b) Social workers should avoid engaging in sexual relationships with colleagues when there is potential for a conflict of interest. Social workers who become involved in, or anticipate becoming involved in, a sexual relationship with a colleague have a duty to transfer professional responsibilities, when necessary, to avoid a conflict of interest.

2.08 Sexual Harassment

Social workers should not sexually harass supervisees, students, trainees, or colleagues. Sexual harassment includes sexual advances, sexual solicitation, requests for sexual favors, and other verbal or physical conduct of a sexual nature.

2.09 Impairment of Colleagues

(a) Social workers who have direct knowledge of a social work colleague's impairment that is due to personal problems, psychosocial distress, substance abuse, or mental health difficulties and that interferes with practice effectiveness should consult with that colleague when feasible and assist the colleague in taking remedial action.

(b) Social workers who believe that a social work colleague's impairment interferes with practice effectiveness and that the colleague has not taken adequate steps to address the impairment should take action through appropriate channels established by employers, agencies, NASW, licensing and regulatory bodies, and other professional organizations.

2.10 Incompetence of Colleagues

(a) Social workers who have direct knowledge of a social work colleague's incompetence should consult with that colleague when feasible and assist the colleague in taking remedial action.

(b) Social workers who believe that a social work colleague is incompetent and has not taken adequate steps to address the incompetence should take action through appropriate channels established by employers, agencies, NASW, licensing and regulatory bodies, and other professional organizations.

2.11 Unethical Conduct of Colleagues

(a) Social workers should take adequate measures to discourage, prevent, expose, and correct the unethical conduct of colleagues.

(b) Social workers should be knowledgeable about established policies and procedures for handling concerns about colleagues' unethical behavior. Social workers should be familiar with national, state, and local procedures for handling ethics complaints. These include policies and procedures created by NASW, licensing and regulatory bodies, employers, agencies, and other professional organizations.

(c) Social workers who believe that a colleague has acted unethically should seek resolution by discussing their concerns with the colleague when feasible and when such discussion is likely to be productive.

(d) When necessary, social workers who believe that a colleague has acted unethically should take action through appropriate formal channels (such as contacting a state licensing board or regulatory body, an NASW committee on inquiry, or other professional ethics committees).

(e) Social workers should defend and assist colleagues who are unjustly charged with unethical conduct.

3. SOCIAL WORKERS' ETHICAL RESPONSIBILITIES IN PRACTICE SETTINGS

3.01 Supervision and Consultation

(a) Social workers who provide supervision or consultation should have the necessary knowledge and skill to supervise or consult appropriately and should do so only within their areas of knowledge and competence.

(b) Social workers who provide supervision or consultation are responsible for setting clear, appropriate, and culturally sensitive boundaries.

(c) Social workers should not engage in any dual or multiple relationships with supervisees in which there is a risk of exploitation of or potential harm to the supervisee.

(d) Social workers who provide supervision should evaluate supervisees' performance in a manner that is fair and respectful.

3.02 Education and Training

(a) Social workers who function as educators, field instructors for students, or trainers should provide instruction only within their areas of knowledge and competence and should provide instruction based on the most current information and knowledge available in the profession.

(b) Social workers who function as educators or field instructors for students should evaluate students' performance in a manner that is fair and respectful.

(c) Social workers who function as educators or field instructors for students should take reasonable steps to ensure that clients are routinely informed when services are being provided by students.

(d) Social workers who function as educators or field instructors for students should not engage in any dual or multiple relationships with students in which there is a risk of exploitation or potential harm to the student. Social work educators and field instructors are responsible for setting clear, appropriate, and culturally sensitive boundaries.

3.03 Performance Evaluation

Social workers who have responsibility for evaluating the performance of others should fulfill such responsibility in a fair and considerate manner and on the basis of clearly stated criteria.

3.04 Client Records

(a) Social workers should take reasonable steps to ensure that documentation in records is accurate and reflects the services provided.

(b) Social workers should include sufficient and timely documentation in records to facilitate the delivery of services and to ensure continuity of services provided to clients in the future.

(c) Social workers' documentation should protect clients' privacy to the extent that is possible and appropriate and should include only information that is directly relevant to the delivery of services.

(d) Social workers should store records following the termination of services to ensure reasonable future access. Records should be maintained for the number of years required by state statutes or relevant contracts.

3.05 Billing

Social workers should establish and maintain billing practices that accurately reflect the nature and extent of services provided and that identify who provided the service in the practice setting.

3.06 Client Transfer

(a) When an individual who is receiving services from another agency or colleague contacts a social worker for services, the social worker should carefully consider the client's needs before agreeing to provide services. To minimize possible confusion and conflict, social workers should discuss with potential clients the nature of the clients' current relationship with other service providers and the implications, including possible benefits or risks, of entering into a relationship with a new service provider.

(b) If a new client has been served by another agency or colleague, social workers should discuss with the client whether consultation with the previous service provider is in the client's best interest.

3.07 Administration

(a) Social work administrators should advocate within and outside their agencies for adequate resources to meet clients' needs.

(b) Social workers should advocate for resource allocation procedures that are open and fair. When not all clients' needs can be met, an allocation procedure should be developed that is nondiscriminatory and based on appropriate and consistently applied principles.

(c) Social workers who are administrators should take reasonable steps to ensure that adequate agency or organizational resources are available to provide appropriate staff supervision.

(d) Social work administrators should take reasonable steps to ensure that the working environment for which they are responsible is consistent with and encourages compliance with the NASW Code of Ethics. Social work administrators should take reasonable steps to eliminate any conditions in their organizations that violate, interfere with, or discourage compliance with the Code.

3.08 Continuing Education and Staff Development

Social work administrators and supervisors should take reasonable steps to provide or arrange for continuing education and staff development for all staff for whom they are responsible. Continuing education and staff development should address current knowledge and emerging developments related to social work practice and ethics.

3.09 Commitments to Employers

(a) Social workers generally should adhere to commitments made to employers and employing organizations.

(b) Social workers should work to improve employing agencies' policies and procedures and the efficiency and effectiveness of their services.

(c) Social workers should take reasonable steps to ensure that employers are aware of social workers' ethical obligations as set forth in the NASW Code of Ethics and of the implications of those obligations for social work practice.

(d) Social workers should not allow an employing organization's policies, procedures, regulations, or administrative orders to interfere with their ethical practice of social work. Social workers should take reasonable steps to ensure that their employing organizations' practices are consistent with the NASW Code of Ethics.

(e) Social workers should act to prevent and eliminate discrimination in the employing organization's work assignments and in its employment policies and practices.

(f) Social workers should accept employment or arrange student field placements only in organizations that exercise fair personnel practices.

(g) Social workers should be diligent stewards of the resources of their employing organizations, wisely conserving funds where appropriate and never misappropriating funds or using them for unintended purposes.

3.10 Labor-Management Disputes

(a) Social workers may engage in organized action, including the formation of and participation in labor unions, to improve services to clients and working conditions.

(b) The actions of social workers who are involved in labor-management disputes, job actions, or labor strikes should be guided by the profession's values, ethical principles, and ethical standards. Reasonable differences of opinion exist among social workers concerning their primary obligation as professionals during an actual or threatened labor strike or job action. Social workers should carefully examine relevant issues and their possible impact on clients before deciding on a course of action.

4. SOCIAL WORKERS' ETHICAL RESPONSIBILITIES AS PROFESSIONALS

4.01 Competence

(a) Social workers should accept responsibility or employment only on the basis of existing competence or the intention to acquire the necessary competence.

(b) Social workers should strive to become and remain proficient in professional practice and the performance of professional functions. Social workers should critically examine and keep current with emerging knowledge relevant to social work. Social workers should routinely review the professional literature and participate in continuing education relevant to social work practice and social work ethics.

(c) Social workers should base practice on recognized knowledge, including empirically based knowledge, relevant to social work and social work ethics.

4.02 Discrimination

Social workers should not practice, condone, facilitate, or collaborate with any form of discrimination on the basis of race, ethnicity, national origin, color, sex, sexual orientation, age, marital status, political belief, religion, or mental or physical disability.

4.03 Private Conduct

Social workers should not permit their private conduct to interfere with their ability to fulfill their professional responsibilities.

4.04 Dishonesty, Fraud, and Deception

Social workers should not participate in, condone, or be associated with dishonesty, fraud, or deception.

4.05 Impairment

(a) Social workers should not allow their own personal problems, psychosocial distress, legal problems, substance abuse, or mental health difficulties to interfere with their professional judgment and performance or to jeopardize the best interests of people for whom they have a professional responsibility.

(b) Social workers whose personal problems, psychosocial distress, legal problems, substance abuse, or mental health difficulties interfere with their professional judgment and performance should immediately seek consultation and take appropriate remedial action by seeking professional help, making adjustments in workload, terminating practice, or taking any other steps necessary to protect clients and others.

4.06 Misrepresentation

(a) Social workers should make clear distinctions between statements made and actions engaged in as a private individual and as a representative of the social work profession, a professional social work organization, or the social worker's employing agency.

(b) Social workers who speak on behalf of professional social work organizations should accurately represent the official and authorized positions of the organizations.

(c) Social workers should ensure that their representations to clients, agencies, and the public of professional qualifications, credentials, education, competence, affiliations, services provided, or results to be achieved are accurate. Social workers should claim only those relevant professional credentials they actually possess and take steps to correct any inaccuracies or misrepresentations of their credentials by others.

4.07 Solicitations

(a) Social workers should not engage in uninvited solicitation of potential clients who, because of their circumstances, are vulnerable to undue influence, manipulation, or coercion.

(b) Social workers should not engage in solicitation of testimonial endorsements (including solicitation of consent to use a client's prior statement as a testimonial endorsement) from current clients or from other people who, because of their particular circumstances, are vulnerable to undue influence.

4.08 Acknowledging Credit

(a) Social workers should take responsibility and credit, including authorship credit, only for work they have actually performed and to which they have contributed.

(b) Social workers should honestly acknowledge the work of and the contributions made by others.

5. SOCIAL WORKERS' ETHICAL RESPONSIBILITIES TO THE SOCIAL WORK PROFESSION

5.01 Integrity of the Profession

(a) Social workers should work toward the maintenance and promotion of high standards of practice.

(b) Social workers should uphold and advance the values, ethics, knowledge, and mission of the profession. Social workers should protect, enhance, and improve the integrity of the profession through appropriate study and research, active discussion, and responsible criticism of the profession.

(c) Social workers should contribute time and professional expertise to activities that promote respect for the value, integrity, and competence of the social work profession. These activities may include teaching, research, consultation, service, legislative testimony, presentations in the community, and participation in their professional organizations.

(d) Social workers should contribute to the knowledge base of social work and share with colleagues their knowledge related to practice, research, and ethics. Social workers should seek to con-tribute to the profession's literature and to share their knowledge at professional meetings and conferences.

(e) Social workers should act to prevent the unauthorized and unqualified practice of social work.

5.02 Evaluation and Research

(a) Social workers should monitor and evaluate policies, the implementation of programs, and practice interventions.

(b) Social workers should promote and facilitate evaluation and research to contribute to the development of knowledge.

(c) Social workers should critically examine and keep current with emerging knowledge relevant to social work and fully use evaluation and research evidence in their professional practice.

(d) Social workers engaged in evaluation or research should carefully consider possible consequences and should follow guidelines developed for the protection of evaluation and research participants. Appropriate institutional review boards should be consulted.

(e) Social workers engaged in evaluation or research should obtain voluntary and written informed consent from participants, when appropriate, without any implied or actual deprivation or penalty for refusal to participate; without undue inducement to participate; and with due regard for participants' well-being, privacy, and dignity. Informed consent should include information about the nature, extent, and duration of the participation requested and disclosure of the risks and benefits of participation in the research.

(f) When evaluation or research participants are incapable of giving informed consent, social workers should provide an appropriate explanation to the participants, obtain the participants' assent to the extent they are able, and obtain written consent from an appropriate proxy.

(g) Social workers should never design or conduct evaluation or research that does not use consent procedures, such as certain forms of naturalistic observation and archival research, unless rigorous and responsible review of the research has found it to be justified because of its prospective scientific, educational, or applied value and unless equally effective alternative procedures that do not involve waiver of consent are not feasible.

(h) Social workers should inform participants of their right to withdraw from evaluation and research at any time without penalty.

(i) Social workers should take appropriate steps to ensure that participants in evaluation and research have access to appropriate supportive services.

(j) Social workers engaged in evaluation or research should protect participants from unwarranted physical or mental distress, harm, danger, or deprivation.

(k) Social workers engaged in the evaluation of services should discuss collected information only for professional purposes and only with people professionally concerned with this information.

(l) Social workers engaged in evaluation or research should ensure the anonymity or confidentiality of participants and of the data obtained from them. Social workers should inform participants of any limits of confidentiality, the measures that will be taken to ensure confidentiality, and when any records containing research data will be destroyed.

(m) Social workers who report evaluation and research results should protect participants' confidentiality by omitting identifying information unless proper consent has been obtained authorizing disclosure.

(n) Social workers should report evaluation and research findings accurately. They should not fabricate or falsify results and should take steps to correct any errors later found in published data using standard publication methods.

(o) Social workers engaged in evaluation or research should be alert to and avoid conflicts of interest and dual relationships with participants, should inform participants when a real or potential conflict of interest arises, and should take steps to resolve the issue in a manner that makes participants' interests primary.

(p) Social workers should educate themselves, their students, and their colleagues about responsible research practices.

6. SOCIAL WORKERS' ETHICAL RESPONSIBILITIES TO THE BROADER SOCIETY

6.01 Social Welfare

Social workers should promote the general welfare of society, from local to global levels, and the development of people, their communities, and their environments. Social workers should advocate for living conditions conducive to the fulfillment of basic human needs and should promote social, economic, political, and cultural values and institutions that are compatible with the realization of social justice.

6.02 Public Participation

Social workers should facilitate informed participation by the public in shaping social policies and institutions.

6.03 Public Emergencies

Social workers should provide appropriate professional services in public emergencies to the greatest extent possible.

6.04 Social and Political Action

(a) Social workers should engage in social and political action that seeks to ensure that all people have equal access to the resources, employment, services, and opportunities they require to meet their basic human needs and to develop fully. Social workers should be aware of the impact of the political arena on practice and should advocate for changes in policy and legislation to improve social conditions in order to meet basic human needs and promote social justice.

(b) Social workers should act to expand choice and opportunity for all people, with special regard for vulnerable, disadvantaged, oppressed, and exploited people and groups.

(c) Social workers should promote conditions that encourage respect for cultural and social diversity within the United States and globally. Social workers should promote policies and practices that demonstrate respect for difference, support the expansion of cultural knowledge and resources, advocate for programs and institutions that demonstrate cultural competence, and promote policies that safeguard the rights of and confirm equity and social justice for all people.

(d) Social workers should act to prevent and eliminate domination of, exploitation of, and discrimination against any person, group, or class on the basis of race, ethnicity, national origin, color, sex, sexual orientation, age, marital status, political belief, religion, or mental or physical disability.

Appendix B

National Association of Black Social Workers (NABSW) Code of Ethics

The Code of Ethics of NABSW, adopted in 1971, is excerpted below:

In America today, no Black person, except the selfish or irrational, can claim neutrality in the quest for Black liberation nor fail to consider the implications of the events taking place in our society. Given the necessity for committing ourselves to the struggle for freedom, we as Black Americans practicing in the field of social welfare set forth this statement of ideals and guiding principles.

If a sense of community awareness is a precondition to humanitarian acts, then we as Black social workers must use our knowledge of the Black community, our commitments to its determination, and our helping skills for the benefit of Black people as we marshal our expertise to improve the quality of life of Black people. Our activities will be guided by our Black consciousness, our determination to protect the security of the Black community, and to serve as advocates to relieve suffering of Black people by any means necessary.

Therefore, as Black social workers we commit ourselves, collectively, to the interests of our Black brethren and as individuals subscribe to the following statements:

- I regard as my primary obligation the welfare of the Black individual, Black family, and Black community and will engage in action for improving social conditions.
- I give preference to this mission over my personal interest.
- I adopt the concept of a Black extended family and embrace all Black people as my brothers and sisters, making no distinction between their destiny and my own.
- I hold myself responsible for the quality and extent of service I perform and the quality and extent of service performed by the agency or

Ethics in Social Work: A Context of Caring
© 2006 by The Haworth Press, Inc. All rights reserved.
doi:10.1300/5577_18

organization in which I am employed, as it relates to the Black community.

- I accept the responsibility to protect the Black community against unethical and hypocritical practice by any individual or organizations engaged in social welfare activities.
- I stand ready to supplement my paid or professional advocacy with voluntary service in the Black public interest.
- I will consciously use my skills, and my whole being as an instrument for social change, with particular attention directed to the establishment of Black social institutions.

Bibliography

American Medical Association (2006). Louisiana State Medical Society. Available online at: http://www.ama-assn.org/ama/pub/category/13346.html.

Amundsen W. D. (1978). *The History of Medical Ethics: Ancient and Medieval Period*. In W. T. Reich (Ed.), *Encyclopedia of Bioethics*, Volume Three. New York: The Free Press.

Ancsel E. (1988). *Szaz Bekezdes az Emberrol* [One Hundred Introductions on Man]. Budapest: Kossuth Publication. In Hungarian.

Annas G. (1989). *The Rights of Patients*. Southern Illinois Press.

Annas J. (2002). Should Virtue Make You Happy? In L. Jost and R. Shiner (Eds.), *Eudaimonia and Well-Being: Ancient and Modern Conceptions. Apeiron*, 35(4): 1-19.

Aristotle (1992). *Eudemian Ethics*, Books I, II, and VIII. Translated by Michael Woods. Oxford, UK: Clarendon Press.

Aristotle (1997). *Ethica Nicomachea* [Nicomachean Ethics]. Translated by Szabo Miklos, Budapest: Europa Publisher. In Hungarian.

Barker R. L. (1987). *The Social Work Dictionary*. Silver Spring, MD: NASW Press.

Barker R. L. (1999). *The Social Work Dictionary*, Fourth Edition. Washington, DC: NASW Press.

Beauchamp T. L. and Childress J. F. (1994). *Principles of Biomedical Ethics*, Fourth Edition. Oxford, UK: Oxford University Press.

Benjamin M. and Curtis J. (1992). *Ethics in Nursing*, Third Edition. Oxford, UK: Oxford University Press.

Bentham J. (1973). An Introduction to the Principles of Morals and Legislation. In *The Utilitarians*, New York: Anchor.

Biestek F. P. (1957). *The Casework Relationship*. Chicago: Loyola University Press.

Billingsley A. (1992). *Climbing Jacob's Ladder: The Enduring Legacy of African American Families*. New York: Simon and Schuster.

Blasszauer B. (1995). *Medical Ethics*. Budapest: Medicina Publisher. In Hungarian.

Boros G. (1997). *Spinoza and the Problem of Philosophical Ethics*. Budapest: Atlantisz Publishers. In Hungarian.

Boxill B. R. (2001). King, Martin Luther, Jr. (1929-1968). In L. C. Becker and C. B. Becker (Eds.), *Encyclopedia of Ethics*, Volume Two (pp. 950-951). New York and London: Routledge.

Brick J. (1999). Judaism and Social Policy. *The Common Opinion*, 17(2): 6-7.

Ethics in Social Work: A Context of Caring
© 2006 by The Haworth Press, Inc. All rights reserved.
doi:10.1300/5577_19

Broderick F. L. (1959). *W. E. B. Du Bois: Negro Leader in a Time of Crisis.* Stanford, CA: Stanford University Press.

Brodsky A. M. (1986). The Distressed Psychologist: Sexual Intimacies and Exploitation. In R. R. Kilburg, P. E. Nathan, and W. Thoreson (Eds.). *Professionals in Distress: Issues, Syndromes, and Solutions in Psychology* (pp. 153-171). Washington, DC: American Psychological Association.

Buber M. (1953). *Good and Evil.* New York: Scribners.

Buchanan J. M. (1989). *The Ethics of Constitutional Order: Essays on the Political Economy.* Honolulu: University of Hawaii Press.

Buda B. (1985). Dillemak az orvosi titoktartasban [Dilemmas in Medical Confidentiality]. Budapest: *Csaladi Lap [Family Pages].* In Hungarian.

Callahan J. (1994). The Ethics of Assisted Suicide. *Health and Social Work,* 19(4): 237-244.

Cameron M. E., Schaffer M., and Park H. A. (2001). Nursing Students Experience of Ethical Problems and Use of Ethical Decision-Making Models. *Nursing Ethics,* 8(5): 432-447.

Carlson B. E. (1991). Domestic Violence. In A. Gitterman (Ed.), *Handbook of Social Work Practice with Vulnerable Populations* (pp. 471-502). New York: Columbia University Press.

Chilman C. S. (1987). Abortion. In A. Minahan (Ed.), *Encyclopedia of Social Work,* Eighteenth Edition (pp. 1-7). Silver Spring, MD: NASW Press.

Cicero M. T. (1909). *De Senectute,* E. S. Schukburg, Ed. New York: St. Martin's Press.

Clarkin T. (2000). Martin Luther King, Jr. In J. K. Roth, C. J. Moose, and R. Wildin, Eds., *World Philosophers and Their Works,* Volume Two (pp. 1017-1024). Pasadena, CA: Salem Press, Inc.

Comte-Sponville A. (1998). *Little Book on the Great Virtues.* Budapest: Osiris Publisher. In Hungarian.

Congress E. P. (1992). Ethical Decision Making of Social Work Supervisors. *The Clinical Supervisor,* 10(1): 157-169.

Cottingham J. (1997). Medicine, Virtues and Consequences. In D. S. Oderberg and J. A. Laing (Eds.), *Human Lives, Critical Essays on Consequentialist Bioethics* (pp. 128-143). London: MacMillan.

Cowen S. (2001). A Statement of the Noahide Laws. *Journal of Judaism and Civilization,* 3: 28-45.

Cwikel J. G. and Cnaan R. A. (1991). Ethical Dilemmas in Applying Second-Wave Information Technology to Social Work Practice. *Social Work,* 36(2): 114-120.

Dalai Lama (1999). *Ethics for the New Millennium.* New York: Riverhead Books.

de Botton A. (2000). *The Consolations of Philosophy.* London: Hamish Hamilton.

de Montaigne M. (1991). *The Complete Essays.* Translated by M. A. Screech. New York: Penguin Books.

Dolgoff R. and Skolnik L. (1992). Ethical Decision Making, the NASW Code of Ethics and Group Work Practice: Beginning Explorations. *Social Work with Groups,* 15(4): 99-112.

Du Bois W. E. B. (1908). *The Negro American Family.* Atlanta: Atlanta University Press.

Edelstein L. (1967). *Ancient Medicine: Selected Papers of Ludwig Edelstein,* O. Temkin and C. L. Temkin (Eds.). Baltimore, MD: The Johns Hopkins University Press.

Einstein A. (1931). *The World as I See It.* Abridged edition. New York: Philosophical Library, distributed by Citadel Press.

Encyclopaedia Hebraica (1960). Aristotele. Volume Five, pp. 838-859.

Ephross P. H. and Reisch M. (1982). The Ideology of Some Social Work Texts. *Social Service Review,* 56(2): 273-291.

Erdemir A. D. (1995). *Lectures on Medical History and Medical Ethics.* Istanbul: Nobel Tip Kitaberleri Ltd.

Erikson E. H. (1959). *Identity and the Life Cycle.* New York: Norton.

Fencsik L. (1986). *Political Dictionary.* Budapest: Kossuth Publisher. In Hungarian.

Fletcher J. (1997). *Situation Ethics: The New Morality.* Westminster, UK: John Knox Press.

Frankena W. K. (1973). *Ethics,* Second Edition. Englewood Cliffs, NJ: Prentice Hall.

Frankl V. E. (1962). *Man's Search for Meaning: An Introduction to Logotherapy,* Second Edition. New York: Touchstone.

Frankl V. E. (1985). *The Will to Meaning.* Translated by Saul Broida. Tel Aviv: Dvir. In Hebrew.

Frankl V. E. (1986). *The Doctor and the Soul: From Psychotherapy to Logotherapy.* New York: Vintage Books.

Friedenwald H. (2003). Oath and Prayer of Maimonides. *Bulletin of Johns Hopkins Hospital,* 28: 260-261.

Fry S. and Johnstone M. J. (2002). *Ethics in Nursing Practice: Guide to Ethical Decision Making,* Second Edition. Oxford: Blackwell Publishing.

Gaizler Gy. (1994). Variations of Medical Oaths. *Lege Artis Medicinae,* 4(4): 394-402. In Hungarian.

Garrett K. J. (1994). Caught in a Bind: Ethical Decision Making in Schools. *Social Work in Education,* 16(2): 97-105.

Gauthier C. C. (2002). The Virtue of Moral Responsibility in Healthcare Decision-making. *Cambridge Quarterly of Healthcare Ethics,* 11: 273-281.

Gewirth A. (1978). *Reason and Morality.* Chicago: University of Chicago Press.

Gil D. G. (1998). *Confronting Injustice and Oppression: Concepts and Strategies for Social Workers.* New York: Columbia University Press.

Glassman C. (1992). Feminist Dilemmas in Practice. *AFFILIA, Journal of Women and Social Work,* 7(2): 160-166.

Goldstein H. (1987). The Neglected Moral Link in Social Work Practice. *Social Work,* 36: 138-144.

Goldstein S. and Rosner I. (2000). *Social Workers Law in Practice*. Tel Aviv: University of Tel Aviv. In Hebrew.

Green A. (1976). A Contemporary Approach to Jewish Sexuality. In M. Stressfeld and S. Stressfeld (Eds.), *The Second Jewish Catalog* (pp. 96-99). Philadelphia: Jewish Publication Society.

Harsanyi J. C. (1978). Economics and Ethics: Altruism, Justice, Power: Discussion. *American Economic Review*, 68(2): 231-232.

Hartman A. (1994). Social Work Practice. In F. G. Riemer (Ed.), *The Foundations of Social Work Knowledge* (pp. 13-50). New York: Columbia University Press.

Hauck G. H. and Louisell D. W. (1978). Malpractice. In S. G. Post (Ed.), *Encyclopedia of Bioethics*, Volume Three. The Free Press.

Heller A. (1994). *General Ethics*. Budapest: Cserepfalvi Press. In Hungarian.

Hippocrates (1967). The Judgment. *Encyclopedia Hebraica: General, Jewish and Israeli*, Volume 14, pp. 342-348. Translated by Jeshayahu Leibowitz. In Hebrew.

Hutchinson D. S. (1988). Doctrines of the Mean and the Debate Concerning Skills in Fourth-Century Medicine, Rhetoric and Ethics. In R. J. Hankinson (Ed.), *Method, Medicine and Metaphysics: Studies in the Philosophy of Ancient Science*, Apeiron 21(2): 17-52.

Hyun I. (2003). Conceptions of Family-Centered Medical Decision-Making and Their Difficulties. *Cambridge Quarterly of Healthcare Ethics*, 12: 196-200.

Jayaratne S., Croxton T., and Mattison D. (1997). Social Work Professional Standards: An Exploratory Study. *Social Work*, 42: 187-198.

Jayaratne S., Croxton T. A., and Mattison D. (2002). Race, Practice Behaviors and the NASW Code of Ethics. *Journal of Social Service Research*, 28(3): 65-89.

Jenei I. (1994). Modern Medical Ethics. *EMMIK*, 3, Debrecen: Kossuth Press. In Hungarian.

Johnson A. (1955). Educating Professional Social Workers for Ethical Practice. *Social Service Review*, 29(2): 125-136.

Johnstone M. J. (1999). *Bioethics: A Nursing Perspective*, Third Edition. Sydney: Harcourt Saunders.

Joseph M. V. (1985). A Model for Ethical Decision-Making in Clinical Practice. In C. B. Germain (Ed.), *Advances in Clinical Social Work Practice* (pp. 207-217). Silver Spring, MD: National Association of Social Workers Press.

Joseph M. V. (1989). Social Work Ethics: Historical and Contemporary Perspectives, *Social Thought*, 15(3/4): 4-17.

Jung C. G. (1954). *The Collected Works of C. G. Jung*, Volume Sixteen, *The Practice of Psychotherapy*. London: Routledge and Kegan Paul.

Kant I. (1991). *Critic of Practical Mind*. Translated by Gabor Berenyi. Budapest: Gondolat Publishers. In Hungarian.

Kelly P. J. (1990). *Utilitarianism and Distributive Justice: Jeremy Bentham and the Civil Law*. Oxford, UK: Clarendon.

King M. L. Jr. (1964). *Why We Can't Wait*. New York: Harper & Row.

Kirk S. A. and Kutchins H. (1988). Deliberate Misdiagnosis in Mental Health Practice. *Social Service Review,* 62 (2): 225-237.

Kloisner J. (1960). Plato. *Encyclopedia Herbraica,* Volume 5, pp. 223-236. In Hebrew.

Kopels S. (1993). Response to 'Confidentiality: A Different Perspective.' *Social Work in Education,* 15(4): 250-252.

Kopels S. (1997). Is the NASW Code of Ethics an Effective Guide for Practitioners? No. In E. Gambrill and R. Prueger (Eds.), *Controversial Issues in Social Work Ethics, Values and Obligations* (pp. 120-125). Needham, MA: Allyn and Bacon.

Kopels S. (1997). Is the NASW Code of Ethics an effective guide for practitioners? No. In E. Gambrill & R. Prueger (Eds.), *Controversial Issues in Social Work Ethics, Values and Obligations.* Needham, MA: Allyn & Bacon.

Kopels S. and Kagle J. D. (1993). Do Social Workers Have a Duty to Warn? *Social Service Review,* 67 (1): 10-26.

Kovacs J. (1998). Guidelines in Lifesaving Functions and Caring for the Dying. *Lege Artis Medicinae,* 8(12): 896-903. In Hungarian.

Kraus N. (1998). *Jewish Ethics and Morals.* Debrecen: Fichmun Publishers. In Hungarian.

Kunzmann P., Burkard F. P. and Wiedmann F. (1999). *Filozofia Atlasz.* Budapest: Holnap Kiado. In Hungarian.

LaNey I. C. (1999), African American Social Work Pioneers' Response to Need. *Social Work,* 44(4): 311-321.

Levinas E. (1981). *Otherwise than Being or Beyond Essence.* Translated by Alphonso Lingis, Boston: Martinus Nijhoff Publishers.

Levy C. (1972). The Context of Social Work Ethics. *Social Work,* 17(2): 95-101.

Levy C. S. (1976). *Social Work Ethics.* New York: Human Sciences Press.

Levy Y. (Ed.) (1995). *Oxford English-Hebrew, Hebrew-English Dictionary.* Oxford, UK: Kernerman-Lonnie Kavn.

Lewis H. (1985). The Whistle-Blower in a Whistle Blowing Profession. *Journal of Clinical Social Work with Children.* Winter Issue.

Loewenberg F. M. (1995). Financing Philanthropic Institutions in Biblical and Talmudic Times. *Nonprofit and Voluntary Sector Quarterly* 24: 307-320.

Loewenberg M. (1992). Notes on Ethical Dilemmas in Wartime: Experience of Israeli Social Workers during Operation Desert Shield. *International Social Work* 35(4): 429-439.

Loewenberg M. and Dolgoff R. (1996). *Ethical Decisions for Social Work Practice,* Fifth Edition. Itasca IL: F. E. Peacock.

Loewy E. H. (1994). Philosophy and its Role in Medicine: Inaugurating a New Section. *Theoretical Medicine,* 15(2): 201-205.

Loudon I. (1994). The Hippocratic Oath. *British Medical Journal,* 309(6951): 414.

Marsh J. C. (2004). Editorial: Social Work in a Multicultural Society. *Social Work,* 49(1): 5-6.

Martin E. P. and Martin, J. M. (2002). *Spirituality and the Black Helping Tradition in Social Work*. Washington, DC: NASW Press.

Mattison M. (2000). Ethical Decision Making: The Person in the Process. *Social Work*, 45(3): 201-212.

McCracken J. (1999). Comic and Tragic Interlocutors and Socratic Method. *Teaching Philosophy*, 22(4): 361-375.

Mill J. S. (1962). *Utilitarianism/On Liberty/Essay on Bentham*. Edited by Mary Warnock. New York: New American Library.

Mill J. S. (1973). On Liberty. In *The Utilitarians*. New York: Anchor.

Minahan A. (Ed.) (1987). *Encyclopedia of Social Work*, Eighteenth Edition. Silver Spring, MD: NASW Press.

Morales A. and Sheafor B. W. (1986). *Social Work: A Profession of Many Faces*, Fourth Edition. Boston: Allyn & Bacon.

Morowitz D. (1993). Malpractice. *The Humanist*, 53(4): 9-14.

Morreim E. H. (1993). Am I My Brother's Warden? Responding to the Unethical or Incompetent Colleague. *Hastings Center Report*, 23(3): 19-27.

Munson R. (2000). *Intervention and Reflection, Basic Issues in Medical Ethics*, Sixth Edition. Belmont, CA: Wadsworth/Thomson Learning.

Munthe A. (1990). *The Novel of San Michele*. Translated by Marcel Benedek. Budapest: Fabula Publisher. In Hungarian.

National Association of Social Workers (1996). *Code of Ethics*. Washington, DC: NASW Press.

National Association of Social Workers (2001). *NASW Standards for Cultural Competence in Social Work Practice*. Washington, DC: NASW Press.

Northen H. (1998). Ethical Dilemmas in Social Work with Groups. *Social Work with Groups*, 21(1/2): 5-17.

O'Neill S. (2002). The Social Worker's View. *Journal of Clinical Ethics*, 13(3): 233, 238-239.

Pakaluk M. (2005). *Aristotle's Nicomachean Ethics: An Introduction*. Cambridge, UK: Cambridge University Press.

Pasnau R. O. (1985). Ten Commandments of Medical Etiquette for Psychiatrists. *Psychosomatics*, 26(2): 128-132.

Pecz V. (1902). *Ancient Lexicon*. Budapest: Franklin Association. In Hungarian.

Pellegrino E. D. (1964). Ethical Implications in Changing Practice. *American Journal of Nursing*, 64(9): 110-112.

Pellegrino E. D. (1985). The Caring Ethic: The Relation of Physician to Patient. In A. H. Bishop and J. R. Scudder Jr. (Eds.), *Caring, Curing, Coping*. Tuscaloosa: The University of Alabama Press.

Pellegrino E. D. (1989). Can Ethics be Taught? An Essay. *The Mount Sinai Journal of Medicine*, 56(6): 490-494.

Pellegrino E. D. (1991). Trust and Distrust in Professional Ethics. In E. D. Pellegrino, R. M. Veatch, and J. P. Langan (Eds.), *Ethics, Trust and the Professions:*

Philosophical and Cultural Aspects (pp. 69-89). Washington, DC: Georgetown University Press.

Pellegrino E. D. and Faden A. I. (1999). *Jewish and Catholic Bioethics: An Ecumenical Dialogue*. Washington DC: Georgetown University Press.

Peternelj-Taylor C. A. and Yonge O. (2003). Exploring Boundaries in the Nurse-Client Relationship: Professional Roles and Responsibilities. *Perspectives in Psychiatric Care*, 39(2): 55-66.

Plato (1987a). *The Last Days of Socrates*. Translated by Hugh Tredennick. New York: Penguin Books.

Plato (1987b). *The Socratic Dialogues—Protagoras and Meno*. Translated by W. K. C. Guthrie. New York: Penguin Books.

Plato (1994). *Gorgias*. Translated by Robin Waterfield. Oxford, UK: Oxford University Press.

Plato (1994). *Szokratesz Vedobeszede. A Lakoma. [The Plea of Socrates and The Feast]*. Translated by G. Devecseri and Z. Telegdi. Szombathely: Europa Publishing Company. In Hungarian.

Pope K. S. (1988). How Clients are Harmed by Sexual Contact with Mental Health Professionals: The Syndrome and its Prevalence. *Journal of Counseling and Development*, 67: 222-226.

Pope K. S., Tabachnik B. G., and Keith-Spiegel P. (1987). The Beliefs and Behaviors of Psychologists as Therapist. *American Psychologist*, 42: 993-1006.

Proctor E. K., Morrow-Howell N., and Lott C. L. (1993). Classification and Correlates of Ethical Dilemmas in Hospital Social Work. *Social Work*, 38(2): 166-177.

Pumphrey M. W. (1959). *The Teaching of Values and Ethics in Social Work Education*, Volume Thirteen. New York: Council on Social Work Education.

Rawls J. (1971). *A Theory of Justice*. Cambridge, MA: Harvard University Press.

Rawls J. (1993). *Political Liberalism*. New York: Columbia University Press.

Reamer F. G. (1992). The Impaired Social Worker. *Social Work*, 37(2): 165-170.

Reamer F. G. (1994). *Social Work Malpractice and Liability*. New York: Columbia University Press.

Reamer F. G. (1995). Malpractice Claims Against Social Workers: First Facts. *Social Work*, 40: 595-601.

Reamer F. G. (1998). The Evolution of Social Work Ethics. *Social Work*, 43(6): 488-500.

Reamer F. G. (1999). *Social Work Values and Ethics*. Second Edition. New York: Columbia University Press.

Rock B. and Congress E. (1999). The New Confidentiality for the 21st Century in a Managed Care Environment. *Social Work*, 44(3): 253-262.

Roy A. (1954). Code of Ethics. *Social Worker*, 23(1): 4-7.

Rozovsky F. A. (1984). *Consent to Treatment: A Practical Guide*. Boston: Little, Brown.

Rozsos E. (2000). *Ethics in Nursing*. Budapest: Medicina Publisher. In Hungarian.

Rozsos E. (2003). Hungary's Black Angel and Her Dragons. *Nursing Ethics*, 10(4): 428-432.

Runes D. (Ed.) (1976). *The Ethics of Spinoza: The Road to Inner Freedom.* Secaucus, NJ: The Citadel Press.

Russell O. R. (1977). *Freedom to Die: Moral and Legal Aspects of Euthanasia.* New York: Human Sciences Press.

Sadler J. Z. (1997). Recognizing Values: A Descriptive-Causal Method for Medical/Scientific Discourses. *The Journal of Medicine and Philosophy*, 22: 541-565.

Samuelson N. M. (2001). Rethinking Ethics in the Light of Jewish Thought and the Life Sciences. *Journal of Religious Ethics*, 29(2): 209-233.

Scally G. (1993). Confidentiality, Contraception, and Young People. *British Medical Journal*, 307: 6.

Schlessinger J. H. and Schlessinger, B. (2000). Moses Maimonides. In J. K. Roth (Ed.), *World Philosophers and Their Works*, Volume Two (pp. 1163-1165). Pasadena, California: Salem Press, Inc.

Schultz D. (2004). Professional Ethics in a Postmodern Society. *Public Integrity*, 6(4): 279-297.

Schutz B. M. (1982). *Legal Liability in Psychotherapy.* San Francisco: Jossey-Bass.

Schwartzschield S. S. (1974). *Justice, in Jewish Values.* Jerusalem: Keter Publishing Company.

Schweitzer A. (1999). *Ehrfurcht vor deer Leben [Respect for Life].* Translated by Dani Laszlo and Klara Balassi. Budapest: Ursus Publisher. In Hungarian.

Seedhouse D. (1986). *Health—The Foundations for Achievement.* Chichester, UK: Wiley.

Sethi J. D. (1979). *Gandhi Today.* Sahibabad, India: Vikas Publishing House.

Siegel-Itzkovich J. (1993). Rabbis and Doctors Sort Out Medical Ethics in Jerusalem. *British Medical Journal* 307(6901): 404.

Simmons L. (1997). On Not Destroying the Health of One's Patients. *Human Lives*, 8(18): 144-160.

Smith T. V. (1944). The Strategy of Virtue. *Ethics*, 55(1):1-8.

Solomon B. B. (1986). Social Work with Afro-Americans. In A. Morales and B. W. Sheafor (Eds.), *Social Work: A Profession of Many Faces* (pp. 501-421). Fourth Edition. Boston MA: Allyn & Bacon.

Spinoza B. (1982). *The Ethics.* Translated by Samuel Shirley. Indianapolis, IN: Hackett Publishing Co.

Spinoza B. (1989). *Theological-Political Treatise.* Translated by Samuel Shirley. Leiden, the Netherlands: Brill.

Spinoza B. (1997). *Spinoza and the Problem of Philosophical Ethics.* Budapest: Atlantisz Publishers. Hungarian translation by Gabor Boros.

Starr B. E. (1999). The Structure of Max Weber's Ethic of Responsibility. *Journal of Religious Ethics*, 27(3): 407-431.

Steinberg A. (Ed.). (1976). *ASSIA: Original Articles, Abstracts and Reports on Matters of Halacha and Medicine.* Jerusalem: The Dr. F. Schlesinger Institute for Medical and Halachic Research, at Shaare-Zedek Hospital.

Strom-Gottfried, K. (1999). When Colleague Accuses Colleague: Adjudicating Personnel Matters through the Filing of Ethics Complaints. *Administration in Social Work,* 23: 1-16.

Szlezak T. A. (2000). *Hogyan Olvassunk Platont [How to Read Plato].* Translated by Peter Lautner. Budapest: Atlantisz. In Hungarian.

Tauber A. (2006). In Search of Medicine's Moral Glue. *American Journal of Bioethics,* 6(1): 41-44.

Teasdale A. and Kent J. (1995). The Use of Deception in Nursing. *Journal of Medical Ethics,* 21: 77-81.

Telushkin J. (1994). *Jewish Wisdom, Ethical, Spiritual and Historical Lessons from the Great Works and Thinkers.* New York: William Morrow and Company.

Texas State Board of Social Worker Examiners (2005). About the Profession: Code of Conduct. Updated July 27, 2005. Available online at: http://www.dshs.state .tx.us/socialwork/sw_conduct.shtm.

Towle C. (1965). *Common Human Needs.* Washington, DC: National Association of Social Workers.

Veatch R. M. (1989). *Medical Ethics.* Boston: Jones and Bartlett.

Vincent C. A. (1993). The Study of Errors and Accidents in Medicine. In C. A. Vincent, M. Ennis, and R. J. Audley (Eds.) *Medical Accidents* (pp. 17-33). Oxford, UK: Oxford University Press.

Walz T. and Ritchie H. (2000). Gandhian Principles in Social Work Practice; Ethics Revisited. *Social Work,* 45(3): 213-222.

Weiss M. (2000). John Rawls. In J. K. Roth, C. J. Moose, and R. Wilden (Eds.), *World Philosophers and Their Works,* Volume 2. Pasadena, CA: Salem Press.

Weiss R. and Butterworth C. (Eds.) (1975). *Ethical Writings of Maimonides.* New York: Dover Publication.

World Medical Association (1949). International Code of Medical Ethics. *World Medical Association Bulletin,* 1(3): 109, 111.

Yeo M. and Moorhouse A. (1996). *Concepts and Cases in Nursing Ethics,* Second Edition. Ontario, Canada: Broadview Press.

Zarday Z. (1987). Ethical Concept in Contemporary Medicine. Unpublished manuscript.

Index

Order a copy of this book with this form or online at:
http://www.haworthpress.com/store/product.asp?sku=5577

ETHICS IN SOCIAL WORK
A Context of Caring

_____in hardbound at $44.95 (ISBN-13: 978-0-7890-2852-5; ISBN-10: 0-7890-2852-2)

_____in softbound at $29.95 (ISBN-13:978-0-7890-2853-2 ; ISBN-10: 0-7890-2853-0)

286 pages plus index

Or order online and use special offer code HEC25 in the shopping cart.

COST OF BOOKS_____

POSTAGE & HANDLING_____
(US: $4.00 for first book & $1.50
for each additional book)
(Outside US: $5.00 for first book
& $2.00 for each additional book)

SUBTOTAL_____

IN CANADA: ADD 7% GST_____

STATE TAX_____
(NJ, NY, OH, MN, CA, IL, IN, PA, & SD
residents, *add appropriate local sales tax)*

FINAL TOTAL_____
(If paying in Canadian funds,
convert using the current
exchange rate, UNESCO
coupons welcome)

☐ **BILL ME LATER:** (Bill-me option is good on US/Canada/Mexico orders only; not good to jobbers, wholesalers, or subscription agencies.)

☐ Check here if billing address is different from shipping address and attach purchase order and billing address information.

Signature_____

☐ **PAYMENT ENCLOSED: $_____**

☐ **PLEASE CHARGE TO MY CREDIT CARD.**

☐ Visa ☐ MasterCard ☐ AmEx ☐ Discover
☐ Diner's Club ☐ Eurocard ☐ JCB

Account #_____

Exp. Date_____

Signature_____

Prices in US dollars and subject to change without notice.

NAME_____
INSTITUTION_____
ADDRESS_____
CITY_____
STATE/ZIP_____
COUNTRY_____ COUNTY (NY residents only)_____
TEL_____ FAX_____
E-MAIL_____

May we use your e-mail address for confirmations and other types of information? ☐ Yes ☐ No
We appreciate receiving your e-mail address and fax number. Haworth would like to e-mail or fax special discount offers to you, as a preferred customer. **We will never share, rent, or exchange your e-mail address or fax number.** We regard such actions as an invasion of your privacy.

Order From Your Local Bookstore or Directly From
The Haworth Press, Inc.
10 Alice Street, Binghamton, New York 13904-1580 • USA
TELEPHONE: 1-800-HAWORTH (1-800-429-6784) / Outside US/Canada: (607) 722-5857
FAX: 1-800-895-0582 / Outside US/Canada: (607) 771-0012
E-mail to: orders@haworthpress.com

For orders outside US and Canada, you may wish to order through your local
sales representative, distributor, or bookseller.
For information, see http://haworthpress.com/distributors

(Discounts are available for individual orders in US and Canada only, not booksellers/distributors.)

PLEASE PHOTOCOPY THIS FORM FOR YOUR PERSONAL USE.
http://www.HaworthPress.com   BOF06